D1558877

SMALL TOWN

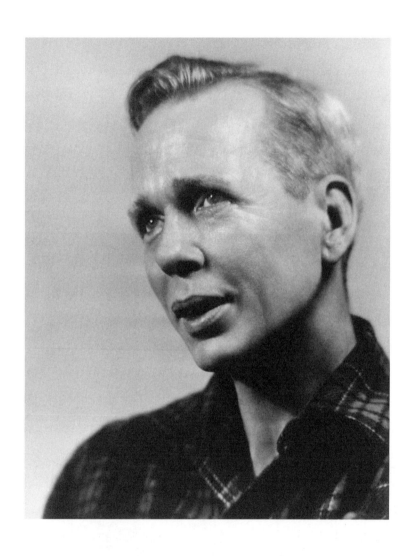

Portrait-photograph of Granville Hicks
taken about 1943 by Lotte Jacobi.

Granville Hicks

SMALL TOWN

FORDHAM UNIVERSITY PRESS

NEW YORK 2004

Library of Congress Cataloging-in-Publication Data

Hicks, Granville, 1901–
Small town / Granville Hicks.—1st Fordham University Press ed.
p. cm.
Includes bibliographical references.
Originally published : New York : Macmillan, 1946.
With new pref. and biographical essay.
ISBN 0-8232-2357-4 (hardcover)
1. City and town life. 2. Intellectuals. 3. Cities and towns—United States.
I. Title.
HT153.H53 2004
307.76—dc22   2004014754

Printed in the United States of America
08 07 06 05 04   5 4 3 2 1

First Macmillan Company edition, 1946
First Fordham University Press edition, 2004

For
Dorothy

Contents

Preface to the Fordham University Press Edition

RON POWERS

Granville Hicks saw it coming. "Has any small town a future in this age of industrialism, urbanism, and specialization?" he asks in his classic work of 1946, which examined a town caught in the decline of small-scale society that even back then was well underway. Nearly 60 years of "future" later, the balefulness of Hicks's question seems sadly to have been enlarged, transmuted, and emphatically justified. For evidence, we need look no farther than the three categories he lists—although, if we did look farther, the evidence would continue to mount.

Industrialism? How about "post-industrialism," tethered to a concept scarcely imaginable in the wary, fractious year after the end of World War II—"globalism?" After manufacturing abandoned towns for centralized locales in the decades following the war, it went overseas—"overseas" itself being a museum piece of a term in the age of cyberspace. Nor is it only America's erstwhile Axis enemies whose workers inherited the factory jobs once happily performed by folks in Smallville, U.S.A. That, too, is stale news, as quaint-sounding as the old toy label, "Made in Occupied Japan." These days, the multinational corporations have targeted countries in a far-distant realm for cheap labor in making designer shoes, electronics, clothing, and automotive parts, a realm unsuspected by any Grafton bobby-soxer or soda-jerk, unless they were sci-fi fans or readers of *Strange Tales* comic books: a realm known as the Third World.

Urbanism? By 1946, urbanism was already a trend "as dead as yesterday's headlines," to quote some fast-talking dame in a black-and-white flick whose name I no longer recall (though I

recall that the dame was a blonde). *Sub*urbanism was replacing it
as the migratory town-killer from the late 1940s onward, as hundreds of thousands of returning white servicemen took advantage
of low-interest G.I. loans to move themselves and their new families away from the dreaded central cities populated by the (equally dreaded) African-American laboring class that had migrated
out of the South just a few years earlier. With the advent of the
interstate highway—another innovation unknown to Granville
Hicks's "Roxborough" (actually, Grafton, New York)—the 'burbs
eventually mutated, or metastasized, into the great, formless,
centerless "edge cities": clusters of office towers and shopping
malls out there on the Crabgrass Frontier, as Kenneth T. Jackson
has called it. The suburbs and the edge cities swallowed up
many existing small towns, and created economic incentives that
drained the youthful workforce from many others.

As for specialization—well, that concept, correctly identified
by Hicks, has also swelled far beyond the boundaries of the term
as it was understood in 1946. Not only have the passing years
seen an erosion in the viability of the old-fashioned jack-of-all-
trades, the yeoman farmer, the family doctor, the carpenter-
builder, the skilled journeyman mechanic, and factory worker;
they have witnessed a radical segmentation, an atomization really, in the way people choose to live their lives. Witness those
tightly compartmentalized office cubicles in those edge-city office towers; witness the gated communities from which those office workers commute (usually in the encapsulated space of the
single-passenger car); witness the commodifying and "niching"
of everything from recreation to sports to ideas in politics,
schools and colleges, literature, music, magazines and newspapers,
the movies. Witness the many stratifications of Internet porn.
(On second thought, don't witness that.)

Within each of these categories cited by Granville Hicks, we
can see myriad dynamics at work that militate against the fate and
fortunes of the small town, and very few, if any, dynamics mili-
tating in the small town's favor. All of them bear heavily on the

value that implicitly underlies Hicks's concern for the Small Town—the value of community.

For instance, "industrialism," or industrialization—its undeniable benefits notwithstanding—has reached into the vitals of town life, extracting not only people and livelihoods, but also the underpinnings of purpose and self-identity for those who remain.

Most small towns are sustained by a surrounding farm economy. America has lost half its farms since 1950, and four-fifths of its farmers. Those who continue today are mostly over 55. Since 1981 alone, 750,000 family farms have yielded to suburbanization, mall development, and agribusiness in America, taking with them a million small-business jobs based in the rural economy. But that's hardly the whole story. In addition to its fertilizer- and pesticide-driven damage to vast stretches of topsoil and groundwater, agribusiness—which the writer Wendell Berry has called "economic genocide"—has vitiated the rural folk-culture on which small-town life depends. The economies of scale, reinforced by the shift of governmental subsidies and other kinds of support from family farms to agribusiness conglomerates, has further diminished the traditional farm's survival prospects. The collateral damage has included the network of interdependency built up over decades, even centuries.

Granville Hicks's Grafton, New York, lies about 15 miles from the southern Vermont border. I live a little more than 100 miles north of the town he studied, in a region where town life is still the norm. Vermont is a surviving cradle of American town culture: a still-operative latticework of small-scale community life, with its nearly 250 towns compacted into 9,609 square miles. Millions of visitors come each year (and leave behind a billion and a half dollars in purchases) seeking to encounter a Brigadoon of 200-year-old villages, tidy dairy farms, town meetings, and glimpses of earflap-wearing oldsters passing on the skills of huntin' and fishin' and doin' the chores to the eagerly receptive small fry. And to shop and ski a little.

The visitors find much of what they are seeking, or persuasive representations thereof, but the day-to-day reality of Vermont has long since ceased to fit with the myth. At the start of the twentieth century, 80 percent of Vermont was indeed farm country, with 32,000 family farms, most of them producing dairy products. Today, only about 6,000 of those remain. The rest were casualties of overwhelming economic competition (see: agribusiness), and the lure of developers' prices. (In 1993, Vermont finally surrendered its stance as the last state in the union to deny access to Wal-Mart. Several "big-box" retailers followed, the corporate-owned ski industry has expanded, and small family-owned stores have boarded up their windows proportionately.) Two-thirds of the surviving farms no longer keep herds of cows, but have adapted to niche products such as salsa and llamas. A growing number of these farms have learned to market themselves to tourists as stylized versions of their functioning pasts— as venues for "agritourism."

The state's small towns and their close-knit community traditions have suffered accordingly. They haven't suffered as much as, say, the towns of the Great Plains, where rural counties are approaching something very close to culture-death after 70 years of population decline; or the stranded river- and railroad-burgs of the Midwest—"stone dead," proclaim the editors of the 2003 anthology *A Place Called Home*; or the failing little communities of the Mississippi Delta, where you can hardly find a joint to go and hear the blues. Vermont remains a wonderful place to live, but youth gangs, heroin addiction, teen pregnancies, and school dropouts—most of these unimaginable even two decades ago— are now as familiar in the state as hayrides, 4-H clubs, and the girl scouts used to be.

Clearly, "the future" has been far less kind to small towns outside the rural New England grid. As industry has centralized, corporatized, and grown distant (except for agribusiness and its noxious waste lagoons, which have not grown distant enough), and as the barges and freight trains have vanished and taken whole economies with them, suburbanization has flowed into the vacuum. Suburbia has reconfigured "town" life in patterns that would have seemed utterly alien to the folks of Granville Hicks's era, just as they seem alienating to many folks of our own time.

Among the many differences between suburban and town life, two or three are critical, as regards the prospects of community.

In the classic town pattern, people generally lived in proximity to where they worked, often in the same building. Thus there tended to be a vital commingling of friends and strangers, day and night, in what the sociologist Ray Oldenburg has called "the Third Place"—the restaurant, the bar, the coffee shop, the green, the bowling alley, the hair salon, the town hall—places easily accessible from both home and office, and conducive to gossip, debate, romance, the revivifying play of wit and ideas—human affirmation. In the suburb, where the home is far removed from work, both home and workplace tend to be evacuated at alternating periods through the day; people go their separate ways, and the humanizing interplay is cauterized.

Another difference is that of proprietorship, as contrasted with employment. Main Street had its shop-owners, restaurateurs, booksellers, self-employed businessmen: people who, with their families, had a direct stake in the community's maintenance and well-being, and whose self-identities are enriched by the awareness of accomplishment and an imprint on the fortunes of the town. The mall, the Cineplex, the Wal-Mart, the Burger King— these have their employees, whose destinies and conditions of work are controlled by others. (Wal Mart is now the largest corporation in America in sales; it has planted almost 3,000 stores in America—mostly post-rural America—with another thousand planned over the next five years.)

Yet a third critical difference lies in the accelerated mobility of suburbanites—their propensity to relocate frequently and across great distances, often as the price for moving upward through the corporate ranks. (Corporations value efficiency in middle-management vacancies far more than they value community cohesion, which value to them may be stated as "zero.") "Corporate re-lo" has spawned its own satellite industry of "assistance" services for the vast army of migrating strangers in America, an army that beggars the migrants of John Steinbeck's purview in *The Grapes of Wrath.* The resulting rootlessness is memorably analyzed in *Habits of the Heart,* Robert Bella's 1985 landmark examination of the burgeoning individualism in American culture. Bella and the members of his Berkeley study group discovered that Americans, though fluent in the idioms of managerial strategy, the therapy movement, and other jargons, tended to fall silent when asked to speak about their lives in moral terms. This silence, Bella argues, indicates a collapse in the concept of the common good, and of the value in acting on behalf of one's community as an enduring extension of oneself. No community, no extension of the self. And thus no compelling impetus toward duty, toward compassion, toward ennobling sacrifice; toward a vision of a life enriched by shared story, shared celebration, shared mourning, shared hope.

In this tight formulation can be found the essence of what Granville Hicks saw coming, and which has long since arrived.

So what is there to be done about the fate of America's small town?

The question implies a dubious proposition in this age of economic determinism, an age in which market-driven trends and forces are generally held to be inherently self-justifying, and self-evidently desirable. It implies that something *needs* to be done. The language of transcendence recedes at quantum speed before the logic of the quantifiable. The accuracy of Robert Bellah's dire prophecy of 1985—that individualism in America "may have grown cancerous," that it may be "destroying . . . social integuments," and "that it may be threatening the survival of freedom itself"—can be measured in part by its very lack of resonant power less than two decades afterward: What is freedom, an acculturated bottom-liner of 2004 might in all sincerity ask, other *than* individualism?

To be sure, an impetus exists in many corners of America to reverse the decline of the small town and restore its status as a fountainhead of the American character. Countless foundations, institutes, alliances, politicians, and others are generating action plans, informational strategies, grant proposals, and appropriations bills toward this end.

A paradigm, at once exalted and a little forlorn, that unites many of these efforts is *social capital.* Social capital refers to the reservoirs of reciprocal support, community norms, associative networks, and collective talents that, when activated, can solve problems and restore those same integuments that Bellah and his colleagues see as withering. Sometimes these reservoirs are called "networks of trust." Ideally, social capital unites private interest with public good. Its effects are most noticeable in small, human-scale environments, such as towns. A concept with roots in Tocqueville's *Democracy in America,* social capital was re-invigorated as a rallying cry in the pages of Robert Putnam's influential book, *Bowling Alone.*

The avatars of social capital have indeed scored successes in hundreds of local venues—communities—across America. However, the paradigm has yet to achieve anything like the critical mass necessary to neutralize, or even slow, the tremendous momentum that is driving Granville Hicks's three categories as they have mutated over these 60 years: (post)-industrialism, (sub)urbanism, and specialization. Social capital remains an abstraction in bottom-line America. Capital—cold, hard, quantifiable capital—is what counts, and is counted.

Until all of that changes, perhaps the best hope for the Small Town will be to recreate itself at a slight postmodern remove from the "Roxborough" that Hicks so warily and provisionally embraced: as a stylized, visitor-friendly replica—call it "interactive museum"—of the functioning hive that it used to be . . . aware of its illusions, at peace with the necessary artifice, but structurally intact, protective of its irreducible sacredness. A Brigadoon in mufti, waiting, waiting.

Granville Hicks: Champion of the Small Town

WARREN F. BRODERICK

Granville Hicks (1901–1982), while best known as an advocate of the small town, was a widely published author, literary critic, and early socialist. After graduating from Harvard University, Hicks married Dorothy Dyer in 1925 and taught briefly at Smith College before accepting a position as an English professor at Rensselaer Polytechnic Institute in 1929. The remainder of his life was devoted to literary pursuits. He counted many literati as his friends and colleagues, including Newton Arvin, Malcolm Cowley, Carson McCullers, Bernard Malamud, Wright Morris, Richard Rovere, and John Unterecker.

Hicks joined the Communist Party in 1935 and was subsequently dismissed from the Rensselaer faculty; he renounced Communism four years later. During this period, he served as literary editor of the *New Masses* and authored two works which presented a Marxist approach to literature (*The Great Tradition: An Interpretation of American Literature Since the Civil War* and *Figures of Transition: A Study of British Literature at the End of the Nineteenth Century*). He also became fascinated with and authored two biographical works on the contemporary activist, John Reed (*John Reed: The Making of a Revolutionary* and *One of Us: The Story of John Reed*).

His other works included a retrospective look at his former interest in Communism and his honest yet unapologetic autobiography (*Part of the Truth*). During these years, Hicks also authored two additional works of modern literary criticism as well as four novels with small-town settings (*The First To Awaken, Only One Storm, Behold Trouble,* and *There Was a Man In Our*

Town). During his career, the prolific Hicks contributed many articles and reviews to a variety of magazines and journals. He removed from Grafton in 1978 because of poor health and died in New Jersey in 1982.

Formerly one of the major industrial and cultural centers in the Northeast, by the 1930s, Troy, New York, had declined to the status of a dingy, depressed former mill city. Hicks found Troy particularly unappealing and began looking for a summer home in the country. Many weekends were devoted to house-hunting in rural Rensselaer County and in nearby Massachusetts and Vermont. In May of 1932, he spotted an advertisement in a newspaper: an eight-room farmhouse for sale on 40 acres of land, only 15 minutes east of Troy.

The farm was located on Shaver Pond Road in the Town of Grafton, Rensselaer County, north of the new "State Road" (Route 2). The story-and-a-half wooden home was nestled among old sugar maples, former agricultural fields, and young forest, and its land extended to Shaver Pond, an unspoiled mountain lake. The old house lacked electricity, and the road was sometimes closed due to snow, ice, or mud, but Granville and Dorothy Hicks soon fell in love with its simple charm. They purchased the farm for $1,750, and Granville and Dorothy soon became very friendly with the nearby Agan family (who had once lived in the house).

Grafton was then a town of fewer than 650 residents, with little or no industry aside from logging. It had once supported subsistence farming and small local industries and was a minor resort community, but now, like much of rural America, the town was experiencing hard times. The town center along Route 2 consisted of a village green surrounded by neat but plain houses, two churches, two stores, and a one-room schoolhouse. The town center struck Hicks as "comfortable and homelike—not dignified, not impressive, certainly not beautiful, but not unattractive."[1] This simple rural "charm," as James Kunstler reaffirmed 60 years later, is far more than a sentimental platitude; it implies a quality "that makes our physical surroundings worth caring for."[2]

The Hickses entertained friends at their summer home, including such literati as Newton Arvin, Robert and Hope Davis, Howard and Frances Wilde, Edith Walton, and Henry Christman. During his first years in Grafton, Granville Hicks was not greatly involved in the Grafton community. "On the whole," he wrote in *Small Town*, "we did not belong to the town. . . . the part of life that was . . . intellectual, professional, and social, had little to do with Roxborough [Grafton]. The manuscripts I read came from New York, and the manuscripts I wrote went there. As a communist I was active in Troy and Albany and New York, but not in Roxborough."[3] Hicks wrote later that the memories of his first summers in Grafton were "wholly pleasant," involving hiking, swimming, entertaining guests, playing croquet, and even opening a path to Shaver Pond.[4] Likewise his wife and parents found this "the home they liked best."[5]

After losing his position at Rensselaer Polytechnic in 1935, Hicks gave up his apartment and began living in Grafton as a full-time resident. He enjoyed walking to town to pick up groceries at the general store, and his daughter, Stephanie, was attending the one-room school on the green. He was treated by the Grafton natives as an outsider, but he was somewhat surprised that they did not greatly resent a communist living in their midst. He was once told that his being a communist was really no different in the minds of natives than his being a liberal or a registered Democrat. He was viewed as a personable, harmless, overeducated eccentric, and he used to enjoy conversations with town residents, later remarking that "nobody seemed to resent my being there."[6]

In 1938, Hicks accepted a Harvard Nieman fellowship, which lasted one year and was highly controversial in the Boston area. Harvard did not renew his contract, and he returned home to Grafton. The following year was eventful for Hicks, whose public resignation from the Communist Party, following the signing of the Warsaw Pact, made national headlines.

Not content with being merely an accomplished writer, biographer, and reviewer living and working at a country retreat like many other authors, Hicks began to take an active interest in his community. With their daughter in the local school, Granville and Dorothy Hicks first became involved with the local Parent Teacher Association, and to some extent with the local fire company, town government, and other town affairs. "We had been drawn a little more into the life of Grafton," Hicks later wrote, and "since I had thought of myself as living apart from the town, I was pleased to find that there were a good many townspeople I knew fairly well."[7]

Animosity toward Hicks began to develop among natives who resented his being a liberal, intellectual, and outsider. On the other hand, his new ideas seemed refreshing to others, and a "pro-Hicks" faction emerged as well. Hicks resented the petty local politics, the ever-present gossip, the resistance by many natives to any kind of change, and the bigotry expressed by some of his neighbors against Jews, Blacks, Catholics, and homosexuals. But at the same time, he came to realize that these prejudices were part of the reality of small-town life that was beyond anyone's power to change markedly. If Hicks were to make any accomplishments in Grafton, change would have to occur within this framework.

America had now become directly involved in World War II, and some of Grafton's sons had gone off to battle. Communities in New York State were now expected to develop war-effort support activities. Granville Hicks was in the forefront in organizing the Grafton Defense Council in 1942, which became involved in collecting scrap metal and paper, monitoring gas rationing, and leading civil defense-related training. Hicks put his literary talents to good use in establishing a small local newsletter, the *Grafton Defender*, which he edited until 1957. The *Defender* contained a wide variety of community and personal news as well as information on the progress of the war and civil-defense efforts. This modestly mimeographed small-town newspaper gained recognition throughout the state. The Grafton Defense Council eventually became the Grafton Community League and sponsored various civic affairs after the war.

Hicks's next major effort involved the establishment of a town library in 1943, first opened in the Methodist Church parsonage with a collection of over 600 volumes that he personally donated. A permanent library building was later constructed and opened to the pubic in 1954. Hicks devoted much of his time working in and promoting the Grafton Free Library (now the Grafton Community Library) and considered its establishment "the achievement of a hope and the fulfillment of an obligation."[8]

Granville Hicks was also active in the establishment of the Grafton Fire Company and the Grafton Fire District, and in the creation of a modern Grafton Elementary School, which opened in 1963. He was always involved in town government, speaking at board meetings and working on town activities, but he never sought elected office as some of his friends and supporters suggested. Grafton was clearly not ready for a supervisor or councilman who was a liberal-minded author and something of a celebrity.

Hicks wrote a number of works while he was a full-time Grafton resident. The first was *I Like America*, an interesting and attractively designed little paperback illustrated by Richard Bennett, in which Hicks explained why being a communist was not un-American. His next two book-related projects involved seeing *The Letters of Lincoln Steffens* through publication, also in 1938, and authoring *Figures of Transition*, a Marxist approach to British literature, which appeared the following year. The next four years saw the publication of the first three of his four novels, *The First to Awaken* (1940), *Only One Storm* (1942), and *Behold Trouble* (1944). All three novels, as well as his later novel, *There Was a Man in Our Town* (1952), received mixed reviews; all were set in a small town resembling Grafton. Some of his neighbors recognized that characters in the novels were based on local residents, and while some resented this association, others were flattered.

Hicks's most significant works to date had been *The Great Tradition: An Interpretation of American Literature Since the Civil War* (1933), still regarded as the most important work of American Marxist literary criticism, and two important biographies of John Reed. *One of Us: The Story of John Reed* (1935), illustrated by Lynd Ward, remains a classic in the genre of revolutionary literature, and *John Reed: The Making of a Revolutionary* (1936) has never been replaced as the gold standard of Reed biography. Hicks's next important nonfiction work, and by far his best-known book, is *Small Town*, published in 1946. By this time, Hicks felt the need to compose a serious nonfiction work on small-town life in the Northeast, based on his personal experiences. Aided by a grant from the Rockefeller Foundation, Hicks produced *Small Town*, now recognized as a pioneering sociological study on the subject.

What distinguished *Small Town* from any of its predecessors (and many of the similar works that followed) was the status of its author. While the other books represented the work of sociologists who came from academia merely to visit the small towns they were studying, *Small Town* was the first to be written by a small-town resident. Hicks declared in *Small Town*, "I could not adopt the point of view of a visiting anthropologist; I am writing from inside."[9] For this reason, Hicks stood apart from most other scholars, who studied small towns from the perspective of aloof outsiders, as sociologist Baker Brownell also noted, who also "fail to evaluate the community of statement and people where good work is done."[10]

Hicks was never disinclined to express his strong opinions. *Small Town* is a highly personal account of his neighbors and his community; neither statistical tables nor a bibliography of academic studies is included. But this work was to become, as Hicks had intended, more than merely "a plea for the small town" but rather "a book about a small town in another kind of world."[11] In other words, the "new" small town, reconstituted by bringing forth its traditional values into a viable modern rural community, might become a bulwark against the rootless and impersonal society which he saw growing rapidly in America.

Small Town became a prototype that other authors would follow, most notably *Democracy in Jonesville* (1949) by William Lloyd Warner and his associates, *Small Town in Mass Society*, by Arthur Vidich and Joseph Bensman (1958), and Joseph Lyford's *The Talk in Vandalia* (1962). Lyford's highly personal work echoes Hicks's emphasis on the importance of "the power of personal word." Lyford concluded that small-town residents "are in some ways in a better position to observe and to feel, sometimes most painfully, the consequences of a changing society" than the suburbanite or the city dweller.[12]

Baker Brownell praised Hicks in *The Human Community* (1950), in fact defining the community as a "small town in which each person can know a number of others as whole persons, not as functional fragments . . . when it becomes so large that the people in it do not know one another, the community disappears."[13] Brownell and Hicks had been corresponding with each other, and Hicks believed that Brownell "states the [small-town] problem well [and is] tackling it the right way.[14] Hicks, in turn, praised *The Human Community* in his review of Brownell's work and David Riesman's *The Lonely Crowd*. Brownell, like Hicks, had observed changes in American culture related to the shift in population and power from the country to the city. "The consequences have been two-fold," Hicks wrote," the isolation of man from nature . . . and the isolation of man from man." In confronting this problem with what Hicks referred to as "remarkable courage," Brownell believed that "the movement away from the human community can be checked, and even reversed."[15]

Brownell had the opportunity to read a manuscript of *Small Town* earlier in 1946, and although pointing out to Hicks specific passages that might need some refinement, was effusive in his overall praise of the work:

It really is not solely on the small town, but on the relation of an intellectual to a small town, each seen in the light of the other, and this is its greatest value. Or, to put it more abstractly, it presents the relationship, the conflict, the modern dilemma of mind and folk, and the sterility and impoverishment of one without the other. It is a regional book in the best sense of the word, presenting . . . a whole human situation. The disciplines of sociology, history, anthropology, psychology, education are synthesized so well in it, that these harsh specialties sink back, unrecognized as such, in the fluid movement of the book as a whole. It would be better to say that it is a masterpiece of plain, human observation deeply interwoven with critical and personal insight.[16]

Margaret Mead, in reviewing *Small Town* for the *New York Times*, praised it as a "perceptive and moving book," and she added that, unlike other works that had appeared recently lamenting the decline of rural life, Hicks's work "lacks the note of disappointment and repudiation that springs of the memories of" a contented rural America of the past, which has been lost "in the realities of the present." Mead continued:

He comments perceptively on Roxborough people, who function in ways to make the intellectual, anxious for the future of mankind, stop, reassess his problems, and soberly lower his sights to conform to the realities of small-town inertia, lack of orientation, and lack of motivation. Interwoven, however, is a genuine, convincing appreciation of what the small town gives not only to the native but to the intellectual. He values the chance to know many kinds of people, in many different contexts, so that people become, not functions, not types, but individuals to be shunned in one situation, but depended on wholly in another.[17]

Robert Lynd, co-author of the "Middletown" books, also praised *Small Town* in his review. "This book derives from a general conviction that I respect deeply," Lynd wrote, "that democracy is worth making an effort for; that the people in all the little communities at the grass roots must be immediately and continuously involved in that effort." Lynd recognized that *Small Town* was far more than merely the latest book in the "city person returns to the country" genre, adding that, despite his reservations, he found "a warmth and perceptiveness about . . . Hicks's approach to his neighbors that makes the book fascinating in its detail." Lynd, however, did not share Granville's optimism in proposing conditions for salvaging the small town. "Hicks is right in recognizing the potential power in the little people of America; but it is sheer moonshine to expect them to find and to exercise this power to build more democracy within the present coercions of monopoly capitalism."[18]

Malcolm Cowley, despite having some serious reservations about life in Grafton, elevated Granville Hicks above other intellectuals who "scatter to the corners of the earth . . . when they become disenchanted" or "take to the woods . . . trying to achieve independence on five acres . . . they want to cut the ties to society and achieve the illusion of leading their own lives."

> Granville Hicks has taken an opposite course, one in which I imagine that comparatively few will follow him, because . . . it involved more day-to-day problems than arctic exploration or beachcombing in the South Seas. He has stayed at home and has plunged into the closely knit community life of an upstate New York town.[19]

Although Grafton is called "Roxborough" in the book (an early name of the town used in the late 1700s), and the names of persons mentioned there are fictional, the events the book details are entirely factual. *Small Town* achieved great popularity and general critical acclaim. Granville Hicks received numerous letters of praise from small-town residents and natives from across the country. As one might expect, some of his Grafton neighbors enjoyed the book, and others detested it. *Small Town* lacked illustrations and was printed by Macmillan on poor-quality paper used during and after war years. Its design and printing were certainly not commensurate with the book's importance.

Small Town was selected by the New York State Education Department for its Educator's Book Club, and as a result the book became immensely popular with teachers and school administrators. Although *Small Town* "does not pretend to treat of formal educational matters," the reviewer noted, it should be "almost required reading for school folks," as important a work as Margaret Mead's *Coming of Age in Samoa* or *The Education of Henry Adams*. "It is as readable as a novel," the reviewer continued, "and as folksy as a gossip column . . . this is the kind of book that can be read for enjoyment and 'pondered' over for understanding."[20]

Granville Hicks delineated seven positive attributes or values of small-town life in *Small Town* and his other writings. First, though his educational background and literary career had been restricted to academia, Hicks soon developed an appreciation of nature, rural scenery and the out-of-doors. Shortly after purchasing his farm, he recognized the scenic beauty of Grafton. Hicks remarks in *Small Town* that Grafton held particular appeal because of "wild country . . . becoming wilder now that abandoned farms are growing up to woods."[21]

The second important attribute of small-town life that Hicks recognized was what he called "the power of personal word." In his article, "The Mind of A Small Town," the issuance of which preceded the publication of *Small Town* by a few months, Hicks discussed this attribute at some length. "Talk between neighbors used to be the only means for the transmission of news and opinions, and it is still an important means wherever neighborly contacts exist" as they did in Grafton. The town, Hicks concluded, "has almost no impersonal spectacles . . . There is every chance for a person . . . to learn about his neighbors, and few distractions to keep him from doing so."[22]

Closely related to the "power of personal word" is small-town neighborliness. In a small town like Grafton, for better or worse, you know your neighbors. In *Small Town,* he commented that Roxborough was composed of "people they know and have known from childhood, people who know them, who know their faults and have got used to them, know their virtues and appreciate them."[23] He later wrote that as "mass society" became larger and larger, "more and more relationships would become impersonal" if the process couldn't be "slowed down." In small towns "most relationships were between person and person, not between function and function." Hicks commented how much he enjoyed trading in the country store "where I am known by name and can meet friends and swap gossip." In a small town, one is "thrown with many kinds of men and not merely with intellectuals. In short I like living in a small town."[24]

Hicks made an interesting observation on social classes in a small town. As many as six social classes might exist in a larger community, but he observed only two social classes in Grafton, and it is was "not easy to define the differences between them": "The lower class," he wrote, "has a few rather disreputable characters, but for the greater part it is made up of people not strikingly different in outward appearance or in income from the bulk of the upper class. It is no wonder that for all the more important affairs of life Roxborough is a classless society."[25] Coming from a former socialist, this is indeed an interesting observation to make about small-town life.

"Efficiency" of life was another value of small-town life that Hicks admired. Life in a small country house was "efficient" and very basic, as he first had noted in *I Like America.* His Grafton home had fresh air, clean water and sunlight, and with firewood as a heat source, one didn't need to "give the superintendent hell about it if you don't get it," as might his "city friends."[26] Life was also "efficient" in a small town because "small-town functions overlap, and as a result one can do two or three strokes of business in a single call."[27] Everett Ladd, in his later study of Putnam,

Connecticut, noted that Hicks, unlike most of the social scientists, was "concerned with what people *don't* talk about."[28] In this regard, Ladd recognized that Hicks had "found the same preoccupation with the concrete and the immediate" in rural America as de Tocqueville had over a century before.[29]

Hicks observed that "there is never a week that is wholly free from community activity of some kind or another."[30] While most of those tasks involved little or no compensation, they did involve various residents working together on an assortment of projects and strengthened a sense of community. "What Toynbee calls 'the link of loyalty' is still very important in Roxborough, and it is my guess that this is a far more significant tie than any other," he wrote in *Small Town*.[31]

The final positive attribute of small-town life that Hicks referred to is the understanding of "community past." "The significant thing about the natives," he wrote in *Small Town*, "is the way they think in terms of the past—not merely the individual past but the community past."[32] He had come to learn that a majority of Grafton residents descended from old families and were in some way related. Hicks had always found Grafton's history interesting. In *I Like America*, he touches on the early history of the town and had come to learn the history of the Francis West family who had established the farm where he resided. He addressed these topics at length in "A Place in the Country." Grafton, Hicks concluded, had still been an "isolated and partly self-sufficient community" into the early 1900s, and this was important because "there are so many people in the town who remember that period and are constantly looking back to it."[33] "Because the past is so close, it seems to the younger people as well as the old-timers that Roxborough life is different from city life."[34]

Following the publication of *Small Town* and the wide acclaim it received, Hicks soon became recognized as one of the nation's principal spokespersons for the virtues of small-town life in rural America. His reputation was greatly enhanced by his participation in a debate on the popular public radio program, *Town Meeting of the Air,* held on December 26, 1946. The debate was held in Schenectady in the studios of WRGB Channel 6. Hicks debated Charles Jackson, who had spent a few disappointing years of his life in Orford, New Hampshire, an even smaller and more isolated town than Grafton. The debate, entitled "Would You Rather Live in a Small Town or a Big City,"? was narrated by George V. Denny, Jr., and lasted nearly an hour. The debate was lively, made even more so when the two "interrogators," the husband-and-wife team of radio personalities, Reagan "Tex" McCarthy and "Jinx" Falkenburg, took strongly opposing positions, each sympathizing with one of the two authors.

When Hicks had written *I Like America* in 1938, he still maintained a fondness for New York City, but he soon realized that although the big city was an interesting place to visit, his home would be in the country. He began to see the many activities the big city offered as "impersonal spectacles" and now distrusted "the judgments of the city intellectuals when they talk about the 'people'—whether they take the line that the people are boobs or refer piously to the common man." He had developed by now a "strong distaste for big cities" and he had proven "that an intellectual remains an intellectual even though he does live in a small town."[35] "Whenever I am in New York City," he proclaimed near the beginning of the Schenectady debate, "I wonder how people can live without quietness and without clean, fresh air. I wonder, too, how they can stand the pressure of anonymous humanity. I know people as individual human beings. I don't like the bitter faces and the sharp elbows of the subway."[36] Granville Hicks is generally acknowledged to have "won" the debate, and the people of Grafton felt that he "had successfully defended the small town." Many urban dwellers, Hicks noted, have "small-town backgrounds, and when urban frustrations grow too severe, they long for quiet and simplicity." Even Charles Jackson admitted that the "American dream" consisted of "a Cape Cod cottage on a village green."[37]

As a result of the broadcast, *Life* magazine decided to run a story contrasting Hicks's life in Grafton and Jackson's life in New York City. Photographer Kosti Rouhomaa shot hundreds of photos in Grafton on a visit that winter, and six of them were used in the article "City vs. Country," which appeared in *Life* on March 17, 1947. Grafton townsfolk delighted in the publicity and attention they were receiving; Hicks's friend, storekeeper Sherman Barnhart, said that the "pictures of this small town . . . will be seen all round the world."[38]

Later in 1947, in an article in *Georgia Review*, "Reflections of a Small-Towner," Hicks commented on the big city versus small town debate he had popularized the previous year:

> I did not set out . . . undertaking a crusade against big cities. . . . First of all, I personally prefer life in a small town to life in a city. Secondly, I believe that the small town is an important part of American life, and should neither be sneered at or neglected. . . . We chose our present residence not because we wanted to live in a small town but because we wanted to live in the country. . . . But in time the people came alive for us, and their affairs became important to us, and we are glad that this happened. They are our people now, our neighbors, our fellow-citizens, our friends and our enemies, and their affairs are our affairs. These people and their affairs have taught us a great deal about human nature and the problems of democratic government.[39]

Reflecting on the now-famous debate, Hicks reminded readers that his purpose "in examining the shortcoming of cities" was "not to call city-dwellers to repentance but rather to awaken in small-towners an appreciation of their advantages, their opportunities and their responsibilities."[40]

Small Town, as Margaret Mead had indicated in her review, stood alone from other books on the subject published before 1946, in part because it not merely lamented the loss of small-town values, but also dealt with the small town's future. "The old basis of the small town has been destroyed and cannot be rebuilt, but I can believe that new foundations can be established," Hicks wrote, upon which the small town can survive as a community, providing that three conditions are satisfied:

> The first essential, obviously, is an economic basis for the existence of the town. The second is the establishment of a standard of living comparable of that of the cities. And the third is the development of forms of activity that will bring the people of the town closer together—that will take the place of a network of personal and economic relationships that once linked the members of the self-sufficient community.[41]

Hicks speculated how the small-town mind, with its resistance to outside authority, would react to regional planning. He advocated "planned decentralization," where county, regional, state and federal government would provide the town assistance, but not interfere with local autonomy, which he considered "a valuable bulwark against totalitarianism."[42]

Because of its small population and the many interpersonal contacts among its residents, Hicks saw the small town as a "school of practical democracy."[43] Despite the problems associated with small-town politics, one's vote counted more in a small-town election, and a small-town resident could more easily participate in the local political process than in a large city. Hicks advocated the "town meeting" form of government as practiced in rural New England, because it led to greater citizen involvement. "In the past, the small community was the seedbed of our American kind of democracy" Hicks wrote. "In the future, if we are wise, the small community may become an experiment station for new democratic processes."[44]

Granville Hicks continued to maintain an interest in the viability of the small town. In 1953, he contributed an article to *Commentary* called "Roxborough, Post-Truman: The New Small-Town Community in the Making." In the intervening years since *Small Town* was published, the population of Grafton had increased by about 200 persons, mostly "newcomers." "Some of them take part in town activities . . . and contribute to town causes. . . . Far from being a disruptive factor, they have helped transform Roxborough into a suburb" of sorts.[45] "If the newcomer is reasonably personable, he will be urged to join two or three organizations as soon as he has made a few friends in town," he continued. These newcomers have "put down roots," and while they will always be treated as "outsiders," they find more "people of congenial tastes and habits, which would not have been true 20 years ago."[46]

As Hicks had predicted in *Small Town*, the "psychological effect of prosperity" had been "tremendous." The stark rural poverty he had observed when house-hunting in 1932, which he mentioned in *I Like America*, had begun to disappear:

> I find it hard to remember how it used to be—the unpainted, ramshackle houses, the yards full of junk and ragged children. Now, there is a television aerial on every roof, of course, and there are refrigerators, washing machines, and electric or bottled-gas ranges in the kitchens. . . . I used to be distressed by the hangdog faces I saw, especially on the women, at school meetings and elections. Now the same women hold their heads up, and when they have something to say, they say it.[47]

The "conversion to suburb status" had benefited the small town, wrote Hicks, "first by making possible prosperity, second by extending the experience of many of the natives, and third by giving it a more varied population."[48] Although much remained to be accomplished in Grafton, Hicks continued to profess that

> . . . there is still much to be said for the small community. At least we are a long way from urban impersonality and anonymity. Face-to-face relationships do prevail, and the individual is not reduced to a function. Furthermore, when, as in Roxborough, one

is so close to a self-sufficient past that it still influences the attitudes of many people, one gains a better perspective on the values and deficiencies of a mass society.[49]

Granville Hicks wrote an article entitled "Is the Small Town Doomed" in 1956, intended for publication in *Woman's Home Companion*. The article never appeared because the magazine ceased publication in 1957, but it survives in typescript drafts in the Granville Hicks Papers at the Syracuse University Library. "While many small towns have been swallowed up," Hicks noted, "the situation is not quite so bleak as some observers maintain." Hicks recognized that the automobile had "made possible a new pattern of living" in which small-town residents could commute to jobs in nearby cities while spending quality time in the small-town community. Hicks also saw the "decentralization of industry" and the development of rural tourism and outdoor recreation as benefiting the small town. He concluded this article with a note of optimism:

> One of the greatest dangers is the belief that the destruction of the small town is inevitable. As we have seen, there are forces working for the small town as well as forces working against it. If no one cared for the small town, the destructive forces would almost certainly prevail but millions of people do care, and their caring can make a difference. When people have succumbed to fatalistic lethargy, there is little hope, but much can be done by intelligent, planned action.[50]

Granville Hicks last commented on the small town in his 1972 *New York Times* reviews of Vance Packard's *A Nation of Strangers* and Edwin Rosskam's *Roosevelt, New Jersey*. As Packard and Rosskam both noted, the progress of technology threatened to doom small-town life, in spite of the best efforts to preserve it. It will either assimilate the small towns into mass society or take them "into the abyss," Hicks lamented. "In the meantime,

xxxiv   *Granville Hicks: Champion of the Small Town*

for many of us, the small town is a better place than most to spend whatever time remains." The newly found social mobility may have been blindly embraced by many, but was feared by both Packard and Hicks, for this mobility led to "rootlessness . . . because of the problems" it caused "in establishing and in keeping identity."[51]

In his later years, Granville Hicks became somewhat less involved in local affairs, to some extent because of his failing health, but also because he wanted to devote additional time to literary criticism. He had stated in *Small Town* that he "hoped to unload" some of his town-related projects, but concentrate on a few, particularly his work with the Grafton Free Library. A "complete withdrawal" from local activities "would be both an admission of defeat and a betrayal of the friends who have worked with us. So long as we live in the town," he concluded, "we cannot do anything to jeopardize the gains that we have helped to win."[52] When the final issue of the *Grafton Defender* appeared in 1957, Hicks remarked that this now ended "fifteen years of intense community effort. . . . I was not disillusioned," he continued, "I was not bitter. I had no regrets. Though less had been accomplished than I had dreamed of [in particular, the lack of a community center] the accomplishments were not to be laughed off."[53]

Malcolm Cowley, his long-time friend and colleague, praised the life and work of Granville Hicks in a long review, appearing in the *New York Times* in 1965, of Hick's autobiography, *Part of the Truth*. Largely as a result of Hicks's untiring efforts, Cowley noted that Grafton not only now had a fire house, library, and modern school, but also "seems to have developed more local pride and a stronger sense of community." Still, as Cowley noted, "Grafton is not a beacon light for the nation." Cowley admired Hicks but regretted "that for 20 years Hicks's talent for leadership, his doggedness, and his social conscience" had been "chiefly confined to that narrow field" of improving life in a small town, which today still only has a population of about 1,950.[54]

Thirty-nine years have passed since Cowley's review, and it has become easier to examine the career and writings of Granville Hicks from a broader perspective. Hicks's interest in studying small-town values and reconstituting small-town life as a viable part of the American experience had a far broader influence than Cowley might have imagined. Baker Brownell elevated Hicks to the status of a benevolent missionary of sorts, who along with Arthur Morgan and some prominent members of the American clergy, "made impressive demonstrations of modern ways to stabilize the community or identity the intellectual life with it.[55]

For Hicks, Grafton was not only his home, but also a representative "little slice of America."[56] As Margaret Mead commented in her review of *Small Town*, Granville Hicks "blazed . . . a path" in the interest in small-town studies. The soft-spoken transplanted New England intellectual, staunch in his beliefs, had left his mark in a field seemingly unrelated to, but equally as revolutionary as American social history or Marxist literary criticism.

Warren F. Broderick
Lansingburgh, New York
March 2004

NOTES

[1] Granville Hicks, *Small Town* (New York: Macmillan, 1946), 3–4.

[2] James Howard Kunstler, *The Geography of Nowhere: The Rise and Decline of America's Man-Made Landscape* (New York: Simon & Schuster, 1993), 168.

[3] Hicks, *Small Town*, 43.

[4] Ibid., *Part of the Truth: An Autobiography* (New York: Harcourt, Brace & World, 1965), 106.

[5] Ibid., 111.

[6] Ibid., 157.

[7] Ibid., 195.

[8] "Dedication," *Grafton Defender* 13, no. 6 (17 July 1954), 1.

[9] Hicks, *Small Town*, 11. Angie Debo's *Prairie City: The Story of An American*

Community (Knopf, 1944) is better classified as a local history (of Marshall, Oklahoma), but covers the modern era and presents an interesting picture of small-town society.

[10] Baker Brownell, *The Human Community, Its Philosophy and Practice for a Time of Crisis* (New York: Harper's, 1950), 220.

[11] Hicks, *Small Town*, p. 274.

[12] Joseph Lyford, *The Talk in Vandalia* (Santa Barbara, CA: Center for the Study of Democratic Institutions, 1962), 99, 102.

[13] Brownell, *Human Community*, 207.

[14] Hicks, *Small Town*, 219.

[15] Ibid., "The American Character Changes," *New Leader*, 12 March 1951, 20–22.

[16] Personal correspondence, Baker Brownell to Granville Hicks, 1 March 1946, Granville Hicks Papers, Syracuse University Library.

[17] Margaret Mead, "Grass Roots and the Intellectual," *New York Times Book Review*, 15 December 1946, 4.

[18] Robert Lynd, "Ivory Village," *Saturday Review* 30, no. 3, (18 January 1947), 14.

[19] Malcolm Cowley, "Hicksborough," *New Republic* 115, 9 December 1946, 766–767.

[20] Personal correspondence, Peter P. Muirhead to Granville Hicks, 15 January 1947, with review attached, Granville Hicks Papers, Syracuse University Library.

[21] Hicks, *Small Town*, 89.

[22] Ibid., 106; ibid., "The Mind of a Small Town," *The American Mercury* LXIII, no. 272 (August 1946), 158.

[23] Ibid., *Small Town*, 90.

[24] Ibid., *Part of the Truth*, 235.

[25] Ibid., *Small Town*, 93–94; see also W. Lloyd Warner and Paul Lunt, *The Status System of a Modern Community* (New Haven: Yale University Press, 1942).

[26] Granville Hicks, *I Like America* (New York: Modern Age Books, 1938), 31–32.

[27] Ibid., *Small Town*, 9.

[28] Everett Ladd, *Ideology in America: Change and Response in a City, a Suburb and a Small Town* (Ithaca, NY: Norton, 1969), 186.

[29] Ibid, 136–137; see also Alexis de Tocqueville, *Democracy in America,* edited by J.P. Maier and Max Lerner (New York: Harper & Row, 1976).

[30] Hicks, *Small Town*, 10.

[31] Ibid., 98.

[32] Ibid., 85.

[33] Ibid., 93.

[34] Ibid., 88.

[35] Ibid., 14.

[36] "Would You Rather Live in a Small Town or a Big City?," *Town Meeting* (Bulletin of America's *Town Meeting of the Air*) 12, no. 35 (26 December, 1946), 4.

[37] Granville Hicks, "Reflections of a Small-Towner," *Georgia Review* I, no. 2 (Summer 1947), 146.

[38] Ibid., *Part of the Truth*, 241.

[39] Ibid., "Reflections of a Small-Towner," 144–145.

[40] Ibid., 150.

[41] Ibid., *Small Town*, 209–210.

[42] Ibid., 234, 245.

[43] Ibid., 219.

[44] Ibid., 274.

[45] Granville Hicks, "Roxborough: Post-Truman," *Commentary* 15, no. 3 (March 1953), 228.

[46] Ibid., 228–229.

[47] Ibid., 229.

[48] Ibid., 234.

[49] Ibid., 235.

[50] Granville Hicks, "Is the Small Town Doomed," unpublished article, 1956, Granville Hicks Papers, Syracuse University Library, 8, 13.

[51] Granville Hicks, "Roosevelt, New Jersey," *New York Times Book Review*, 30 July 1972, 7; ibid., "A Nation of Strangers," *New York Times Book Review*, 10 September 1972, 2–3, 50–51.

[52] Ibid., *Small Town*, 55.

[53] Ibid., *Part of the Truth*, 283.

[54] Malcolm Cowley, "Yankee Crusader on the Left," *New York Times Book Review*, 1 August 1965, 1.

[55] Brownell, *Human Community*, 184.

[55] Hicks, *I Like America*, 84.

Author's Preface

Because it would be impossible to conceal from any resolute investigator the identity of the town about which this book is written, I have employed only the flimsiest of disguises. If I do not use the name that the town bears on the map, that is to remind my neighbors that most readers will not care what the town is called or where it is located.

No living resident of the town, except for myself and my family, is given the name he actually bears. I do not therefore assume that my neighbors will be unable to identify some of the men and women who are mentioned. However, I warn them to be careful, for I have not hesitated to mix things up when it served my purpose.

A book of this kind is valueless unless it is honest. I have set down nothing in malice, but I may as well admit that the book could never have been written if I had stopped on every page to worry about the possibility of hurting someone's feelings. I have not wanted to hurt anybody's feelings, and if feelings are hurt, I'm sorry, but that was a chance I had to take.

There are some of my fellow townsmen who wouldn't like anything I did, and the fact that they won't like this book doesn't particularly bother me. On the other hand, there are many neighbors whom I should be loath to offend. I don't think they will be offended. I think they will see that I have written about their town and mine because one has to start with what he knows. After all, from the point of view of the general reader this isn't a book about the particular town in which my neighbors and I live; it is a study of a small fragment of American life—small but, I hope, significant.

The book was begun in the summer of 1944, and a first draft was finished a year later. The manuscript was completely rewritten between September 1, 1945, and February 1, 1946, and the point of view throughout is that of the months following V-J Day.

I am grateful to the Rockefeller Foundation for making possible the writing of the book, and to John Marshall, Associate Director of the Humanities Division of the Foundation, for his help and encouragement. I am grateful to all the friends who have read and criticized the manuscript at various stages, and particularly to Baker Brownell. I thank Rollee Herbert, Rachelle Lubar, Jane Metzger, Alice Rabe, and Jeanne Watson for letting me examine the results of their studies of public opinion in a small town. And Lee Levenson is once more to be thanked for her typing.

I

Starting Out From Roxborough

This was a week, a not unrepresentative week, in the autumn of 1945.

Sunday was memorable because I finished reading Volume VI of Arnold Toynbee's *Study of History*. That, however, was late in the evening, after a day that was for the most part spent out of doors.

We got up moderately early for a Sunday, and after breakfast I did the chores; that is, I brought in a couple of baskets of wood for the kitchen stove, chopped a little kindling, and filled the water-storage tank. I listened to the news on the radio, and set out for the village.

We live on a dirt road almost exactly a mile north of the highway, a road that is a pleasure six months of the year and a problem the other six. I passed the Cutters' home, just out of sight from our house, and the new home of the younger Cutters across the road. I passed the rundown farmhouse where Wilbur North lived for so many years. I crossed the brook, drove along the flats, which are so often blocked with snow in winter, and eased the car down Allen's Hill to the cement highway.

From the corner one sees half a dozen houses. Three of the places were being actively farmed when we came to Roxborough in the summer of 1932. One of them has now been sold to city people. On the second most of the stock was disposed of and some fields taken out of cultivation when the young man of the family was drafted. The owner of the third went to work in a defense plant soon after Pearl Harbor, though he has managed to do a considerable amount of farming in his spare time.

It is a mile from the corner to the center of the village. At first the houses are spread out, but soon one comes to a little settlement—eight or ten neat but unpretentious houses close together—and then one is in the village proper. There are no beautiful old houses, such as one sees in so many New England towns, but most of the residences are substantial and well taken care of. One passes an abandoned store on the left, the town's honor roll on the right, and one is at the four corners. Mark Betterton's general store occupies the northeast corner, and diagonally opposite it is the Methodist church. Across from the church there is a pleasant little park, beyond which one sees the Baptist church and a white, one-room schoolhouse. Beyond the church there is Al Black's store and grill. At the top of the hill, just visible from the four corners, is the town hall.

There were two or three cars in front of each store and four or five behind the church. After I had bought my Sunday papers from Al Black, he followed me to the door, and I knew from the glow in his eyes that he had a piece of political gossip. His story, confirming and amplifying a rumor I had already heard, seemed to both of us to indicate that the Republican boss had made a first-rate blunder, and we were both pleased.

In the soft, unseasonable warmth the village seemed comfortable and homelike—not dignified, not impressive, certainly not beautiful, but not unattractive. One saw few signs either of private wealth or of public spirit. Not only was there nothing ostentatious; the whole look of the place was informal and a little unkempt—like the kitchen of an easy-going but really not slovenly housekeeper. A city person might even have found the scene rather sordid, but to me it suggested comfort and a certain indifference to appearances.

As I came out of Al's store, people were leaving the Methodist church—not many of them—and I spoke to them all and paused to talk with Lucy Sheldon about the library. I went into Mark Betterton's store, not only to do some shopping but also to discuss the tax rolls with Mark, who was collector of School District 1, of which I was trustee. Mark was talking with Sergeant Higgins, who had flown home from India the preceding week, and of course I joined in the conversation.

There was something I wanted to ask Steve Porter, and I stopped at his house on the way home. That particular stop is almost habitual, for the Porters are usually eating breakfast just as I come back with the papers, and I can count on a cup of coffee. Over the coffee this particular morning we discussed the square dance the night before, made plans for the next Saturday night's dance, examined and reexamined the story I had got from Al Black, and commented—with some malice and yet with some friendliness, too—on the behavior of an acquaintance.

When I picked up our daily jar of cream at the Cutters', a carful of relatives had just arrived, and I spoke to those whom I had previously met and was introduced to the others. Across the road Stan Cutter was working on the pump he had recently installed, and we talked about that.

It was too good a day to stay inside, and I had a job that needed doing. I glanced at the papers, and went to work. The day before I had started to remove from the lawn a rock on which I had repeatedly nicked my mower. In the course of digging around that rock I had uncovered four others that weighed a hundred pounds or more apiece, and I had found myself confronted in the end with a hole five feet in diameter and two feet deep—and at least two hundred and fifty pounds of Rensselaer grit in the middle of it. With the sledge hammer I had borrowed from Mr. Cutter I tried to break the rock, but I succeeded only in chipping off small pieces. Finally I called on Dorothy, who was working in the flower garden and didn't want to be bothered. While I pried the boulder up with a crowbar, she placed rocks underneath it, and at last, after prying from this side and that for a matter of two hours, we rolled it out. I spent the remainder of the afternoon filling the hole and planting grass. So it was late when I got to Toynbee and later when I finished my reading.

Monday morning I wrote letters until nearly eleven, which is the deadline for outgoing mail at the post office. After I had mailed my letters, I loaded my car with boxes of waste paper at Betterton's store and took them to the salvage station. I spent the remainder of the morning and the first part of the afternoon taking notes on Toynbee. The weather was still fine, and for a couple of hours before dinner Dorothy and I worked on a banking that had been an eyesore ever since we had the place.

The evening, so far as I knew, was free for me, but Dorothy had to see the president of the PTA. The chairman of the Community League's nominating committee telephoned my mother to ask if she could attend a meeting, and the friends who brought her home came in and stayed until past midnight. We talked about many things: the harvest dance, a supper for the National War Fund, and various personal matters. But chiefly we discussed the latest Republican maneuver—the matter I had already discussed with Al Black and with the Porters—and a question of policy that was disturbing the members of the fire company.

Because of that interruption, my notes on Toynbee had to be finished in a hurry the next morning. I drove to Troy, did some errands, had lunch with friends, and went on to Albany, where I worked for several hours in the library. I was home at five, and chopped wood before dinner.

Our plans for the evening were complicated, for Dorothy had a PTA meeting, I had a meeting of the board of fire commissioners, and Mother was scheduled to serve at the library. Fortunately, the library is next to the church hall, where the PTA was meeting, and Mother was able to share the PTA covered-dish supper and still open the library at seven. I ate at home, and was just about to leave for my meeting when friends called to discuss a real estate deal. They knew, of course, that I had a meeting at eight, and they did not stay long.

Assembling at the church about ten, the three of us came home and spent the hour before bedtime talking about what we had done. The PTA meeting had been a success, but there were the usual clashes, and some problems had been left unsettled. Mother had had a busy evening, partly because some PTA members, coming into the Center for the meeting, had visited the library for the first time. As for my meeting, it had gone quietly enough until the committee on rules and regulations made its report, and then there had been an argument in which tempers were lost. The chairman had succeeded in quieting the combatants, but I could see that there were tiresome sessions ahead.

Wednesday was almost entirely my own, although it is true that I delivered some tickets for the harvest dance as I was going for the mail. After a moderately productive day, I took time off in the evening to work on a skit for presentation at the dance. Dorothy, meanwhile, was involved in a series of telephone calls regarding the purchase of a new piano for the town hall. This was a PTA project, but since the support of both the Community League and the fire company was being sought, I was called on for advice.

Thursday also promised to be a comparatively free day for me, but not for Dorothy. Members of the PTA were assisting with the annual medical examination of school children, and that took half of her morning and the whole of the afternoon. I finished reading a manuscript in the morning, and, having written my report on it before lunch, I counted on some two hours of writing and two hours of outdoor work in the afternoon. But almost before I had a sheet of paper in the typewriter, Walter Gaynor, one of my colleagues on the board of fire commissioners, called to discuss the issue that had caused so much dissension at our Tuesday's meeting. The problem concerned the dismissal of members of the fire company. State law gives the power of removal to the commissioners, but the chief and one commissioner had insisted that certain ironclad rules should be established with regard to attendance at meetings and drills, whereas Walt and I believed that the commissioners should be allowed to exercise their discretion. At the meeting I had shown some willingness to compromise, but Walt had stood firm. He came to see me that

Thursday afternoon because he wanted to reconsider the whole matter, and it was good that he did, for, in the course of a long review of the problem, we saw some elements that we had hitherto overlooked, and we ended with a proposal that seemed likely to bring the maximum of agreement with a minimum of time spent in committee meetings. If, however, time was saved in the long run, half that afternoon was gone, and I spent an hour working at my desk and an hour working on a stonewall.

That evening we had a rehearsal at the Porters for our skit. The Porters are young and, as I have already indicated, hospitable, and Jane served coffee and toasted cheese sandwiches. Somehow the seven of us got to telling stories, and then one of the stories led into a serious discussion of anti-Semitism. It was eleven-thirty when we came home.

The school children's health examination, as it turned out, had consequences for me that I had not anticipated. In the first place, the examiner reported that one of the children needed immediate medical attention, and Thursday evening his mother took him to her own doctor, who confirmed the diagnosis. As a result she telephoned me on Friday to say that she could not take part, as she had planned to do, in the National War Fund campaign. In the second place, tests showed some eyestrain among the children of School District 1, and the use of a meter in the schoolroom revealed that the lighting was inadequate. This was my responsibility as trustee, and on Friday I went to the school to see what could be done.

In a small town functions often overlap, and as a result one can do two or three strokes of business in a single call. Friday evening, while making some purchases at the store, I got Mark Betterton to countersign several school district checks. One of these checks I took to the janitor, and since he is also a member of the board of assessors, I was able to raise the question of the exemption of a lot owned by the Community League. I stopped at the library to discuss with Lucy Sheldon not only library business but also the accompaniments she was to provide for our sketch the next night. Then, when I picked Dorothy up at the town hall, which she and the Porters were decorating for the dance, Jane Porter, as an insurance agent, handed to me, as secretary of the fire district, a liability policy covering members of the fire company.

Saturday morning, after a couple of hours' work, I took Jane Porter to the hall to finish the decorations. While she was working, I hunted up a delinquent member of the cast and made sure he would be present that evening. En route I encountered a local contractor and asked him some questions about the lights at the school.

In view of all I have said about preparations, it is satisfying to report that the dance was successful. There were approximately a hundred and fifty persons there, and though I may be biased, as co-author and one of the performers, I think they liked the entertainment. And when the caller shouted, "Fill up the floor," it did fill up. There were so many squares, in fact, that Dorothy and I were quite willing to forego dancing, and in any case I had a couple of Chinese auctions to take care of and some persons to see about the National War Fund campaign. The four of us—we had taken one of the Cutter boys with us—left before the dance was over, but not before we knew that more than a hundred dollars had been raised for the Christmas present fund. That was the night the clocks were set back, and though we like daylight-saving time, we weren't sorry to have an extra hour for sleep.

—⁂—

Not all weeks are as bad as that, but there have been weeks that were worse, and there is never a week that is wholly free from community activity of one kind or another. A list of jobs will show why that is so. Dorothy is a former president of the PTA and currently chairman of one of its committees. Mother and I are also members, though I—in common with most male members—rarely attend meetings. All three of us belong to the Community League, and Dorothy is vice-president while I am one of the directors. I am chairman of the library committee, and Mother is an assistant librarian. I am a member of the volunteer fire company and also secretary of the fire district. I am editor (and mimeographer) of a bi-weekly town bulletin. And I am trustee of School District 1.

I am not bragging. When the town board was appointing fire commissioners, I overheard one of the members say, "No. Not him. He's into everything." I knew whom he meant, and I sympathized. I didn't want to be a fire commissioner, for I knew that the job, at least at the outset, would involve frequent meetings, tedious records and reports, and unlimited criticism. Some of us, however, had worked hard to build up a fire company in the first place and, in the second place, to create the fire district, and we were unwilling to have our work undone. Roxborough, as I shall have to point out again and again, has no large supply of citizens who will serve the interests of the community without pay. (I was going to say "gratis," but money is commoner than thanks.) If I had declined to be a candidate, there were others, just as loath as I to be involved, who would have had reason to refuse. As it happened, four commissioners were chosen before my name was considered, and then it seemed likely that another man, a man I should have been glad to see appointed, would be given the post. It was my bad luck that a member of the board had a political grudge against this man that outweighed his personal distaste for me.

I do not list these offices because I want to be considered a big shot in Roxborough or be regarded elsewhere as a public-minded citizen. I mention them only because it is necessary to make clear at the outset that whatever I have to say about the town of Roxborough grows out of constant participation in its life. I also want to make it clear that in a small town participation is never a matter merely of official relationships. The individuals I encounter on committees or in organizations are usually personal friends and often are men and women with whom I have business relations as well. As I have already indicated, Mark Betterton, the school district's collector-treasurer, owns the store in which we do most of our local buying. Harvey Dakin, who was at the fire commissioners' meeting on Tuesday, the rehearsal on Thursday, and the dance on Saturday, is the man from whom I buy my firewood. Indeed, there is almost no one mentioned in the chronicle of that autumn week whom I did not meet at least twice during the seven days and in at least two different roles.

From the point of view, then, of one who wants to know how a community functions, the time I spend on Roxborough affairs is not wasted. "What does he get out of all this?" some of my neighbors suspiciously ask. Would they believe me if I told them that I am getting an education? This book is concerned with what I have learned thus far.

In writing about Roxborough I cannot adopt the point of view of a visiting anthropologist; I am writing from inside, and, try as I may to eliminate personal bias, I do not assume that I can achieve scientific objectivity. What I propose to do first, therefore, is to reveal my point of view by giving some account of myself: how I came to be an intellectual and how I came to be an intellectual who is deeply involved in the life of a small town. Then I shall talk about Roxborough, its history, its structure, and particularly its people. Finally I shall consider some of the general problems that are raised by my experiences here: the problem of the future of the small town in an urban-industrial civilization, the problem of human control over society, the problem of education, and the problem of the relationship of the intellectuals to the rest of mankind.

Perhaps, unless I am fortunate, it will seem that I have written two books—one about small-town life and the other about various controversial topics that are national or international in their scope. I can only say that it would be relatively easy to write either a book about Roxborough as an isolated unit or a book about what is wrong with the world. What I want to do, however, is not only to see Roxborough clearly but also to see it in perspective, and at the same time I want to check my ideas about the nation and the world by discovering how they apply to a group of people I know reasonably well, my fellow townsmen. After all, I do find myself thinking about both the big problems and the little ones, and they do seem to have some bearing on one another. I suppose no one will deny that it is necessary to understand the great movements of history in order to understand what goes on in Roxborough. Perhaps it is also true that understanding the Roxboroughs helps one to understand the world.

To say this raises at once the question of Roxborough's representativeness. My guess is that Roxborough is in many ways representative of towns of from five hundred to a thousand inhabitants in the Northeast—worse than some but perhaps better than others. In fewer ways it is representative of all small towns in the United States, and later on I shall speak of resemblances and differences. I am not much interested, however, in the exact degree of representativeness, and I do not feel apologetic because I cannot tell you how many towns of this size there are in the country. It is a different kind of representativeness that seems important to me. I do not believe that what I have learned about small-towners has no application to big-city people. For one thing, the big cities have plenty of men and women from the small towns, and however much they may have changed on the surface, many of them are small-towners at heart. For another, it was not so long ago that the United States was a nation of small towns, and we have not outgrown our small-town heritage. No one can write about such a place as Roxborough without emphasizing patterns of thought and action that distinguish small-town from urban life, but I should be less interested than I am in Roxborough if I did not believe that it has something to teach us about the American character.

It is probable that some readers will find these claims ridiculous. They have never known people like my neighbors, and they may conclude that such people exist only in stagnant back-waters and there only in insignificant numbers. I believe that, quite literally, these readers do not know what they are talking about.

One of the most obvious characteristics of urban life is the way in which little groups are segregated according to occupational interests or social tastes. In the small town you know everybody or nearly everybody, and, what is more, you know a considerable number of persons in a considerable number of ways. The city dweller, on the other hand, rarely has intimate friends in any social or economic group but that to which he belongs, and this is peculiarly true of the intellectuals. The average urban intellectual knows other urban intellectuals, and that is all. If the urban intellectual knew the postman and the elevator operator and the exterminator and the corner grocer—if, that is, he talked with them in his home and in theirs, if he encountered them at church and on election day and in meetings of various organizations— he might find that they have a good deal in common with my Roxborough neighbors.

Two of my preconceptions must already have become clear. In the first place, I have grown to distrust the judgments of the city intellectuals when they talk about "the people"—whether they take the line that the people are boobs or refer piously to the common man. In the second place, I personally have a strong distaste for the big cities. Not only do I believe that they are manifestations of the disease of our civilization; I cannot understand why anyone wants to live in New York or Chicago or Washington or San Francisco. However, I am not seeking to win converts to small-town life, and I shall not be disappointed if there is no penitent exodus from our megalopolitan monstrosities. My purpose is not argument but description, the story of an intellectual in a small town, from which the reader can draw his own conclusions.

What must be recalled is that an intellectual remains an intellectual even though he does live in a small town. In so far as this is an account of the development of a point of view, it draws upon the world of ideas and not merely upon my experiences in Roxborough. My life as a member of the Roxborough community is not the only life I lead, and my story cannot be told merely in Roxborough terms. Two kinds of experience are important in my life, and the book is an attempt to bring them to bear upon each other.

Argument, as I have said, is not my purpose. Eight years ago I wrote a book that also was based in part on personal experience, but then I thought that I knew the remedy for all the world's ills, and the book was intended to make converts or at any rate sympathizers. Now I am not so sure of anything as I was of almost everything then. I do not know what should be done to save Roxborough, much less the world. I am not unaware, however, that the world is in a bad way and that each of us is, in his own tiny measure, responsible for what happens to it. The aims of the book, in other words, are modest, but the intentions are serious.

II

The Natural History
of an Intellectual

Of his transposition from Brook Farm and Concord to the Salem Custom House Nathaniel Hawthorne wrote, "I took it in good part, at the hands of Providence, that I was thrown into a position so little akin to my past habits, and set myself seriously to gather from it whatever profit was to be had." That is a note that runs through our literature, and it is the rare intellectual who has not at some time been flattered because he felt that he was being accepted as an equal by men of action, whether they were soldiers or sportsmen or Wall Street speculators or so-called common men.

I confess that I, too, take pleasure in the fact that I seem to be able to get along with men whose way of life is rather different from my own, and I think that I have gathered no small profit from the association. Yet the mere consciousness of pleasure is evidence of a persisting sense of isolation. There are barriers, and it would be foolish to pretend the contrary.

When we came to Roxborough, we were summer people, and summer people are tolerated, for they bring money into the town and they don't, as a rule, mix in its affairs. I was then teaching at an institution that was known by name to most of the natives, and my being a teacher no doubt served to explain everything about me, including traits of behavior and speech that were regarded as foreign and funny. I had status—as an outsider.

In 1935 we became all-the-year residents, and the circumstances were blatantly public. A few citizens were distressed by the presence of a prominent Red in their midst, but I do not think the disapproval was either acute or widespread. In Roxborough anyone who is not a Republican is an oddity, and in the

days of bitterness against the New Deal a communist seemed
only slightly more dangerous and slightly more bizarre than a
Democrat. We paid our bills and minded our business, and curiosity dwindled. My position was more ambiguous than it had
been when I was a teacher, for people could not make out how I
earned my living, and I am now sure that there was far more talk
than I supposed at the time, but if I was a problem, I was not a
problem that people had to do anything about.

When, however, I began to take some part in the life of the
town, my fellow townsmen naturally ceased to think of me as a
harmless freak. I became their problem then, and one about
which some of them did a deal of worrying. By that time I was
no longer a member of the Communist Party nor in any sense a
sympathizer with its program, but of course that was regarded as
a mere technicality, and I was generally supposed to be some sort
of radical. I doubt, however, if my radicalism had much to do
with the hostility that developed. My reputation as a Red was a
good peg on which to hang criticisms, but there would have
been disapproval in any case. I was different, and the difference
lay not in my having been a radical but in my being an intellectual. One day a friend of mine and an enemy were having an argument about me, and after the friend had beaten down a series
of unwarranted criticisms, the enemy said in desperation, "He
knows too damned much."

My real participation in the life of the town, as I shall tell later
on, began with the organization of civilian protection in the early
months of the war. There were some persons who objected to my
appointment as chief air-raid warden, and ever since then there
has been what I can only describe, however immodestly, as an
anti-Hicks faction. But there has also been a pro-Hicks faction,
composed of those with whom I have worked. Some were well-
disposed at the outset; others were more or less hostile and only
came slowly to the conclusion that I was neither a complete dope
nor a dangerous character. In time, at any rate, I was generally
accepted as one of the group.

Yet, though I have come to be taken largely for granted in this particular circle, I am again and again made conscious—and so, I suppose, are the others—of the barriers that do exist between the intellectuals and the rest of society. Except for myself, the members of the group can easily account for themselves. One of them, for instance, works in a garage, another is a factory mechanic, another is a welder, another sells pulpwood. That is all perfectly clear, clear to them and clear to me. But then I come along and say, "I read manuscripts for a publisher, and I write books," and it touches nothing in their experience. When I hear them discussing the idiosyncrasies of internal combustion engines, I am bewildered by the extent of their technical information, but I do know in a general way what they are talking about. I am afraid that they would be not merely bewildered but completely lost and hopelessly bored if they were to listen to the shoptalk of intellectuals.

I have often wondered how it would be if I were a doctor or a lawyer. Medicine and law are familiar to them in a way that literature is not, but I have an idea that the difference is only one of degree. Doctors and lawyers have bodies of specialized information of which the layman can make specific use, whereas the value of my particular equipment is made apparent to my friends chiefly in the fact that it earns me a living. Yet medicine and law are also mysteries—and, as Shaw has pointed out, conspiracies. Of course we are all at the mercy of a multitude of specialists nowadays, and I think I have been more thoroughly bamboozled by garage mechanics than I have ever been by doctors, but a specialist who is also the practitioner of a mystery does have the edge.

The non-intellectual thinks of the intellectual, "He has something that I haven't got, and I don't even know what it is." That is what hurts. And it does hurt. There is pain and there is resentment. I was momentarily bewildered when I heard that someone had referred to me as "that damned lazy pauper who sits on his ass all day." I am not a pauper, and I work more hours a day than my critic does. But he refuses to admit that what I do is work, and it seems to him the rankest injustice that I should be paid for loafing. I have known farmers and craftsmen, mostly of an older generation, who honestly believed that a man wasn't a man unless he did a day's work with his hands, and they were secure in their sense of superiority. My critic, however, has been corrupted not only by jealousy but also by a suspicion that I may have more than a financial advantage over him.

Resentment against the intellectuals enters in a surprising way into anti-Semitism. "Have you ever known a Jew who was a farmer or a factory worker?" a man will ask. "They always want the soft jobs." Note that the charge goes beyond the conventional assumption that Jews are out to make money; they are accused of avoiding manual labor. I have heard a man say, as if he were describing a crime, "Jews will do anything to send their kids to college so they can be doctors or lawyers or teachers."

I am not saying that the barrier has not been crossed by individuals. Apparently I get across it now and then, for some of the mechanics and farmers in Roxborough seem willing to admit at least that an intellectual can be a human being and even that he can sometimes be useful *qua* intellectual. Moreover, some of my friends cross it, coming over to my side and discussing things in my terms. But the barrier is there, and I am constantly running up against it.

The question that various Roxborough people, both friends and enemies, might like to put to me is, "How did you get that way?" It is a more than legitimate question. I am not an intellectual[1] by inheritance. My grandparents and great-grandparents

---

[1] I do not like the word "intellectual," which seems to me both pretentious and ambiguous, but there is no convenient substitute, and I can only explain what I mean by it. When I speak of an intellectual in this chapter, I am thinking of a person who is temperamentally, as well as professionally, concerned with ideas. The Concise Oxford Dictionary of 1934 defines "intelligentsia" as "the part of a nation . . . that aspires to independent thinking," and this is more or less what I have in mind. Arthur Koestler's "The Intelligentsia" (in *The Yogi and the Commissar*) is a suggestive but not wholly satisfactory discussion of some of the characteristics of the group that I call the intellectuals. On the other hand, both "intellectuals" and "intelligentsia" are sometimes so defined as to embrace almost all persons of more than average education. Konrad Heiden (in *Der Fuehrer*, p. 12, fn.) explains that he means by

were farmers or skilled mechanics, and my father was an office worker. By what process was I alienated from the kind of people who produced me?

—ᴡᴡ—

More than anything else, my parents were responsible. They were Unitarians or Universalists, according to the church facilities available, but what they really believed in was education. In their minds education was economically, socially, and morally imperative. It was the means of avoiding the insecurity and indignity of manual labor, but it was also a path to self-fulfillment and the good life. They could not say, in paraphrase of Aunt Mary Moody Emerson, "All Hickses are born to be educated," but they had not the least doubt that this particular Hicks was. They were not well-to-do, and during some periods in my boyhood they were down-right poor, but the conviction never flagged that I should go to college. To that end, I was given to understand, they would make any sacrifice, and no less was expected of their only son.

Nature conspired with nurture to give them what they wanted, though of course it is hard to tell where one leaves off and the other begins. I was not a robust child, and I was conspicuously bad at games. Not very intelligent teachers convinced me that I was incompetent with my hands, thus robbing me of skills that I was afterwards able to cultivate in some degree and also fostering in me the conviction that manual dexterity was unimportant. Inevitably I attached chief importance to those subjects

---

"intellectual" "the pragmatical and mechanistically minded modern man, product of mass education." In effect, however, he classes as intellectuals the professionals, the literati, the managers, the bureaucrats—in short, virtually all "brain" workers. Arnold Toynbee makes "intelligentsia" almost as inclusive *(A Study of History, V,* 154ff.). The more inclusive definition has the advantage of being less subjective, and later on in the book, especially in the last chapter, I use the term in its broader rather than its narrower sense. The trouble is that the two meanings of the term can never be separated with perfect clarity, and the difficulty is not merely semantic, for the phenomena to which they refer are constantly shifting. However, after this warning—and I apologize for its pedanticism—I think the reader can decide which way the emphasis is falling.

in which I could excel. As inevitably I took refuge in the habit of constant and indiscriminate reading. My father, who had no serious quarrel with the world as he found it and was not inclined to question many of its values, would have been glad if I had been less of a sissy, but he saw that I was moving straight ahead on the path that had been laid out for me, and that was what counted.

Like most intellectuals I know, I look back on my boyhood as a period of acute unhappiness. It was natural that I should be miserable because I did badly in games, but I was also unhappy in school. I got good grades (except in drawing and penmanship) but I was bored, so bored in one class, I remember, that I habitually checked off as it passed each of the twenty fifteen-minute periods into which the school day could be divided. Actually, I suppose, I was unhappy only a small part of the time. Certainly I was happy when I was reading, and for that matter I have more pleasant than unpleasant memories of play with my contemporaries. But the impression of unhappiness persists, and I think it is dependable.

I was born in Exeter, New Hampshire, a medium-sized town, agreeably laid out and, as I recall it, full of agreeable people. When I was seven, my family moved to a bleak, treeless suburb of Boston, where we lived on a street of uniform two-family houses. My father, my mother, and my older sister were never comfortable in Quincy, and I, too, felt the difference between the friendliness of Exeter and the impersonality of a real estate development for commuters. Four years of Quincy were more than enough. The very day that we arrived in Framingham a man spoke to me on the street, and I came home and reported that it was just like Exeter. That was not quite true, but it was pleasanter than Quincy, and in time we all became attached to the town.

I was eleven when we moved to Framingham, and I can see now what a variety of dogmas I had already acquired. Not only had I picked up the rudiments of intellectual snobbishness; in moral matters I was a dogmatic and inflexible little boy. My parents had given the usual warnings against tough boys and bad language, and I had accepted the admonitions at face value, presumably because I didn't like the tough boys anyway. I couldn't compete with them and it was a satisfaction to push them out of my world on the two charges of stupidity and badness. That didn't take care of them in practice, of course, but it was a consolation none the less.

The friends I made were good boys, not good enough, to be sure, to figure in Sunday school literature and not good enough to do themselves any harm, but good enough for me and my parents. That is to say, they were the sons of respectable, thrifty, church-going, middle-class Americans. One or two were less docile, or at any rate more curious, than I was, but probably all of them believed as implicitly as I did that boys whose fathers got drunk, boys whose fathers beat their wives, boys who hung around pool rooms, boys who smoked publicly and with bravado—such boys would come to bad ends. When I was six or seven, I had been shocked to learn that a favorite uncle not only was a Democrat and Free Mason but drank beer and even whiskey. This was incredible, for my father was a Republican, an Odd Fellow, and a total abstainer. At fourteen I could laugh at my naïveté in supposing that Odd Fellows were good and Free Masons bad, but I was still not quite sure about Democrats, and I had the gravest doubts about men who drank beer.[2]

As I have said, I was not happy in grammar school, either in Quincy or in Framingham. Only one of my teachers, it seems to me, had any pride in her profession, and even in her room I was consistently bored. High school was different. It was not a large school—probably there were fewer than four hundred pupils at the time I entered—and even in 1915 it was not first-rate. But

---

[2]When I was recently bringing a couple of seven-year-olds home from school, one of them said, "I think that Billy drinks beer. He stinks. Anyway his mother and father are beer-drinkers." The accents seemed to me to be my own. I observed that the other seven-year-old, who knows very well that his parents drink beer and that so do I, made no comment. Perhaps there is a kind of conspiracy in favor of self-righteousness.

fortunately for me, though unfortunately for the majority of pupils, it was strongest in its college preparatory course. I think gratefully of a good mathematics teacher, two good history teachers, a good science teacher, a good Latin teacher, and a rather extraordinary English teacher.

The teachers, however, didn't make all the difference. There was a change in the atmosphere, and if a scholar was still less highly regarded than a football player, he was not positively scorned. More than that, high school placed a high value on executive ability, and this was a talent I was discovering in myself. Hitherto I had exercised it only in the boy scouts and in the young people's society of the church—organizations that my contemporaries were beginning to regard with a sophisticated scorn. In high school, however, a good administrator won almost as much public approval as an athlete, and by the time I was a senior I held nearly as many offices as I now hold in Roxborough—and enjoyed a good many more honors.

I imagine my elders thought of me as a good boy. Certainly I was an active one. I worked summers, on a newspaper counter, on farms, in a hardware store. I worked during the school year, too, mowing lawns, taking care of furnaces, sweeping offices, beating rugs, and reporting high school events for the local paper. With all my high school activities, I continued to be a mainstay of the Sunday school and the young people's society. Yet somehow there was time for swimming in the summer and skating in the winter, for games of whist, for Sunday afternoon walks, for occasional dates, and for a great deal of reading.

During my senior year I decided to go to Harvard, partly because the principal of the school had gone there and his son—my closest friend—would follow him, partly because a cousin of mine, who had worked his way through, said that Harvard was the college for a poor boy. What was my equipment for college? I passed the college board examinations, and so I presumably knew the academic subjects about which a college entrant is supposed to be informed. I knew as much about current affairs as anyone who was wholly dependent on the Boston press could be expected to know. (I had been interested in politics since the triangular election of 1912, when my father followed Theodore Roosevelt out of the Republican party, and I had watched with excitement the progress of the first World War, which ended in the autumn of my senior year.) I had read hundreds of popular novels and seen scores of moving pictures. Over many college freshmen I had an advantage, in that I knew how to work, both with my hands and with my brain, and I had seen several kinds of business from the inside. On the other hand, my social experiences had been rigidly limited, and I knew almost nothing about people outside the lower middle class.

In so far as my mind had been awakened to things that lay outside the routine of my busy days, the credit goes to a minister and an English teacher. The minister, who had studied psychology under G. Stanley Hall, was by local standards a poor preacher and a poorer pastor, but whether he did anything for anyone else in the little church, he gave me the beginnings of a systematic philosophy. Reading Charles and Mary Beard's *The American Spirit* when it appeared in 1942, I realized that here was a biography of the complex of ideas that was handed over to me in my late teens. Basic was the idea of progress. The Universalists do not include in their articles of faith, as the Unitarians do, "the progress of mankind onward and upward forever," but most of them accept the doctrine—or did in 1919—and certainly Mr. Mooney preached progress, with Darwinism as example and reinforcement. The idea of progress, humanitarianism, a religious faith in democracy, trust in education, and individualism in the Emersonian sense of courageous nonconformity—these were the elements in the synthesis that I took over. Something of a pacifist, the young minister had reconciled himself to support of the war by dwelling on the possibilities of a just peace, and I, his one disciple, became a passionate Wilsonian, convinced that the League of Nations represented a new climax in humanity's eternal march onward and upward.

From Miss Treat came a different set of ideas. The Miss Treats of American education have figured so prominently in autobiographies and novels that everyone knows the type: the motherly teacher, reconciled to single life, anxiously scrutinizing each new class in the hope of finding genius that will justify her career or, at the least, talent that will make her days endurable. What she gave me was chiefly encouragement to read books different in kind from those I habitually read. I continued to read—and to enjoy—the Tarzan books, the western novels of Zane Grey and Clarence Mulford, the historical romances of Robert Chambers and Jeffrey Farnol, the detective stories of Conan Doyle and Louis Joseph Vance. But, as I look over the reading lists I kept in those days, I begin to find surprising titles: *Sartor Resartus, Chesterton's Orthodoxy,* the poetry of Alfred Noyes, the poems and the letters of Alan Seeger, novels by Arnold Bennett, Henry James, H. G. Wells, and Edith Wharton. I find *The Winning of Barbara Worth* sandwiched between *Eugenie Grandet* and Galsworthy's *The Mob,* and I note that after I finished the *Alcestis*—in what inept translation, I wonder—I read Curwood's *Barre, Son of Kazan* before tackling the *Medea.* What Balzac and de Maupassant, to say nothing of Euripides, meant to me I cannot say, but I can remember my response to the tenseness of *Ethan Frome,* the music of *Riders to the Sea,* the magnificent bombast of *Cyrano.* If I entered college with some slight awareness that reading could be more than a pleasant way of passing the time, Miss Treat deserves the credit.

I was valedictorian of my class. My speech was a series of platitudes, and I knew it, but the sentences sounded rather impressive as I rolled them off. I wonder what the people in the audience thought—if, indeed, they had thoughts for anyone but the sons and daughters of their own who were being graduated. I imagine some of them thought of me as conceited, a smart boy who knew he was smart. Others may have regarded me as a troublemaker—though such a judgment would have had to be almost purely intuitive at that point. The majority, I feel sure, looked on me as a bright, hard-working boy who was likely to do well for himself. That night, on that platform, I was one of theirs, and they were moderately proud. But they all took it for granted, as I did, that I would not be one of theirs much longer. They had no feeling that I would come back after college to their community. No, they knew that I would be out and away—like all the other bright boys of the towns and the smaller cities of America. And of course they were right.

—∞—

But for a time I was out and away only in spirit. Of my first two years at Harvard the most important thing to say is that I was a commuter. Until J. P. Marquand wrote *So Little Time*, no one had mentioned "the grim and underprivileged group that appeared in the Yard each morning with small leather bags containing books and papers." Like Mr. Marquand's Jeffrey Wilson, I was not so sorry for myself then as I became later on, but it was a grim and unsatisfactory business. One thing was fortunate: I was even less conscious than Jeffrey of all the ramifications of the other world with which I was so abruptly brought into contact. I saw the boys running about in gray flannel pants and blue shirts, and I knew that this had something to do with initiation into an organization variously called Dickey and the Institute, but I had been an alumnus for some years before I ever heard of such a thing as a finishing club. Only one resident of that other world—he holds an important political office—made any effort to pull me out of the social abyss. It was no use, and he gave up, but we remained friends.

The truth is that I had seen almost at a glance that Harvard was too much for me. Against such competition I could not hope to repeat the successes I had enjoyed—and how I had enjoyed them—in high school. I had to have scholarships to stay in college, and I therefore devoted myself to getting good grades. But for social life and a kind of self-expression I turned to the young people's organization of the Universalist church. There was a paper on which I could work, thus making a little money, and there were conferences and conventions to attend. Moreover, the young people I met were my own kind, solid sons and daughters of the middle class, not Harvard snobs and sophisticates.[3]

I enjoyed most of my courses in my first two college years, and if I thought I was learning more than I was, I was at least laying a foundation that has proven reasonably useful. Yet I was not much influenced by any of my teachers, not anywhere near as much as I was by a hometown eccentric who called himself Old Doc Kay in recognition of the unpronounceability of his Teutonic surname. He had been a printer, an editor, a ship's surgeon, and heaven knows what else, and was currently earning his living as a janitor while playing the role of gadfly in the town of his adoption. He was an imperfect Socrates, devoted in theory to the urbane question but capable of hot-tempered outbursts. What he did for me was not merely to point out the iniquity of the Treaty of Versailles, ridicule the prevailing view of the Boston police strike, and otherwise provide an unorthodox commentary on passing events. No, and it was not merely to suggest that every institution from town meeting to Congress, from kindergarten to graduate school, from corner grocery to Wall Street, would be better off for a general overhauling. What Old Doc Kay gave me was a sense of the intoxicating excitement that could come from contact with ideas. After a Sunday in Boston, spent at four or possibly five forums, the old man gave off a positive aroma of exhilaration. Doubtless there was something ridiculous in his pursuit of argument for argument's sake, but he was no mere hunter of fads, and in any case his zeal for new ideas was a valuable antidote to the caution and suspiciousness of my middle-class environment.

Old Doc Kay drifted out of town as he had drifted into it, and his only material legacy to me was a little bundle of reactionary bulletins demonstrating, by virtue of a typographical error in the

---

[3] Nineteen years later, serving at Harvard as a counselor in American history, I marveled that I could have found the college so formidable, but the fact remains, and it is a perfectly intelligible fact.

addresses, the self-evident fact that various conservative organizations exchanged mailing lists. He drifted away, and some time
later word came back that he had died. The mere fact that I spent
my junior and senior years in a college dormitory was a testimony to his influence. (I felt that residence at college must be even
more important than I had supposed if so unconventional a person as Doc Kay insisted upon it.) A more significant tribute was
my joining the Harvard Liberal Club. As I listened to socialists,
communists, single taxers, internationalists, prison reformers,
trade-union organizers, birth-control advocates, vegetarians,
nudists, genteel organizers of British cooperatives, passionate
leaders of German youth movements, rich men's sons in overalls
(figuratively speaking), and poor men's sons with Oxford accents, I often thought of the sharp-eyed old man with his trim
beard and his spotless flannel shirts. I did not go to these meetings because I knew he would have wanted me to, but it was
good to feel that what I was doing would have had his approval.

What did I actually believe at that time? I could not easily say
if I did not have a paper that I wrote, for purposes of clarification,
in the summer of 1922. The paper begins with an affirmation of
faith in the scientific method—which I had read about in James
Harvey Robinson's *Mind in the Making* and other books, not
discovered for myself in scientific courses. In fact, I had a little
trinity: the scientific mind, the social mind, and the open mind.
Continuing to be active in church work, I was naturally concerned to define my attitude toward religion. I did not see how
one could either affirm or deny the existence of God in a philo-
sophic sense, but in any case I could not accept the traditionally
Christian conceptions of God, even those held by the liberal
churches. For me, it appears, religion was essentially a faith in the
possibilities of the human race, and the function of the church
was properly to create what I called the social mind, i.e., a recognition of more than purely personal interests. In view of the
number of extremists I had heard, my program of social and
political reform was surprisingly mild, a watering down of an

already diluted Fabianism. Robinson, R. H. Tawney, Graham Wallas, Bernard Shaw, and Glenn Frank were the men who had influenced me. (I had also been influenced at just that point by Lothrop Stoddard, but six months later I scribbled on the margin of the manuscript an indignant repudiation of Stoddard's racism.) The whole essay I called, in imitation of Glenn Frank, "The Evangelical Mind."

Re-reading this portrait of the young man as evangelist more than twenty years after it was written, I was troubled to see just how wrapped up I had been in theories and abstractions. It was a comfort, therefore, to discover another document that came from the same summer, a collection of sketches of men and women with whom I was working. The summer of 1922 was the second I had spent in a factory, and it was much pleasanter, I recall, than the first, perhaps because I succeeded in looking at my experiences as literary material. What I am glad to find, as I look the sketches over, is not merely creditable powers of observation but also evidence of a friendly interest in people of many kinds. Like Hawthorne, I welcome this suggestion of "a system naturally well balanced," this reminder that I was not wholly a slave of the printed page.

The last of my college years was, as it should have been, the pleasantest. Yet when it was over I looked back at Harvard with little of the enthusiasm that is supposed to fill the heart of a young alumnus. It had proved to be, as my cousin had said, the college for a poor boy, and I was thankful for the scholarships that had taken me through without undue hardship. I had missed much that seemed valuable to my fellows, but Harvard was not to blame for that, and there had been compensations. What I felt then and feel now is that, quite purely on the intellectual side, the side on which I had a right to considerable expectations, Harvard's gifts had been meager. I had taken chiefly English courses, and I had read a good share of the masterpieces of English literature, and that was all to the good. What I missed was what I was later to find in the writings of various non-academic critics—a feeling for the excitement of the literary experience, for its grandeur, and for its importance. None of my teachers ever got excited about books or angry about them or had any feeling, so far as I can recall, stronger than a scholarly curiosity or a genteel satisfaction. It was quite natural, I now realize, that the greatest scholar of them all should have spent his spare time reading detective stories. Some of my contemporaries did better than I, but I think that is because they had access to literary groups in Cambridge and Boston of which I knew nothing. They owed no more to the college than I did.

—⚭—

I came close to graduation without having decided what I was to do thereafter. I had said that I wanted to teach English, and the appointment office had brought me an offer from a small college, but I was listening to the naggings of my evangelical mind. It pointed out to me that for four years I had spent much of my time in church work. Was that merely because I enjoyed editing any kind of paper and speaking to any kind of audience? I was not prepared to make such an admission. Then, said the evangelical mind, if church work is worth doing at all, is it not worth devoting your life to? I was shaken. I had no interest in preaching to people about God and heaven, but I was interested in preaching to them about a better life on earth. As a member of the elite—and, skeptical as I was about the value of college education, I never doubted that it entitled me to such a position—I had a duty. There were many institutions through which a man could work for the betterment of mankind, but surely the church was one of them, and one that badly needed the services of intelligent young men—I was not unduly modest—like myself. The evangelical mind won, and I enrolled at the Theological School in Harvard University.

Thus began a two years' detour, pleasant and profitable as detours sometimes are. I have never regretted that I studied the history of religions, church history, and the Old and New Testaments, and studied them under first-rate men. If it took two years to demonstrate to me that I didn't want to be a minister, that was because the intellectual atmosphere of the theological school was so congenial. Two years, however, was enough. Formally, at least, the decision was made by a reversal of the logic that had sent me to the school: I became convinced that the church was no longer an effective instrument for the purposes I believed in. Historically, it seemed to me, the church had been a means of personal salvation, and when it ceased to be that, it ceased to be anything that mattered much, as the ineffectiveness of the liberal denominations proved. When I told the dean my decision, he said, "I never believed that you would make a good parish minister, but I thought you might find yourself in some executive position." Quite unreasonably I was surprised and a little hurt.

Having made my decision, I wanted to find a job as quickly as possible. For a little while I was considered for a position on a liberal weekly, and later on it seemed to me that my life might have been quite different if I hadn't been turned down. In a way it would have been, for I should have been tossed abruptly and with wholly inadequate preparation into the melee of New York literary life. (I was afraid of that, and rather relieved when the editor sent his regrets.) Yet within five years I was contributing regularly to that journal and others of its kind, and in the perspective of twenty years my failure to get the job seems to have made no considerable difference at all.

By then it was fairly clear to me that I wanted to be a writer, but I didn't go to New York, and I didn't go to Paris and start a little magazine. I took the safe way. I became an instructor at Smith College. But if I wanted security in the financial sense, I was not looking for an academic sanctuary from the world and its ideas, and certainly I did not find one. My three years at Smith were not only so agreeable as to take on, in retrospect, an idyllic quality; they were crucial in my education.

This was the middle twenties, and the spirit of the period was handsomely embodied on the Smith campus. Among certain conspicuous members of the faculty a pattern of ideas and values was accepted and promulgated that seems to me now the very essence of the decade. They all subscribed to at least three articles of faith. They believed, first, that science would prove the salvation of humanity, and they had unlimited confidence in the ability of the human reason—and specifically the human reason as manifested in them—to solve any problem. Second, they proudly called themselves liberals, which meant that they advocated freedom of speech and laughed at Calvin Coolidge, but they were not democrats, for they shared H. L. Mencken's contempt for the booboisie. Mencken was, of course, the source or at any rate the spokesman of many of their ideas. Third, they thought of themselves as the civilized minority. "Civilized" was a favorite word with them. It meant one who (a) drank in defiance of the Prohibition amendment, (b) looked with tolerance on violation of the marriage vows, (c) was supercilious towards all religion, (d) regarded politicians as rogues and patriotism as a bad joke invented by the American Legion and the Daughters of the American Revolution, and (e) took pleasure in shocking less sophisticated members of society.

This is an unattractive picture, and not quite true. All of these men were kindly and generous. Some were scholars of distinction and some were able teachers. To a menial instructor like myself they were friendly and consistently helpful. Yet I look back on their species of so-called liberalism with a very uncomfortable feeling. I was influenced by it; make no mistake about that; and I think it was good for me to be brought so abruptly into contact with a school of thought that at just that time had to be reckoned with. Under its influence I sloughed off a good deal of foolish prudishness, and I think I acquired a new facility in dealing with ideas. But it was a bad business, an almost grotesque exaggeration of the attitudes that isolate the intellectuals from the rest of society.

Fortunately, not all my colleagues were Menckenians, and if some were worse, some were better. There was one person, Newton Arvin, whose whole world-view was opposed to the

Menckenian liberalism of the twenties, though at that time he was only somewhat better able than I to see how sharp the opposition was. He, too, believed in science and reason, and he was a rebel against Babbittry, but his beliefs went so much deeper than the slogans of the devout Menckenians that they became in effect different beliefs. Science he saw not as the source of superiority, material or intellectual, for a privileged few, but as the foundation of a decent life for all the people. The right to use Anglo-Saxon monosyllables seemed to him less important than the right to speak out against injustice. And literature he refused to regard either as the base raw material of scholarship or, as Mencken would have it, as mere hen-cackling self-expression. He knew what I only suspected, and believed with assurance what I scarcely dared express.

When I returned to Harvard for a year of graduate work in the fall of 1928, the making of an intellectual was nearly complete. All that remained was to see what kind of intellectual I would turn out to be. That year settled one question: I was not going to become a scholar. I wound up my graduate school career with a sprinkling of articles and edited documents in learned journals, just to show that I could do it, and turned my attention to literary criticism.

Three years later we bought the house in Roxborough. During those three years I had taught English at an engineering school, had written many reviews and articles, had become adviser to a publishing house, and had made a substantial start on a book about American literature. More important, so far as the course of my life is concerned, I had become a convert to communism, though not, as yet, a member of the Communist Party. I do not think my conversion to communism is an essential part of this story.[4] Enough has been said to suggest why, in the horrible years of the depression, I should feel that something had to

---

[4] The matter is touched on again in Chapter X. If anyone has any further interest, there is an account in an essay of mine called "Communism and the Intellectuals," which appears in *Whose Revolution?* edited by I. D. Talmadge.

be done, and my reasons for concluding that what I had to do was to support the communists need not be gone into. Nor shall I comment on my activities between 1932 and 1939, though I do believe, on the one hand, that my thinking as a communist was not quite so distorted as I am often tempted to assume and, on the other, that I did disseminate, with the best will in the world, more half-truths than the rest of my life can atone for.

—⁂—

Let us go back to the spring of 1927, when I was finishing my second year at Smith. Many different things entered into the pleasantness of my life in Northampton, but not the least important was my sense of belonging to—of being accepted by—a group of people I liked. This, I think, is the crucial experience for the intellectual, that moment when he finds his milieu. These were men with lively minds, and my mind acquired a faster tempo. New interests budded daily, and whatever interested me interested others. A casual meeting on the campus could be like an electric shock, and long sessions of talk left me drunk with ideas. This was life as I had dreamed it might be led.

But the moment when the intellectual feels that at last he belongs is the moment when his divorce from society becomes absolute, and I had it proven to me that spring if I had been wise enough to read the lesson. We were all wondering whether Governor Fuller would appoint a committee to review the evidence in the case of Nicola Sacco and Bartolomeo Vanzetti, and some of us decided that there should be a meeting for the purpose of asserting the innocence of the two Italians and passing a resolution to be sent to the governor. The civilized liberals supported the project, and so did many men and women of good will whom the civilized liberals looked down upon as Christers. President Neilson agreed to act as chairman, and Felix Frankfurter was invited to speak. The very large audience listened to James Landis, who had taken Frankfurter's place, and when the address was finished, I read the resolution to be sent to Fuller. As the local paper said, "Bedlam broke loose." The townspeople had come in great numbers, determined that the resolution should not be adopted, and their spokesmen—politicians, Legionnaires, business men— took the floor to argue that Sacco and Vanzetti ought to be elec- trocuted and that in any case it was none of the town's business. Because Mr. Neilson ruled, quite properly, that college students were not citizens and therefore had no right to vote, the resolu- tion was defeated.

Of my part in the episode it is enough to say that I am proud of it, only wishing that I had had the courage and the ability to demonstrate more effectively my sympathy with the men Judge Thayer called "those anarchist bastards." I have no doubt that Sacco and Vanzetti were done to death because they were for- eigners and radicals, because a great section of Massachusetts respectability wanted foreigners and radicals to be given a lesson, because the Massachusetts of Calvin Coolidge was determined that its kind of law and its kind of order should be upheld. In the voices that spoke for the death of Sacco and Vanzetti were hatred and cruelty and viciousness triumphant. When John Dos Passos wrote, "all right we are two nations," I knew that this was what I had felt when my diplomatic little resolution—so tactfully, so politely, so meechingly worded—had been roared down. You didn't fool the other nation with careful words, and you didn't overcome it with noble sentiments.

Yet what was this other nation? Was it the rich and powerful of the state? Certainly it was. But it was also the doctors, the lawyers, the shopkeepers, the farmers, the workers. In Northampton—and it was not so different throughout the state—the battle was between the intellectuals and everybody else. It did not seem so strange to me then, for I was still a little under the influence of the civilized liberals, with their talk about the booboisie. But I was troubled just the same, troubled when the good old man across the road, a retired workman of some kind, stared at me in bewildered disapproval, troubled when a crippled newsdealer broke into abuse, troubled when my Italian landlord confessed over a glass of wine that he dared not admit anywhere else in the city his sympathy for his fellow countrymen. What might have troubled me even more, if I had thought about it, was the fact that these were my only contacts, or at any rate typical of what few contacts I had, with the community in which I had lived for almost two years.

Of course we were right and the others wrong, but was being right enough? I do not want to exaggerate the gulf between the Smith faculty and the citizenry of Northampton, for there were pleasant enough relations between some professors and some townsmen, but on the whole the faculty was isolated and particularly the group that initiated the protest meeting. Say that the citizens were moved by the blindest of prejudice, whereas the intellectuals acted on the purest of humanitarian motives; the fact remains that the intellectuals had no chance of convincing the citizens because they couldn't talk to them. From the point of view of the citizens, a bunch of outsiders, who ordinarily ignored the town and all its people, were trying to stir up trouble. Far from responding to any appeal to re-examine their beliefs, they stiffened their backs, fought for all they were worth, and won the battle.

Only eight years had passed since, wrapped in class honors, I had delivered a diatribe against Bolshevism that was what my audience wanted to hear. Now I was being called a Bolshevik. I felt then that the change represented progress, and I would say so now, but I can now see some implications that I wasn't aware of then. In the first community in which I had set myself up as a householder, a husband, and, just that spring, a father, I was an outsider, even an enemy. Eight years had served so to specialize my interests and character that I belonged to another nation.

III

What Came With the House

When we went farm hunting in the spring of 1932, it was simply a house we were looking for, a house in which we could spend our summers. In a general way we knew what we wanted: privacy, a view, open fields, some woods, perhaps a brook. The house, we assumed, would be run down, or else we could not afford it, but an advanced stage of decay would put an impossible strain on our budget and on my meager skills. Taking Troy as a center, we drew a circle with a fifty-mile radius and began to explore the northeast quadrant, which included the southern end of Vermont and the western end of Massachusetts. If we had happened to find our house in a New England state, this would have been a different story, though perhaps the conclusions to be drawn from it would have been substantially the same. As it turned out, we discovered what we were looking for—everything but the brook—fifteen miles from Troy.

The importance of a house should not be underestimated. To people of the middle class owning a house is security and proof of success of life. My parents had never owned a house, and now I owned one. I might be an intellectual, and a radical intellectual at that, but I took the same kind of pleasure in the ownership of property that my mother and father would have taken. And, as a matter of fact, they shared that pleasure, for in time the house became a home for them, too.

There is more to be said about it, however, than that. In 1932 it seemed completely clear to me that the capitalist system was collapsing and that communism was going to take its place. Today I think we are a long way from the kind of communism I envisaged in 1932, but I am not sure that I was wrong about the breakdown of capitalism. At any rate a house and land seemed relatively permanent at a time when banks were closing and factories were going into bankruptcy and even great institutions of learning thinned out their faculties. In the immediate future, I felt, a house might enable a young writer to survive without the salary he had been receiving as a teacher. And in the more distant future, the future that I could not very concretely visualize, when production stagnated and disorder grew, when there were barricades in city streets and the army of the proletariat braced itself for the final conflict, the house and land would still be there. I did not assume that I could or would want to absent myself from the battle, but I had a family to think about, and, even beyond such considerations, there was a feeling that in the house something valid in the world of the past might survive into the world of the future.

My attitude toward the house seems to indicate that I was not reconciled within myself to the detachment of the intellectual class to which I belonged. I wanted roots. The house, it is true, was still only a house, a shelter, an arrangement of rooms; it was not, even potentially, so far as we were concerned, part of a community. But just as a house, a house with land around it, just as seven rooms and a porch and a garden and a lawn and a well and a woodshed and a garage, it deepened our lives as individuals and our life as a family. We lived in it only in the summer and on occasional weekends throughout the rest of the year, but it was there all the time, and we were always conscious of its being there. As more and more of our wishes, our work, and our money went into it, it became our home in a sense that the rented house in which we spent the greater part of the year could not be.

Roxborough, on the other hand, was a post office address and nothing more. The house had to be located within some political framework, and Roxborough happened to be it. There were neighbors, yes, and neighbors who rather quickly became friends,

but otherwise the people of the town were little more than functions: a postmaster, two storekeepers, a man who sold gasoline, a
tax collector, and so forth. And we, on our side, had no more
existence for the natives than they had for us; we were summer
people, and that was that.

When we became all-the-year residents after three years of
being summer people, our status was less changed than might be
supposed. Life was changed, though, and very deeply. We didn't,
I hasten to say, take up farming. We have never had any stock except a few hens, and we have cultivated only a good-sized kitchen
garden together with a potato patch that has sometimes yielded
a salable surplus. I could not have done much farming without
giving up work that was bringing in needed cash, but even on a
part-time basis we might have had more stock and raised somewhat larger crops. The truth is that I felt no inclination to go beyond the minimum of farming that provided a healthy amount of
exercise, and the rocky soil provided a convenient excuse.

It was in less drastic ways that we felt the change. Much that
we, like all city dwellers, had taken for granted now demanded
urgent attention. Preparations for winter, which subsequently
became merely an arduous routine, were something to be
thought and worried. about that first autumn: storm windows to
be bought and painted and put on, the foundation to be banked,
the water system to be protected against frost, wood to be
bought and split and stored. With its kerosene lamps, its wood
and oil stoves, its supplies of food and fuel, the little house became a fortress against winter, and if it was not an impregnable
fortress, there was always Mark Cutter, our experienced and re-
sourceful neighbor, to be called on for reinforcements.

Mark Cutter, who was then in his early sixties, was born in our
house, which had been the home of his mother's family. (This is
a story I shall tell later on.) He went to New York City as a young
man, worked in the ice business, married, and sired five daughters. After his first son was born, he returned to Roxborough,
bought a place near his old home, and took to farming. The

daughters had all married and left home long before we knew the Cutters, and the older son, Stan, was married in 1933. A younger son was at home in the winter of 1935, but he was soon to leave.

One of the friendliest and most generous men I have ever known—and also one of the least astute in the furthering of his own interests—Mr. Cutter took us in hand from the very beginning. It was he who made the repairs the house needed and later undertook more extensive changes, but his help went far beyond the labor for which he charged so modestly. If the pump broke down or the car wouldn't start or a storm window wouldn't fit, I had only to let him know and in no time he had set matters right and merely as a neighborly deed. More than that, he pitied our ignorance, and time and again he came into our kitchen, his blue eyes bright with excitement or his mouth twitching with amusement, and began, "You know, I been thinkin' . . ." And what he had been thinking about was something, we immediately realized, that we should have thought about ourselves.

We might have done badly that winter if it hadn't been for Mr. Cutter, for it was worse than most, and even an average winter is tough enough. We found ourselves thinking a lot about the weather, not the way real farmers do, of course, but in the fashion of country people. With a child to be taken to school, with the getting and sending of mail an important part of my business, with trips to be made to Troy and occasionally to New York, weather mattered. I learned to look at the eastern sky before I was out of bed, almost before I was awake, and I went to the thermometer as soon as I came downstairs. If the temperature was below zero, there was always a question whether the car would start. If snow had fallen, it had to be studied to see whether chains would serve to take the car to the highway. Even if the plow had been through, one had to try to guess from the condition of the snow and the direction and velocity of the wind whether the whole length of the road would be passable. Only a few years earlier the town had had no plow, but in 1935 the least reconstructed old-timer expected his road to be kept open. It was one of the great sights for us, the way the caterpillar would come rolling up the hill, the tumbling drifts brilliant in its lights. But with many miles of road to be taken care of, the plow did not always come, and once that winter we were snowed in for a week—snowed in, that is, so far as the car was concerned; I went on skis each day for the mail and groceries.

It was on my daily trips that year, and especially on the trips that I made on skis, when I would arrive at the post office early enough for the mail to go out and then wait until the incoming mail had arrived and been sorted, that I began to see a little way inside the life of Roxborough. Mostly it was the old men who sat around the post office, men who are dead now. I remember one in particular, a man of more than ordinary dignity, though his shoulders were bent and he walked with a cane. He would sit patiently in the post office, a look of complete composure on his face, and would talk in the most deliberate of voices about past and present. Except for polite greetings and commonplace remarks about the weather, he seldom spoke directly to me, but he clearly had no objection to my listening when he and his contemporaries were gossiping, and sometimes there were explanatory phrases that seemed to be interjected for my benefit. He would ask now and then about the Cutters, who seldom got to the center in the wintertime, or about Wilbur North, who lived on my road, but if I said that Mrs. Cutter had a bad cold or that Wilbur North had cut his foot, it was with the other men that he discussed the news. There was no awkwardness and certainly no intentional discourtesy in this; I was cast in the role of listener, and I made the most of my opportunities.

One direct contact we had with the life of the town, and one obvious stake in its affairs—the education of our daughter. The eight-year-old was enrolled that autumn in the one-room school of which much later I became trustee, and we carried her to and from school, usually twice a day. We attended the annual school meeting the next spring, as we did every spring thereafter, and we lent our support to such improvements as came within the limits of possibility. We both joined the PTA when it was formed, and in time Dorothy became its president.

On the whole, however, we did not belong to the town. The physical setting of our lives was pure Roxborough—rather austere, rather exciting. Roxborough snows, the colors of a bright winter day, spring mud, the stony soil, summer droughts, cool nights for sleeping and warm nights for growing corn, the depth of frost in the ground, the depth of water in the well, the flashing tails of frightened deer, the fox tracks on a snowy morning, the red of maple buds in April, the shad blow storm—all this became the shape and substance of existence. But the part of life that was not physical, that was intellectual and professional and social, had little to do with Roxborough. The manuscripts I read came from New York, and the manuscripts I wrote went there. As a communist I was active in Troy and Albany and New York, but not in Roxborough. Friends came, all summer long and sometimes in the winter too, and they came from the cities, full of the talk that we were so eager for. In all the more important ways I was still leading the life of the isolated intellectual, and I was not dissatisfied. If I stopped to think about the matter at all, I realized that Roxborough could scarcely be expected to welcome a communist with enthusiasm, and I asked only to be left alone.

—⁓—

When Russia signed its pact with Germany and war broke out, we had a houseful of friends with whom we could discuss these events. What Roxborough thought we did not know and did not greatly care. It was a bad time for me, for I could not reconcile myself to the Communist Party's defense of the pact with fascism, but, deeply concerned as I was with a difficult decision, I had practical matters to attend to. There was a cistern to be built, and thus it happened that when two ardent young comrades arrived one morning to labor with me, their arguments were accompanied by the sound of cement being mixed and poured into the cellar beneath us. One of the workers down below was Mark

Cutter, and when the newspapers carried the story of my resignation from the party, he grinned and said, "I knew it was coming."

If my friends from the city felt at once that their mission was
hopeless, I think it was the cement-mixing that convinced them.
Actually, of course, the building of a cistern had nothing to do
with my decision. I had worked steadily on the house during all
the years in which I had been a supporter and then a member of
the Communist Party, and I knew that such work would go on
until I chose or was forced to abandon the place. But what could
these city people make of a man who was having a cistern built
at what was not only a crucial moment in history but also the
turning point of his life? They had never had to think about such
matters as heat and light and water, and my preoccupation with
these things seemed proof that I was fundamentally a petty bour-
geois. No doubt I was, but so in point of fact were my visitors.
The difference lay in the degree of urbanization.

Perhaps revolutionary movements have always depended
largely on detached individuals, whether proletarians who had
nothing to lose but their chains or intellectuals who were without strong social ties. And perhaps one of the things a successful
revolutionary movement does is to give these individuals not
only a cause but also the sense of belonging to a group. Certainly as a communist I had a feeling of identification with the proletariat. It was ninety-nine per cent illusion, as I now realize, for
there were few enough bona fide proletarians in the party, and I
had little contact with those few, but it was a comforting feeling
while it lasted, and I missed it when it was gone.

No doubt the fact that I was one of the "lonely hearts," as an
ex-comrade of an earlier vintage called us, had a good deal to do
with my taking a greater interest in Roxborough. In the fall of
1939 one of the older boys in the village school—now a veteran
of three years' service in the navy—asked me to lead a boys' club.
It was a rudimentary affair, with Friday afternoon hikes and
games and occasional parties and little trips, but it may have had
some value in a community with almost no recreational facilities.

A friend of mine, another ex-communist, wrote to ask what I was doing. With studied masochism I replied, "I am doing a lot of thinking these days, but my sole activity is taking a group of grammar school kids on a weekly hike." Immediately the friend wrote back, "Good for you! At least your boys' club isn't doing any harm, and I grow increasingly doubtful whether this can be said of our activities in the past five years."

Perhaps the great thing was that I had more time. No longer asked to write more and more articles and make more and more speeches, and no longer convinced that I knew how to save the world and would be personally responsible if it were damned, I began to look around. Physically Roxborough was a lovely place to have a house, but I began to wonder whether much could be said for it as a community. It was the only town in the county that had neither a volunteer fire company nor a library. Its people talked openly and without indignation of the corrupt practices of some of its officials. Squalid poverty could be found along some of its roads. Its Catholic church was open only in the summer, and its two Protestant churches were small and rent by quarrelsome factions. Its seven schools were poorly equipped, and some—not all—of its teachers were incompetent.

These are matters that will be discussed later on, and I mention them now only because I was becoming more conscious of them in 1939 and 1940 than I had been before. If at some earlier stage I had had the time to think about Roxborough's shortcomings, I might have plunged into a one-man crusade to remedy them, but I was a chastened man, and I was saved from such folly.[1] I knew that I was powerless to make more than the mildest reforms and that I could achieve these only if I were lucky. I had once thought that I could make the world over, but

---

[1] In 1942 an acquaintance of mine bought a place in a nearby town, and soon reported with likable enthusiasm the half-dozen enterprises he had undertaken for the benefit of the community. This was a man with manifest advantages: a native of the area, well known for his distinguished services in the first World War and for his professional career, a staunch Republican, a born mixer. Yet within a year he had washed his hands of the whole business: the people were stubborn, ungrateful, lost in sin.

I was now prepared to be satisfied with very moderate changes in Roxborough.

It was at that time that I began to write *Only One Storm*. Of course there were autobiographical elements in it and some material of local origin, but I tried to depict a situation different from my own, if only because my own seemed unrepresentative. Fifty miles away, on the other side of the Berkshires, a man I knew was running for selectman of a town about the size of Roxborough. Attending the annual town meeting and celebrating my friend's victory, I felt that here was my theme. The town was less run down than Roxborough, and the New England form of government was more interesting—and, I think, much better—than New York's mongrel system. Moreover, the new selectman had fewer liabilities than I. But the problem, though it posed itself in a form that made solution easier, was the same problem: could a person bring to a small community some benefit from the knowledge and experience he had gained in college, in an urban career, in a world of ideas beyond the small town's life?

Comment on the novel indicated that the problem, at least, was real to one segment of the intellectuals and to many persons who would not lay claim to that title. One of the most thoughtful students of American life wrote me: "You struck a note that will not be forgotten when you made the town the center of the story. That will be an open sesame for the next crop of intellectuals, and you've probably provided hundreds of them with a new direction already. . . . If the intellectuals are off-center, it's because this always was the center—or should have been—when the highbrows were living in a world of abstractions." But on the other hand there were critics who saw little point in writing seriously about small-town politics and no sense at all in writing about town politics and world politics in the same book. "The idea," said one of them in effect, "seems to be that you can help fight fascism on the world level by going into town politics. Paraphrased in that way, it sounds silly—and it does in the book too." I was ready to admit that the achievement of better town government wouldn't in itself offer much protection against fascism, but, I asked myself, if we can't solve the problems of democracy as they present themselves concretely and intimately in our own immediate environment, how much chance have we of winning the larger fight?

—◊—

I was by now convinced that a community had come with the house as well as some handsome scenery, but I was still outside, and I seemed likely to stay outside. It was the war that made the difference. I was in New York City—and that was perhaps symbolic—when Pearl Harbor was attacked, and I do not know how Roxborough took the news, but I shall not forget the sober meeting in the town hall some ten days later. More than a hundred persons were there, and it probably was the most representative gathering Roxborough had seen in a quarter of a century. The old-timers came, stolid or garrulous as the case might be, but eager to know what was going on and, for the moment, willing to help. The less respectable sections of the citizenry were represented, and their representatives, for once, were sober or at any rate quiet. Outsiders came, some of them men and women rarely seen at town affairs. And the back-bone of the town was there—the middle and younger generations, sons and daughters of the old-timers, self-reliant to the point of lawlessness, some of them usually a little shy and some of them usually a little rowdy but all of them now resolute and cooperative.

It was not an inspiring meeting. There were two speeches, one rather bad and the other fairly good, in the course of which we learned that we were to elect a chairman and co-chairman of civilian defense. The Republican boss was tip-toeing about, whispering in this ear and that, and everyone knew that he was picking out the candidates. I know now better than I knew then how many considerations entered into his choice. He could not choose his own associates, for that would provoke criticism and would be, moreover, an assumption of responsibility, which he temperamentally feared. On the other hand, he would not choose prominent Democrats, for they might draw some political advantage from the positions. There was an outsider present, Professor Stonecraft, a stranger to almost everyone, though he had owned a house in town for two or three years. He would make the ideal chairman, for no one knew anything about him and therefore no one could have anything against him. Furthermore, as the politician understood, the townspeople would feel that it was right to entrust such responsibilities to a man of some standing, even though they had no great respect for teachers as such, and for his own part, believing himself to be a practical man and a shrewd one, he had no doubt that he could manage any professor. The position of co-chairman was less important, but it was necessary to find some woman who would take care of the paper work. The politician's eye traveled the hall, and Dorothy's name was whispered to the members of the nominating committee, along with the professor's. The committee duly presented the two names to the citizens, and the citizens apathetically voted for them.

Over across the Massachusetts line, where my friend was serving as selectman, things were done better. The mood of the inhabitants, from what I heard, was much like the mood of my neighbors—somewhat bewildered, somewhat apprehensive, but predominantly courageous and affirmative. The people were no better than the Roxborough people, but because they were in the habit of coming together periodically and discussing their collective affairs, they knew how to conduct themselves when a special town meeting was called for the purpose of electing defense officials and appropriating money. There was an active minority, of course, but the leaders were more representative of the people, and there was more general participation in the making of decisions. As a result of the New England system, civilian defense was well organized in the Massachusetts town at a time when Roxborough and its neighbors were still blundering through a tangle of conflicting authorities and contradictory directives.

It was a pity. For once a goodly number of Roxborough citizens had shown themselves willing to work together, but the politicians had taken matters out of their hands, and they dropped back into their usual lethargy. That is, most of them did. A few of us decided to put up a fight. Perhaps it seems ridiculous now that we—and so many millions of other people—believed in the importance of preparing against air raids. As a matter of fact, we never did suppose that bombs would fall on Roxborough. But we believed in the general program of civilian defense, and we believed that the job ought to be done properly, even in our little town, if only as a patriotic duty and for the sake of morale. Why the politicians wanted to control the defense organization, I have never known. They may have thought that there would be something in it for them, but my guess is that they were tempted by power for power's sake. At any rate they plotted to set things up their way, and we worked against them.

What really committed us to the struggle was a conversation we had with Harvey Dakin. We knew that he had been suggested for the post of chief of the auxiliary police, and we went to ask him if he planned to accept. It was in the early evening, and he was taking a nap after a day in the woods and a hearty supper. He roused himself and sat on the couch, his hair rumpled and his lumberman's shirt full of wrinkles. He knew as well as we why he was being considered: because he was fearless and because he was universally respected in the town, though not universally liked. The politicians realized that he could do the job, and there was almost no one else who could, and though they must have lamented the necessity, they were willing to appoint him. He smoked and scowled and looked up at us. Did we know what would happen, he asked. Sooner or later the politicians would double-cross him, there would be one hell of a row, and the whole organization would break up. We insisted that the politicians could be beaten, and he began telling us stories of dirty politics in the town, stories that seemed incredible then though we have since come to know that they were true. Again and again we assured him that we wanted to fight, no matter what the odds. He brought out the list of men whom the politicians had recommended as auxiliary policemen and characterized certain of them with profane eloquence. We promised to support him if he made his acceptance conditional on his being given the right to select his own men. And when in the end he agreed to take the job, we knew that we should never be forgiven if we let him down.

The fight against the politicians proved less difficult than we had anticipated, but the tasks of civilian protection turned out to be endless. I found myself organizing and attending first aid classes, running square dances to raise funds, waiting on table at suppers, mimeographing a bi-weekly bulletin, collecting salvage, holding forums. Dakin and I evolved an alarm system for blackouts, assigned wardens and policemen to their duties, educated the people. In every blackout I went rushing down the highway, siren screaming, and then did traffic duty until the all clear came. (That, admittedly, was fun. "I'd just as soon have a blackout every night," Dakin said.) To begin with, there were two or three meetings a week, and each new problem involved letters, telephone calls, and personal interviews.

Since I felt as futile as most other civilians in those days, there was satisfaction in doing reasonably well a job that had some connection with the war, but a more abiding satisfaction came from the sense of being part of a group. It was a small group but an active one, and it was held together by a kind of loyalty rare enough anywhere but unprecedented in Roxborough. The members had been chosen by Dakin, who in time became deputy director of civilian protection, and chosen with great wisdom. Some fell away, but the remainder formed a congenial, enthusiastic, and compact group, which held together throughout the war, and even before the war ended had taken its peace-time form as the Community League.

—⁓—

I was no longer on the outside. I was not accepted as a native is accepted, and of course I never shall be. Among the natives, indeed, my activities had probably made me more enemies than friends. But I had become, rather abruptly, a person to be reckoned with in community affairs. In a small town so extraordinary an affair as civilian protection could not come into existence without affecting almost every aspect of the community's life. The wardens and policemen were not strangers who suddenly appeared on the streets when the blackout sirens sounded; they were the same Bill and Jack and Joe that one ran across daily.[2] Moreover, the Defense Council quickly took on secondary functions. The dances and suppers that we held to raise money for equipment made us an important new factor in the social life of Roxborough. Our activity in National War Fund and Red Cross campaigns and our special drive for Christmas presents for servicemen brought us in touch with every family in town, and our bi-weekly bulletin, which Professor Stonecraft and I had lightly undertaken as a way of letting people know what they were supposed to do in blackouts, became a kind of community newspaper. Finally, we were in politics whether we wanted to be or not. Our group had come into existence in the course of a struggle with the local political leaders, and again and again we found ourselves entangled with them. We had a little trouble when new state laws went into effect, but the greatest battle was over the setting up of an honor roll. We proposed to finance construction, but we wanted the town board to provide the site, and in the resulting conflict the town was sharply divided into two factions. Indeed, the existence of such a group as ours inevitably split the passive majority into supporters and opponents. In a town in which politics had always been acutely partisan we became a kind of third entity, as one citizen recognized when he said, speaking of a community project in which he was interested, "We want

---

[2] The personal element sometimes impaired efficiency: "I'm not going to have Hank Dickinson's boy coming round here and telling me whether I can keep my lights on or not." But such difficulties were handled by Dakin's combination of tact and implacable determination.

everybody to be represented—Republicans, Democrats, and Defense Council."

I should be less than candid if I did not admit that I welcomed my new opportunities for participating in town affairs, but having gone as far as I had, I was bound to be drawn into other community enterprises whether I wanted to be or not. When, in the spring of 1944, the establishment of a volunteer fire company was being discussed, Dakin and I were necessarily consulted, for our group included a considerable proportion of the potential firemen. My role in the fire company, as in the Defense Council, was, to think up ideas and take care of the organizational odd jobs. In time it seemed clear to most of us that we could have efficient protection only if we organized a fire district so that we could raise money by taxation. State laws on the subject of fire districts are exceedingly complex, and I had to do more than my share of drawing up forms and securing signatures. As it turned out, there was virtually no opposition, and all that was necessary was a little persistence. When the district was created, I would have been more than willing to consider my job done, but, as I have already told, chance put me on the board of fire commissioners and professional qualifications made me its secretary.

If I was loath to become a fire commissioner, that was not because I had lost my appetite for participation in community affairs but because there were other jobs in which I was rather more interested. In the summer of 1945, when the district was being organized, a free library was being established, and that seemed to me the particular enterprise on which I ought to be spending my energies. The library had been our baby from the first. The suggestion was originally put forward by my mother, and, after it had been approved by the PTA, the idea was passed on to the town board. The members said politely that it was a nice idea, but months went by and they did nothing. ("If Hicks wants a place to store his father's old books," one of them said, "he can put them in my barn.") Seeing no hope of official support, we turned to the Community League, and eventually the league rented half of a private home for the library. With a hard-working librarian and a staff of volunteers, with some surprising gifts of books, and with a much livelier public interest than we had anticipated, the library seemed to deserve all the time that I could spare for it.

By that time also I was entering upon my second year as trustee of common school district number one. This was a job that came to me in the first place by default. In the spring of 1943 Bert Savage, who had been trustee for as many years as we could re-member, was defeated for re-election. The next spring his succes-sor, Bill Garvey, having discovered that the job was arduous and unpaid, refused to run again, and Bert, whose feelings were hurt, also declined to be a candidate. After virtually every other man in the room had been considered, my name was mentioned. It is sometimes so difficult to find trustees that state law provides a fine for a man who refuses to perform the duties once he has been elected, but even with no material rewards and so little honor at stake, there were people in the district who were sore at my being chosen and said they would have come to the meeting if they had had any idea of such a thing's happening. For my part, I entered the office with a certain enthusiasm, feeling that this was the kind of thing I could probably do rather well, and, having spent one year in learning the ropes, I was not sorry to be re-elected.

There was still another reason why I was not eager to become a fire commissioner. There is nothing Roxborough needs more than some place in which the young people can amuse them-selves, and after V-J Day the members of the league began to dis-cuss the possibility of building some kind of community center as a war memorial. But how could any of us, burdened as we all were, undertake the raising of funds?

That is how deeply I found myself involved less than four years after the beginning of civilian defense. There was only one way I could plunge deeper, and that was to hold political office. And in the summer of 1945 a maverick Republican suggested my entering my name in his caucus as a candidate for town supervisor, while a Democratic committeeman seriously proposed my seeking the Democratic endorsement. If I had thought there was a chance of winning the Republican nomination, or if any Democratic candidate had not been foredoomed to defeat, I might have been tempted, but the situation saved me from this particular expense of time. That is not to say, however, that I wasn't "in" politics: in both the primaries and the election word went about that this candidate or that was or was not a Hicks man, and votes were allegedly given or withheld on that basis.

Sometimes we look back with a certain nostalgia to the days when Roxborough was only a post office address, but we know that we cannot return to them. Certainly we might be less involved than we are now, and I hope to unload some of my jobs before very long, but anything like complete withdrawal would be both an admission of defeat and a betrayal of the friends who have worked with us. So long as we live in the town, we cannot do anything to jeopardize the gains that we have helped to win.

Friends ask us why we do it. As I have already intimated, there are selfish reasons, and it is just as well that there are. If we thought we were acting out of pure altruism, we should be unbearable, and if we were looking for appreciation and praise, we should become hopelessly embittered. Our reward comes in the friendships we have made, in the pleasures of belonging to a group, and in the increase of understanding. But there is no sense in our pretending to be more hard-boiled than we are. Along with everything else, we do have a feeling of responsibility to the community. What we get is, indeed, a by-product of what we give. We did not set out to see what we could learn but to see what we could do.

The reader should understand not only that our labors were not received with humble gratitude as the favors of superior beings but also that we did not perform them with Olympian detachment. We have had to fight hard for whatever we have accomplished, and we fought, as often as not, because we were good and mad. In writing about our experiences, I have tried to discount my irritations, my elation over victories, my discouragement and anger in defeat, but don't for a moment believe that I wasn't irritated and discouraged and elated and angry while things were happening. I have said that the author of this book is a person who is deeply involved in the life of a small town, and I should now add that he is also a person who feels strongly about it.

IV

The Rise and Fall
of a Country Town

This town of ours straddles a range of hills lying between the valley of the Hudson and the valley of the Little Hoosac. Going west from Troy, one climbs steadily and crosses the Roxborough border at an elevation of approximately one thousand feet. The climb steepens, and at Roxborough Center the elevation is over fifteen hundred. Just beyond the center the highway begins its descent to the Little Hoosac, and the eastern boundary is some twelve hundred feet above sea level. The highest points in town are better than eighteen hundred. The ridge drops off sharply to the north, but on the south it continues into the adjoining town.

From our house, which has an elevation of sixteen hundred feet, we look eastward across the valley to the Taconics, a thousand feet higher than we are, and beyond them we can see Greylock. The Massachusetts line runs close to the top of the Taconics, only twelve miles away, and a little to the north it gives way to the Vermont line.

This area became the frontier in the latter third of the eighteenth century. I have always been amazed by the rapidity with which the colonies expanded into what Frederick Turner called the Old West. By 1645 the frontier of the Massachusetts Bay Colony was twenty miles west of Boston, and at the close of King Philip's War in 1676 it had been pushed another thirty or forty miles. (Only a little later my father's ancestors began to establish themselves on another frontier—down east in Maine.) From the Connecticut Valley the settlers moved on to the Housatonic: Litchfield (1720), Sheffield (1725), Great Barrington (1730). In King George's War, Fort Massachusetts—just across the Taconics at the foot of Greylock—held the Hoosac gateway, and after 1763 the Berkshire towns were established. By the time the Revolution began, New Englanders had spilled over into York State. Towns near Roxborough had come into existence, and Roxborough itself probably had a few squatters.

In a sense, however, Roxborough's history had begun a century and a half earlier, when Henry Hudson sailed up the river that is named after him and established the Dutch claim to the region. Twenty years after Hudson's voyage, the Dutch East India Company tried to encourage settlement by offering manorial estates and some degree of feudal status to any Dutchman who would plant a colony of at least fifty persons within the next four years. Several Dutch merchants were tempted by the offer, but the people of Holland were not interested in emigration, and only one of the incipient patroons succeeded in maintaining his estate. This was Kiliaen Van Rensselaer, whose million-acre domain embraced the hills on which Roxborough was eventually founded. New York became a British crown colony in 1664, but the patroon system remained.

The expansion of New England brought clashes between Yankees and Yorkers. In the middle of the eighteenth century Massachusetts and New York battled over border territory not far south of Roxborough, and a little later there was fighting in the New Hampshire Grants to the north. In our county, however, the Yankee conquest was peaceful. Troy became a Yankee city, and in the eighteen-twenties Captain Marryat predicted that it would surpass Dutch Albany across the river. Most of the old families in Roxborough have Yankee names, though there are Boomhowers and Barnharts and Schermerhorns to remind us that this soil once belonged to Holland.

No one can be surprised that the Roxborough hillsides were settled only after the less forbidding sections of the Van Rensselaer domain had been put under cultivation. What is surprising is the speed with which settlement progressed once it had begun. A map made in 1767 does not show a single house within what

were to be Roxborough's boundaries. Just forty years later, when
the township was established, it had a population of some fourteen hundred persons.

How hungry for land these New Englanders must have been
to have accepted Stephen Van Rensselaer's terms for his hillside
acres! Many of them came from Rhode Island, a congested area
by their standards. They crossed the Berkshires and the Taconics,
and followed the Little Hoosac northward. The richer acres
were all taken, and at last they turned west and climbed the
ridge. The soil was heavy and filled with boulders. The climate
was severe and the growing season short. But there was land,
and a man could have it for a small outlay. Forgetting that there
would be rent to pay forever and ever, they began to clear their
acres and build their homes. Soon there were enough of them
to petition for the creation of a separate township, and in 1807
they held a town meeting, New England fashion, and elected
their town officers.

—␣␣—

The population of Roxborough continued to grow until, in 1850,
the census showed two thousand residents. But that was the
peak. There was a falling off in 1855, and another in 1860. After
the Civil War the decline became more rapid, and the population
had dropped below fifteen hundred by 1890, below one thousand
by 1915. In 1930 it was down to 633, but the depression years
checked the decline, and the 1940 census showed a population
of 836.

The history of the town is not well documented, but one can
discern three periods. The first, which ended in the eighteen-
fifties, was the period in which Roxborough was essentially a self-
sufficient farming community. The second, extending from the
Civil War to the first World War, was a period of gradual decline.
The establishment of small industries partly offset the decay of
agriculture, but the trend was downward. Roxborough became
less self-sufficient, but it was still isolated. In the third period,

which began with the building of better roads and the more general use of the automobile, the town became a summer resort
and in some degree a suburb. Both self-sufficiency and isolation
had vanished.

I have looked in vain for accounts of life in Roxborough in the
early days, but the State Library has a diary kept by a farmer in a
nearby town, and I doubt if life in Stephentown was very different from life in Roxborough. This George Holcomb, beginning
in 1805, when he was thirteen years old, set down the most factual kind of daily record in his own somewhat eccentric spelling.
In June he "hode" corn, beans, potatoes. In July he did the haying, and. began to "wrip" the oats and rye. On August 7 he
wrote: "I wrip oats and took up oats and finished harvesting."
For a couple of weeks he was laying up stone walls, and then he
drew and husked corn. Corn, potatoes, and apples occupied him
in September and October, and early in November he accompanied his father to Troy to sell the surplus produce. School began
in November, but George found time to thrash oats and rye and
to cut wood. School closed at the end of March, and in April
plowing began. In May he was planting, and in June he "hode"
corn, beans, potatoes.

So year after year went by. Each Sunday George went to
church, sampling all the varieties of preaching to be found in the
vicinity. Occasionally he made a trip to the store. In the winter he
attended school when it did not interfere with his work. Of the
observance of holidays there is no record in the early years: school
was. held on December 25 as on other days. Only illness—and he
was not a robust youth—interrupted the routine, and only funerals offered diversion. The great event of each year seems to have
been the autumnal trip to Troy with produce. It took two and
sometimes three days to make the journey and carry on the necessary business, and the Holcombs returned with a small collection of manufactured and imported goods and a little cash.

As George grew older, his life became a little more varied. He
began to attend quiltings and balls now and then, and once in a

while he undertook a trading expedition on his own account. On October 9, 1810, he writes: "I went to Dr. Griggs' to see the Magic Lantern." That same month an uncle, a sea captain from Boston, came to visit the Holcombs. The following winter at least two balls took place, and in the early spring there was a singing school. The great event of 1811, however, was a hanging in Troy. After briefly stating the details of the crime, George writes: "The people that went to see Russell hung was estimated about ten and some say twelve thousand. I spent two shillings."

On June 27, 1812, George noted in a postscript that Congress had declared war on Great Britain. The event was to have some effect on his life. He had already been exempted from service in the militia on the ground of deafness, but he was not sure that the exemption would be continued, and he quietly crossed the border into Massachusetts. That winter he worked for an uncle who lived near Worcester. In the spring he went to Boston to look for work—staying with the aunt whose husband was a sea captain. Unable to find a job, he returned to his uncle's, and then sought employment in a cotton factory. At last he found work on a farm, his employer agreeing to pay him $95 for six months, "and he is to find me in Sperits in the time of haying and harvest and no other time except more than common work for farmers." George worked his six months and two days extra, and returned to Stephentown in November of 1813.

As a young man in his early twenties, George Holcomb was clearly a person of considerable enterprise, for his diary is full of references, sometimes rather obscure, to trading ventures, loans, and partnerships. One partnership involved him in a brawl and eventually a law suit, and he had a whole series of unfortunate experiences with blacksmiths whom he imported from neighboring towns. An expedition on foot to Boston, apparently with the intention of purchasing shoes to be sold in Stephentown, ended in serious illness. Other deals and excursions, however, were more successful. In 1815 he obtained a license to distill cider brandy, and his product seems to have been popular. He often sold cider at muster days and town meetings not only in Stephentown but also in Lebanon, Hancock, and Pittsfield. Trips to Troy and Albany became more frequent, and the produce he carried became more specialized—a load of apples, a load of cider, so many dozen live geese.

Invariably George took the trouble to set down the price of what he bought and sold. On December 2, 1814, for example, he reported that he had paid $1.15½ for three drinking glasses and forty-seven cents for three pints of cider brandy. A few days later he bought a toasting iron that was priced at $1.50; he gave for it a bushel and a half of corn and 18½ cents. The next February he and his brother sold ten and a half bushels of apples for $11, and fifteen "ded" geese for $6.45. On that occasion he recorded only that they "traded considerable," but a year later he set down purchases as well as sales. After receiving $18.50 for four barrels of cider, he bought two and a half bushels of salt at 88 cents a bushel, a pound and a half of green tea at $1.37½ a pound, three pounds of brown sugar at 18¾ cents a pound, a gallon of linseed oil for $1.12½, a silk bonnet for his sister for three dollars, and some iron for the wagon for 84 cents.

Looking through the ten thousand pages of the diaries, one feels that almost the dominant motif is the eagerness for cash. Although George Holcomb was able to raise most of what he needed and could secure some additional supplies by bartering his produce for them at the local stores, he was always conscious of what could be bought if he had money. The diary records dozens of enterprises that he undertook with more or less success. But he remained a farmer to the end, and he never got very far from a subsistence economy. The record of the summer of 1855—the summer before his death—sounds much like the record of fifty years earlier except that now it is "I and my two sons" who "hoad" corn, beans, potatoes.

George Holcomb was not an imaginative diarist, and yet, for all the bareness of his chronicle, it gives a picture of the man and his times. The man was hard-working, a little inclined to self-righteousness, deeply secretive. (Although he frequently names the candidates in an election, he never tells for whom he voted.) He was not only a regular church-goer but had some speculative interest in religion, for among the few books he purchased were works of theological controversy. On the other hand, he could not have been a sectarian, since he attended all the churches in the vicinity with complete impartiality. Judging from quarrels and law suits he mentions, one thinks of him as a man determined to stand on his rights and one not likely to be popular, but he retained certain close friends throughout his lifetime. Although his diary shows that he was interested in what went on in Stephentown, he played only a meager part in the life of the community, and the only political office he held was that of assessor. He portrays himself as a practical man, not greedy but attentive to the main chance. The only mystery is why he began and so faithfully maintained his chronicle of days that were so largely uneventful.

As for the times, their austerity makes itself felt sharply enough on these yellowed ledger pages. It was a period when a man worked hard and minded his own business.

Yet George speaks often of "changing" work with his neighbors, and he rarely went to the village without having a drink or two with friends. Church services, political meetings, and funerals served as social occasions, and the unmarried set had its gayer gatherings. There was a surprising amount of travel, in view of its difficulties, and relatives were constantly visiting or being visited. The center of life was the farm, and its demands came first, but beyond that there was the community, and much further on, but still within the limits of consciousness, was the nation. George Holcomb was no man to set down his political philosophy, but there are references enough to indicate that he knew what was going on.

That Holcomb was representative of his age can be gathered from the meager documents that survive here in Roxborough. I have seen, for instance, the day books for 1844 of a general store operated in this town by Ebenezer Stevens and Daniel Saunders. Both men were prominent citizens, and each served several terms as town supervisor. Stevens, according to the county history, came to Roxborough from a neighboring town at the age of twenty, worked diligently, and in due season owned fourteen hundred acres of land, three sawmills, a half interest in the store, and shares in a couple of turnpikes. Saunders also had a farm, a sawmill, and other enterprises.

It was the custom of Saunders and Stevens to enter in the day book every transaction involving either debt or credit. Each customer was assigned a number, and I assume that the entries in the day books were transferred at some point to customers' accounts. The cost of each item was set down in shillings and pence, though the amount due was given in dollars and cents:

Daniel Saunders	Dr.	
to 5 lb. rice at /4	20	
1 yd. calico at 1/	13	33
Truman Burdick	Dr.	
to 30 3/4 sheeting at 1/	3.84	
3 yds, pant cloath at 1/9	66	
1/2 lb. tea at 2/6	31	4.81

Coffee, tea, salt, pepper, and molasses were the principal groceries, with rice, codfish, sugar, and candy not uncommon items. Pork was apparently the only meat the store carried, and was of local origin. Butter, apples, and potatoes were also purchased locally, the sellers being given credit on the day books. The store sold a good deal of cloth and thread, a variety of pills and plasters, almanacs, spelling books, bed cords, chamber pots, mittens, axes, and combs. Prices of imported goods had dropped in the past two or three decades. Tea, for example, sold at from sixty-five to eighty-five cents a pound, whereas George Holcomb in the twenties had paid from $1.25 to $1.50. Some manufactured goods were cheaper, too, notably all kinds of cloth.

Saunders and Stevens bought kegs, hooppoles, and staves. For each keg they paid five and a half, five and three-quarters, or six cents according to size. I do not know how many kegs a man could make in a day, but I have an idea that ten or twelve was a good day's work. I note that a man was paid sixty-eight cents for "one day's work bolting and board himself." When either Saunders or Stevens boarded one of their workmen, the usual charge was $1.25 a week. Local produce did not bring much: twelve and a half cents a pound for butter, fifty cents a bushel for corn, $2.50 a cord for dry wood.

Many transactions were carried on without benefit of cash. If a man owed money, he would ask Saunders and Stevens to assign to his creditor's account the price of the butter or the corn he sold to the store. One particularly complicated transaction appears on the books. A man had dressed 7900 staves at the mill at nine shillings a thousand, and was credited with $8.89. He had also done five and a half days' work at six shillings a day, earning $4.15, and six days' haying at eight shillings a day, earning $6. However, he was charged with $7.59 for thirty-six days' board, and Saunders was credited with $2.53 for twelve of these days and Stevens with $5.06 for the other twenty-four.

Almost any of the old families would serve to epitomize the history of Roxborough. The man who settled our farm was Ezra Easton, a Mayflower descendant, who migrated from Rhode Island about 1790. He was fifty-five years of age at the time, and grown sons came with him, bringing their wives and children. One son pushed further west almost immediately, but others took up nearby farms. Two of them sold out, however, and went west after the death of their father in 1803, and eventually only David Easton was left in the town, occupying the home place. He had married the daughter of another pioneer, and in 1807, when the township was set up, he was one of twenty-two men chosen as overseers of highways and fence viewers. In 1821 he was appointed justice of the peace by the governor, and he was several times elected to the same office. From 1833 to 1835 he served as town supervisor. His sons, like his brothers, grew impatient with Roxborough soil, and all but one of them went west. This one—also a David—lived with his father and inherited the place. But he had no sons who lived to manhood, and the name of Easton died out in Roxborough, though in a western county annual reunions attract Eastons by the score.

Neither the elder nor the younger David Easton is mentioned in any records of industrial or commercial activity. Apparently they were farmers and nothing else, and one can assume from the prominence of the elder David that he at least was a successful farmer by the standards of the times. The fact that his brothers sold their farms and went west may be regarded as evidence of the obduracy of the soil, but it would seem that a hard worker could manage to make a living. I assume that the two Davids, like George Holcomb and his father, made annual or semi-annual pilgrimages to Troy with surplus produce and that the small amount of cash they received was sufficient to their needs and those of their families.

In 1856, two years before his death, the elder David Easton, "being weak and sickly in body but perfect in mind and memory," made his will. To the younger David he bequeathed the house and forty-three acres of land, including the orchard, the remainder of the land to be divided among the other three sons. David also was to inherit "my pair of work horses and two horse waggon and two horse harness sleigh and cutter, and all my chains and iron bar, and two large iron kettles and my scraper, and my clock and all my farming tools." Certain livestock was to be sold so that one hundred dollars could be paid to one son and fifty dollars to another. From the last items in the will one can discover what of David Easton's possessions, aside from the farm itself and the farm equipment, were considered of value: "Twelfthly, I bequeath to my sons David, Lester, William, and Moses my three beds and bedding, table linnen and towels and window curtains, to be equally divided between the four after my decease. Thirteenthly, I bequeath to my son Moses my new

trunk and wearing apparel. Fourteenthly, I bequeath the pro-
ceeds of a lot of wool of two hundred pounds now in the hands
of Almon Green for him to make sale of, for me, for which I hold
the receipt for the same, to be equally divided between my four
children provided I don't use the same before my decease. Fif-
teenthly, I bequeath to my son David my large brass kettle, after
my decease. Sixteenthly, I bequeath to my son William my small
brass kettle, after my decease. Seventeenthly, I bequeath to my sons
Lester and Moses the value of the two brass kettles equally between
them in money from my personal property, after my decease."

The county history lists some of the principal events of the
first fifty years of the town's existence. In 1813 ten school districts
were set up under the new state law. In 1819 a doctor settled in
the town, and became a social and political leader. Many of the
early settlers, coming as they did from Rhode Island, were Baptists,
and groups seem to have met in various parts of the town from
the earliest years. It was not until 1827, however, that a Baptist
society was formed and held regular services in the church built
by Stephen Van Rensselaer, the good patroon, for all denominations. In 1828 the Methodists formed a society, building a church
in the western part of the town and also holding services in the
patroon's church. There were notable Methodist revivals in 1843-
44, and meetings were held in the Patroon Hotel, the landlord
being among the converts. In 1850-51 there were successful Baptist revivals, and the next year the Baptists built their present
place of worship. It was not until 1877 that the Methodists had a
church in the center of town.

It is reported that the patroon built a gristmill as early as 1802.
The assessment rolls of 1813 show four cider mills, three sawmills,
a gristmill, two cheese houses, a blacksmith shop, a shoe shop,
and two stores. About 1830 a paint factory was started in the
southwest corner of the town, and about 1850 a rival concern was
established in the settlement near the western boundary. Aside
from farming, however, lumber was the principal source of income, and countless sawmills were set up in the first half of the

century, the many fast-running streams providing ample power. Charcoal and tan bark were sold in considerable quantities, and so, as we have seen, were kegs and hooppoles. In 1880 the county historian could lament the destruction of "the immense forests of the town."

The assault on the forests, as the historian notes, was accelerated by the necessity of paying an annual rent to the patroon. The rent system imposed a peculiar hardship on the farmers in the hilly country on both sides of the Hudson, and it is not surprising that the anti-rent movement was popular in Roxborough.[1] The town produced none of the leaders of the movement, though the town doctor was an active participant. There was a single flare-up of violence: in 1844, when anti-renters in the customary Indian disguise were demonstrating against a notorious up-renter, a shot was fired and the up-renter was killed. It was generally believed that the murderer was settling a private grudge, but the incident was one of several that helped to discredit the anti-rent cause and at the same time served to call attention to the need for reform. A hundred years later back rent was still a problem to plague the lawyers whenever property changed hands.

In spite of the rent system and all the other obstacles that Roxborough set in the way of its people, the population, as we have seen, continued to grow throughout the first half of the century. There was a falling off in 1845, when the agitation against the patroons was strong, but five years later the town reached its peak. All this time there was a constant emigration, but the birth rate was high, and there was always a newcomer to purchase a farm as soon as it was offered for sale. In Roxborough, as elsewhere, men sought eagerly for ways of augmenting their cash income, but the opportunities were few, and a subsistence economy prevailed. I imagine that some families did very badly,

---

[1] For a complete account of the rent system and the anti-rent wars, see Henry Christman's *Tin Horns and Calico*.

and the cemeteries testify to the high rate of infant mortality, but men did make a living, and sons and daughters did grow up. Moreover, the people managed to build schools and churches and to maintain roads, and several storekeepers seem to have prospered. By modern standards, even by the standards of modern Roxborough, the life was meager enough, and there is no sense in trying to idealize it, but the people had shelter and food and fuel and a comforting degree of security.

—∿—

By 1850 the situation had changed. Thanks to the railroads, wheat could be imported from the West more cheaply than it could be raised in New England or in the Hudson Valley, and butter and cheese from western New York were underselling the local products. At the same time the growth of industrialism was providing new opportunities. In earlier years men had left Roxborough to take up farming in more fertile regions, but now it was the factories that tempted them. Roxborough could still offer a hard-working man a livelihood, but it was not likely to provide him with much cash. Sons of Roxborough farmers went to work in the factories of Troy and other cities, and daughters entered domestic service. The decline of the population was slow, but it was relentlessly steady.

Industrialism contributed in another and more direct way to the abandonment of the subsistence economy. In the early eighteen-fifties Walter Middleton took a contract with a New York City firm for the making of shirt bosoms and collars. At first the work was put out into families and the sewing done by hand, but Middleton soon introduced the sewing machine, and its use became general. In 1856 he began the manufacture of shirts, and a factory was subsequently built. By the end of the Civil War, Roxborough had a flourishing industry of its own.

The Civil War accelerated the advance of industrialism and thus had an important influence on the destinies of Roxborough. Its immediate effect, however, was to take out of the town some seventy-five men, thirteen of whom lost their lives. Among the men who returned was John Cutter, father of our neighbor. John Cutter wrote home with some regularity—or, rather, got his slightly more literate companions to write for him—and his son has preserved the letters. Mostly John complained about the food, the weather, and the marching, but he wrote with some jubilation after Gettysburg: "We left Centerville the 25th of June and have been chasing up old Lee's army ever since, and we found them up to Getisburg Pa, and we gave them one of the worst whippings they have had since this war broke out. We piled them up in winroes. The rebbels loss killed wounded and taken prisoner is 40,000 and our loss is only 10,000. . . . We mean to go through the rebs like a dose of salts, we have been fooling with them long enough."

Occasionally he indulged in a patriotic outburst. "You wrote in your letter that the folks was going to resist the draft and fight at home. I think it is a shame fir them to talk so, and every man that talks like that ought to be shot, and I should like to be the man that was to do it. Do they think they are any better to come and fight than the rest of us? I am willing to die fir my country if necessary, and every man that tries to resist it had ought to be shot without judge or jury. This rebellion must be put down or our country is ruined. I had rather be shot today than to see the Confederate flag flying over our northern states, which if not put down must be ruled by the Confederates. There is a number of men in Roxborough I should like to see here on this draft. Tell G.R. not to be scart, it is nothing but fun. Tell him if he is drafted to come without trying to resist it. He can learn more here in two months than he ever learnt in his life."

Now and then he had a piece of luck: "Today has been a very beautiful and pleasant day as I ever saw, we have had exelent wether here all winter. I am living highly this winter. You see I am cook for the captain and he keeps a barrel of beer on hand all the time and I have all I want to drink and all the apple dumplings that I want to eat too." He could achieve a cocky note, even in writing to his father. "Wall old man, you ought to be here in our camp and hear the balls whistle around our heads. I think if you was you would stick up your ears like a scart mule and scamper for life, but we have got so accustomed to it that we care little about them. . . . I want you to write and tell me all the news that is flying about and what is going on in the neighborhood and so on. . . . How does the men feel about election this fall and who does the majority talk of, Abe or McClellen? We think we shall elect old Abe again this fall for we all like to fight and Abe is the man to fight it out and make Peace that will stand firm and lasting." Often he asked for news of the girls at home and was piqued by their silence: "If any of my old sparks wish to know anything about me tell them that I have come acrost a rich young widow down here and shall marry her if nothing don't happen. They can all kiss my ass if they wish to, for I ask as little odds of them as they do of me. But I think I shall go north on my wedding tour and show them a Va. beauty and heiress, so please to give them all my compliments and say goodbye to all of them for me." Once in a long while he—or his amanuensis— struck a poetic note: "We all are very anxious to return to our friends and home again. Yes, I shall hail with unbounded joy the life and freedom of a Citizen again. I think I have been away long enough to appreciate it." His last letter, written after Lee's surrender, describes a personal exploit: "I suppose you have heard before this time that I have been promoted to Sergt. Wall I will tell you how it happened. In the charge on a fort near the south side of the road the color sergt. fell out sick and I picked up the colors and unfurled them and went on into the charge, and the colonel promoted me there on the field and I have carried the colors ever since."

So John Cutter returned to civilian life with his share of military glory though without the Virginia heiress. He married Elizabeth Easton, daughter of the second David, and eventually bought the Easton place. Of his three sons, only two lived to manhood, and one of these died in middle age without issue.

The third, however, our Mr. Cutter, was to do his share for pos-
terity. As for John, he lived until 1917, and the old-timers remember him as a man fond of company and drink and full of
stories about the Civil War. "He was a card," an old-timer said to
me once, adding, "A good card." He must have worked reasonably hard to make any living at all out of the hill farm, but more
industrious men thought of him as self-indulgent.

Some Roxborough farmers did moderately well in the seventies and eighties. "The soil is chiefly clay," wrote the county historian in 1880, "underlaid by hard pan, and is wet, cold, and hard
of cultivation. Yet, under proper management, excellent crops of
oats, potatoes, and grass are produced. The raising of sheep and
cattle is extensively carried on, and the produce of the dairy is of
considerable value." As far as I can make out, however, neither
dairying nor sheep-raising was ever practiced on a large scale, and
though there was almost certainly an increase in cash crops, farming was done chiefly for the sake of subsistence.

The county history gives a concise account of the town in the
late seventies, when it had a population of some sixteen hundred.
There were three villages. East Roxborough at the time was a
small hamlet of half a dozen houses, a store, a blacksmith shop,
and a wagon shop. The hotel serving passengers on the stagecoach line, was said to be prosperous. West Roxborough also had
a hotel as well as a blacksmith shop and a post office. It was here
that the larger of the two paint factories—"an enterprise of considerable magnitude"—was located. Roxborough Center had
two churches, a school, three stores, two hotels, a post office,
two blacksmith shops, a wagon shop, two shoe shops, a chair
factory, and two shirt factories.

Roxborough Center in this period was dominated by the two
sons of the Walter Middleton who had started the shirt business.
Between them they operated the shirt factory, two stores, a hotel,
and the post office. The factory is said to have employed as many
as three hundred persons, though some of them probably did
their work in their homes. The Middletons also owned large

farms, and their standard rate of pay for men was a dollar a day, a man to work either on the farm or in the factory according to the weather and the will of the owners. Most of the factory employees were women, and the story goes that the men would drive their wives to the factory and then sit around the stores all day until it was time to drive them home again. Doubtless there were men who did this, but for most families the Middleton enterprises must have provided just that margin of cash that made life endurable. The Middletons prolonged the transition from a subsistence to a money economy and rendered it less painful for the people of the town.

The Middletons—three generations of them—dominated the sixty years that constitute the second period of Roxborough history. One Middleton or another was town supervisor during about a third of that time, and they had a good deal to say about other occupants of the office. They owned the principal hotel, the principal store, and, most important of all, the principal factory. It was their town, and they seem to have ruled it reasonably well.

Toward the end of the century Roxborough discovered a second source of income—summer visitors. The town had lakes, woods, and mountain air, and for the working-class people of Troy it seemed the ideal place, only a cheap stagecoach ride away, for a week's or two weeks' vacation. The Middletons got their share of the trade and more, but almost anyone who had spare rooms could find boarders eager to take them.

But in spite of all these new opportunities, the population dwindled, and with increasing rapidity after 1900. The Middletons tried to counteract the tendency by making the town more attractive: they set aside a park for the use of the citizens, provided kerosene lights in the center of town, encouraged the holding of ball games and band concerts. Old-timers and some men and women who are not so old tell me that life was very pleasant here in the first decade of the twentieth century. Wages were low, but there was plenty of work, and farmers found a market for their surpluses. The town was full of life all summer long, and even the winters were busy for those who lived near the center. But the population continued to fall.

When I first moved to Roxborough, I was surprised to discover a considerable number of men in their sixties or early seventies who had worked for a decade or two in New York City. Mark Cutter was one of them, and Wilbur North down the road was another. The dignified old man I used to talk to in the post office, the man from whom I bought my butter, the man I went to see about building a chimney—all had worked in New York and all in the ice business. It appeared that a certain family had found the ice business profitable, and one ambitious Roxborough boy after another had set out for the city. It is remarkable that so many returned, and, as I shall point out later on, the fact that they did return has had a strong effect on the town, but of course there were many more that went away and didn't come back.

In 1915 Roxborough had only half as many people as it had had in 1850, but it still seemed to be a prosperous, self-sufficient little town. If people wanted more out of life than their stony soil could yield, there was a factory in which a man or his wife could work, and there were summer visitors to board. A man could have the security that subsistence farming gives and still enjoy a standard of living comparable to that of the cities. He could live with fair comfort in a compact, comprehensible, neighborly community.

—ɷ—

The second and third periods overlapped. In a sense the third period began when a state highway was built between Troy and Roxborough about 1912. On the other hand, the second period didn't come to a full stop until the closing of the shirt factory about 1922. Rather surprisingly the factory wasn't forced out of business; the eccentric heir of the Middletons arbitrarily decided to close it. Other Middleton enterprises went the same way. The big hotel was still standing when we moved to Roxborough, but it had not been used for many years, and it was subsequently taken down. Robert Middleton operated a store in the early thirties, but that, too, closed its doors some years ago. All the Middleton land went for taxes, much of it falling into the hands of Mark Betterton, the town's leading merchant. It was by courtesy of Betterton that Robert Middleton continued to live—quite by himself—in the pretentious family house on the highway.

The decline of the Middleton fortunes accelerated the decay of Roxborough as a place where a living could be made, but at best the decay could only have been retarded. In some neighboring communities small factories managed to hold on through the thirties, and some of them prospered in the early forties, but the movement of population was not much affected. Roxborough might be better off today if it had had some kind of industrial enterprise during the past twenty-five years, but these small-town businesses usually survive by virtue of the low wages they pay, and it is a question whether they do more good than harm. If city jobs are available, the small-town factory cannot compete. It may help the families that for one reason or another cannot or will not leave, but it does not dam the main stream of emigration.

Such reasoning, however, would not have given much comfort to the people of Roxborough back in 1922, for it must have seemed to them that the foundations of the town had crumbled. And, indeed, it is true that the population suddenly slumped. What people did not realize was that the improvement of the highway and the availability of cheap cars had changed the whole character of Roxborough's problem. Winter driving was still hazardous, and in the twenties only a venturesome few commuted to jobs in Troy and the vicinity. In the thirties, on the other hand, only a lucky few had jobs to commute to. But in the forties it suddenly became clear to everyone that Roxborough had become a suburb of Troy.

If the automobile made it possible for people to go on living in Roxborough, it speeded the decay of the community, for families with cars—and a car quickly became a major necessity—were drawn closer to Troy. People went to Troy for recreation, chiefly the movies, and they began to do more and more of their shopping there. Babies were born in Troy hospitals rather than in Roxborough homes, and patients were taken to Troy doctors. Boys and girls, transported by bus, attended the Troy high school. The automobile also increased mobility within the town, enabling the families that lived in remote sections to take part in village affairs, but it was less important as a unifying than as a disintegrating force.

Moreover, the automobile changed the character of Roxborough's summer population. Before 1915 summer visitors had congregated in boarding houses near the center of town, but in the twenties private homes were built on the shores of several lakes. Old-timers tell me that in the earlier period there were friendly relations between the summer people and the natives, but by 1932 the summer people were largely a race apart. They drove through the town, their cars loaded with supplies they had bought in Troy, and were scarcely aware of its existence. Economically they were an asset, for even the small proportion of buying they did in Roxborough was important to the storekeepers. Furthermore, they paid disproportionately high taxes, and they sometimes employed local workmen. By and large, however, they had no contact with townspeople and no interest in the town. Catholics were and are a partial exception, for they attend the local church—which really exists for their benefit—and support its money-raising affairs.

The career of Mark Cutter illustrates the transition from the second period to the third. Mark, it may be recalled, was one of the Roxborough men who went to New York to try his hand at the ice business. The prosperous Madisons, who were friends and in some degree relatives of his, found him a boarding house that was kept by emigrants from Roxborough, and got him a job. They had a maid, a girl from just such a town as Roxborough, and Mark married her. In the next ten years, while his wife bore

him five daughters, he managed to save enough—from wages of
$12 a week—to buy a two-family house over in New Jersey and
one of the first automobiles on the market. At last a son was
born, and perhaps it was reluctance to bring up a boy in the city
that made Mark think about Roxborough. What he always says
is that it was spring and he just got homesick. With financial aid
from the Madisons he bought a farm adjoining the old Easton
place, our present home, where he was born and where his father
was still living.

For ten years or so Mark contrived to make a living by farming, but I gather that he never cared much for farm work. John
Cutter died in 1917, and Mark, who had inherited the Easton
place, sold it to a man who wanted to cut off the lumber. A few
years later the place, shorn of its trees, was sold to a college professor, the man from whom we bought it in 1932. Meanwhile a
doctor had built a summer camp nearby, and he and the professor hired Mark to do carpentering, plumbing, gardening, road-
building, and anything else they needed done, for he has the
versatility of the traditional Yankee. We came along in our turn,
and, as I have told, quickly learned to depend on Mark Cutter.
More and more he abandoned farming, until he had no horse,
only one cow, a few hens, and a garden patch.

Down the road was another farmer who had gone to New
York in his youth. (A persistent legend said that he had made a
small fortune, but it was not to be found on his death.) More energetic than his neighbor and also less versatile, he did as much
farming as his age would permit. He had a pair of horses and a
cow, raised potatoes for the market, and harvested his hay.
("Them fields ain't gonna grow up to alder so long as I can set
my ass on a mowing machine.") He worked hard, and all things
considered did wonders. The great part of his cash income, however, came from a batch of one-room cottages that he rented to
summer people.

Cash income bulked small in many budgets during the early
thirties. A few men had jobs in Troy all through the depression,

but the majority had to take what they could find in Roxbor-ough. They farmed, they worked on the town and county roads, they cut wood (at two dollars or less a cord), and they did odd jobs for the summer people. There were no WPA projects in Roxborough, and only small amounts of direct relief were dis-tributed, but people seemed to get along. Moreover, they were less unhappy than the urban unemployed, for they could always find things to do, and almost everybody was in the same boat. I remember a story that Stan Cutter told me about the early de-pression days. He was single then and living at home, and he had no trouble getting by with two or three days' work a week. In fact, he managed to accumulate enough cash to make a down payment on a car that he coveted. And then his troubles began. Each time an installment was due, it would seem that he couldn't possibly raise the money, but month after month he managed to get just enough work to pay what he owed. Finally, however, his luck failed him, and the company had flatly refused an ex-tension. He went to one of the old-timers, a frugal man who had accumulated some capital in the ice business and had done rather well as a farmer and craftsman in Roxborough. He lent Stan the money. "And after that," Stan said, "it was plain sail-ing. I got a regular job, met the payments on the car, and paid Walt what I'd borrowed. But, boy, I thought I'd lost that Chevrolet!"

The depression forced people back on the town, and the population rose in the thirties. This gain was not lost in the early forties, perhaps because of the housing shortage in the cities. What happened was that Roxborough became a commuting town. In the summer of 1945 I could account for nearly a hun-dred men who had jobs in Troy and other nearby cities, and less than a third of these had had city jobs before 1940. Some of the others had been forced to work in the city because of the decline of the tourist trade, but most of them had given up uncertain and poorly paid employment in the country for the sake of de-fense factories' high wages. At the same time the demand for pulpwood was providing a boom in Roxborough's one industry, and men were being imported to cut wood.[2]

It was against this background of prosperity that most of the events described in this book took place. With the end of the war, people in Roxborough, like people everywhere else, were wondering what was going to happen. The future of the town is something to be talked about later on, but the immediate effects of the cessation of hostilities deserve to be noted here. Thirty or thirty-five men that I know of were thrown out of work almost as soon as Japan surrendered, and most of them had no trouble in finding jobs. A few of them went to work in Roxborough, and many others could have found work here, not only in the pulp industry but also in private construction. A good many, however, including several who had not worked in Troy before the war, have taken city jobs. I doubt if they prefer to work in the city; on the contrary; but that is where they think security lies.

If employment remains at a high level in this region, Roxborough will become more and more a combination of suburb and summer resort. If there is a general depression, people will be forced back on the town as they were in the thirties. If, on the other hand, the Capital District is less prosperous than other parts of the nation, the more ambitious Roxborough youths will go where prosperity is. One thing the town's hills and lakes do seem to guarantee—an enduring future as summer resort. And perhaps some day a planning board will consign the whole township to this role. Already a government survey map indicates that the greater part of Roxborough is fit only for reforestation.

---

[2] The woodchoppers were mostly floaters, who lived in shacks provided by their employers and appeared in the village only on periodic drunks. On the other hand, their food and drink were usually purchased locally and represented a considerable amount of money. Furthermore, the owners and operators were chiefly local men, and other residents were employed as truck drivers or helpers at higher wages than they had ever received before. Farmers and other self-employed workers cut and drew pulpwood as a subsidiary source of income.

V

The Influence of a Ghost

Prosperity reached Roxborough in the middle forties, but the town didn't change much. People wore better clothes when they bothered to get dressed up, and there seemed to be more drinking, but it is hard to think of other changes. Of course war conditions prevented people from spending money in what might be characteristic ways—for new cars, for instance, or in travel, or on domestic improvements. But deeper than that, I feel sure, was a basic conservatism, a positive resistance to change. Whatever their income, the majority of natives had no intention of adopting city ways.

As Roxborough's old-timers had once been concentrated in the New York City ice business, so a considerable number of war workers were concentrated in a particular chain factory in Troy. In a way this concentration was an accident. The manager was married to a Roxborough girl, and her brother was given a job there. He told his friends of the high wages paid to those who could learn the craft and the good wages paid for unskilled labor. But it was not merely money that attracted the men of Roxborough, for they could have made as much elsewhere. What appealed to them was the traditional independence of the chainmaker. Conditions in the plant were the opposite of those to be found in any Taylorized factory, and the Roxborough men knew it. Other Roxborough men worked in garages and small plants. Few subjected themselves to the discipline of the automatic machine and the production belt.

Our civilian protection group included two chainmakers, a factory maintenance man, a first-rate garage mechanic, and two men in the wood business. The stamp of the town was on them all. According to Arnold Toynbee, medieval England "was a congeries of village communities—interspersed with boroughs as a cake is sprinkled with plums. . . . The people with whom any given subject of the King was likely to have a common political interest were the people whose homes lay within a day's walking or riding distance of his own." But thanks to industrialism, Toynbee continues, "the link of locality has lost its significance for political as well as for most other social purposes. . . . The true constituency has ceased to be local and has become occupational." This is what has *not* happened to my friends in Roxborough: occupational ties are for them far less important than local ties. They go into the world of industrialism, but their hearts stay in Roxborough. Of course they are affected by their urban experiences, but the effects are marginal; at the core they are unchanged.

This means that in spite of everything Roxborough has remained Roxborough. Like every other outsider, I have long been conscious of the massive strength of the natives. In the local vocabulary a native is a person who was born in the town or—to take care of the children the old-timers had while they were in New York—a person who was born elsewhere of Roxborough parents and grew up in the town. The term may be stretched further to include persons who have lived in the town from childhood or youth, especially if they came from small towns and more especially if they have married into Roxborough families.[1]

As nearly as I can make out, approximately three out of four heads of families are actually natives or are regarded as such. In other words, there must be four or five hundred persons in the

---

[1] Harvey Dakin was born in Troy, but he came to Roxborough in his teens, and though he subsequently worked in distant states, he returned to the town and married a local girl. Even so, his independence of mind sometimes reminds his enemies that he isn't an honest-to-God native. As a matter of fact, I have sometimes heard one old man say of another, "He ain't a real old-timer." This is by no means so invidious as calling a person an outsider; it is merely a way of recalling that the individual, though he may have lived in the town for fifty or sixty years and may be universally accepted as a native, nevertheless was not born in Roxborough. A man who has lived here thirty or thirty-five years tells me that you can't become a naturalized citizen in less than a century.

town who have been living together for all or most of their lives. And of course there are many ties of blood. I once told the outsider bride of a young native, "You can say anything you want to about us to anybody in town, but everybody else is somebody else's cousin." That is not quite true, but there are few families—not more than thirty-five or forty I should guess—that do not have relatives in town. And so many persons can trace their ancestry back to half a dozen of the original settlers that an inclusive chart of town relationships would be a genealogist's joy.

Against the solid weight of the natives, outsiders are a feeble force. Some of the outsiders are persons of foreign birth or parentage, and though there is no active prejudice against them—they are hard-working men and women who mind their own business—they play no part in the life of the community except that they vote, and are strenuously urged to vote, on election day. The other outsiders—those of older American stock—do play a part in community life and, for that matter, a disproportionately large part. They hold the principal offices in the PTA, the Community League, and the fire company, and they are generously represented on the town board. Outwardly they have a great influence on the town—on its organizational life, so to speak—but on its inner life their effect is limited. Again and again an outsider, freshly elected to office, sets out to impose his ideas—city ideas—upon the town, but eventually he either withdraws in disgust or adapts himself to Roxborough ways. The town's chief politician, himself an outsider, once said to me, "I've tried to educate 'em, but it doesn't do any good."

The significant thing about the natives, of course, is the way they think in terms of the past—not merely the individual past but the community past. In the spring of 1945, when we were getting signatures on a petition for a fire district, Stan Cutter and I called on Walt Morgan. Only three years earlier Walt had called my attention to a large iron bar he was willing to give to the salvage committee, "Better bring a gang with you," he said. "Course I could put it on the truck myself, but I'm not going to try."

At eighty-one Walt is still capable of doing a day's work in a hay-field, and he hasn't much respect for men of any age who are less vigorous than himself. Though he likes Stan, he received us that evening with unconcealed hostility, glaring at us under his heavy eyebrows and barking out his words. In time he signed the petition, but even after he had scrawled his signature, he had to tell us why we were wrong. "Things are going too fast," he said. "You say it won't cost much. That's what they always say. But it's a little more here and a little more there, and it counts up. When I bought this place forty years ago, my school taxes were two dollars a year and my road taxes five. People were economical back in those days. There was a pathmaster for every stretch of road, and he saw to it that the work was done right and done cheap. Now nobody's economical, from the President down. Maybe it's all right, but it's hard on a man who's tried to save a little money to live on in his old age. I might come to be a public charge yet. I made my money when money came hard—dollar a day or less. And now other people are spending it for me." He began to talk about the past. Forty years ago, he said, he could see nothing but farm and pasture land from his doorstep; now he was living in a regular forest. "Went over to the crossroads a couple of summers ago, and thought I'd get lost." As he saw it, the economic life of the town was steadily declining while the expenses of government constantly mounted. It was no wonder he was gloomy about the future. Not all the old-timers are so sure that the past was better than the present. In fact, the majority of them, if asked out-right, will staunchly assert that life is more satisfying today than it was ten, twenty-five, or fifty years ago. (They feel, I suspect, that it would be un-American and vaguely blasphemous to suggest the contrary.) But the fact is that their minds are constantly occupied with the past, and no one can miss the note of nostalgia in their talk. Mr. Cutter, for example, a firm believer in progress if there ever was one, is never happier than when he is unfolding some long and devious saga of his youth. To be sure, such reminiscences are to be expected from any septuagenarian anywhere. What is significant is the fact that these are Roxborough sagas that Mr. Cutter tells. He is no Iowan transported to California telling men from half a dozen states stories of places they have never seen and persons in whom they have no interest. When he talks to us, he can identify the places and the persons. ("You know Bill Gibbs down on the Wolf Hollow road? Well, this Mizz Cargill had two daughters, or maybe it was three. Anyway, Bill's first wife was her oldest girl, and Sherman Gibbs, the one that's in the army and been wounded or something, he's her grandson.") When he talks to his contemporaries, or even to much younger natives, there is no such necessity for identification. They have the past in common.

Mark Betterton, who subscribes to two or three business magazines and thinks of himself as completely up-to-date, lives in the past almost as much as Mr. Cutter, who is twenty years his senior. He talks to me now and then, and talks rather well, about current economic problems, but his real talents as a conversationalist display themselves only when some occurrence in the store has touched his memory. So it is with Rodney Brothers, one of our town officials. Seeing him in public, one would think him shy and taciturn, but he can be loquacious and dramatic and very funny on the subject of the past. I remember one night when he began to talk about the decline of the Middleton family, an episode in which tragedy and comedy nudge each other. He told the story beautifully, but the real point is that it had so much meaning for his listeners. To some of those present it was a familiar story, though I could see that the vividness with which he told it brightened memories that had grown dim. For the rest of us it explained situations in the town that we had never understood, situations that had become part of our lives.

Most of the talk that I used to listen to in the post office concerned the past, and that is the usual theme of the endless conversations that go on in the barber shop and the stores. Anyone who has listened to old grads at a reunion knows that their recollections, however boring they may be to an outsider, are deeply satisfying to the men who are doing the talking. In Roxborough people have not four years in common but fifty or sixty or seventy. And if they, unlike the old grads, have frequent opportunities to swap stories, they also have memories so stocked as to be almost inexhaustible. "Why, I haven't thought of him in years," an old-timer will say, and then, with a kind of joyous surprise, he will open out his full store of recollections as a lover of music might play a record that had once been a favorite but for a long time had lain neglected.

—∿—

The town has changed, as we have seen, but it has changed slowly. Roxborough was neither a ghost town in the depression nor a boom town in wartime. It has never been swamped by commuters as some of its neighbors have. (The adjoining town on the west is classed by the United States census as part of a metropolitan area.) In thinking of the past, then, the older men and women are conscious of no sharp break. They know perfectly well that Roxborough is less of a community than it was thirty years ago, but there is continuity between past and present. I constantly have to remind myself that one doesn't need to be an octogenarian to remember the days when Roxborough people worked in Roxborough and Troy was a good many hours away. If I had spent my whole life in the town, I would remember the stage coaches that came out every summer, crowded with people who were taking a considerable journey to spend their vacations in the hills. I would have traveled by stage coach myself, if I had traveled at all before I was nine or ten years old. And I might have been one of the persons who were employed by the Middletons, in their factory or on their farms.

Because the past is so close, it seems to the younger people as well as to the old-timers that Roxborough life is different from city life. I notice this when the Cutters' daughters come to visit them. Four of the five girls married out of the town, but they have remained in the vicinity, and the parental farm has continued to be a second home for them and their children. For some of the families it was a refuge during the depression—the elder Cutters at least had milk and eggs and potatoes and a roof over their heads—and in prosperous times it has the attraction of familiarity and stability. The younger Cutters move about, but the parents stay put. All five of the daughters were born in New York City, and the older ones left home soon after the return to Roxborough, but their roots are here.

As for the boys, Arthur, the youngest child, having married a city girl and settled down to a lower-middle-class existence in the city, seems to have alienated himself from Roxborough more completely than any of the other children. Stan, on the other hand, is to me the quintessence of Roxborough. Leaving school at the age of fourteen, he helped his father, worked on town and county roads, and acquired a knack with machinery and a reputation as a hellion. He went his easy-going, independent way until he married, and then he made only the modifications that his code required. That is to say, he got and held jobs reasonably commensurate with his ability, and brought in an income more or less adequate to the demands of his family. On the other hand, he refuses to live anywhere but in Roxborough, and he boasts of what he calls his hill-billy speech and manners. Big and boyish, with friendly, inquisitive eyes and a mouth that can tighten when he yaps at a child or a dog or speaks of someone he doesn't like, he is an ingenious mechanic, a first-rate marksman, a graceful square dancer, an obliging neighbor, and a witty story-teller. With his cap on the side of his head and his hands in the pockets of his greasy pants, he says to the world, "This is what I am, take it or leave it."

I try to think what the appeal of Roxborough is for Stan. In no small measure it is the country, wild country and becoming wilder now that the abandoned farms are growing up to woods. He wouldn't be happy if he couldn't roam around with a gun and shoot game, and he wants plenty of space. I doubt if he will ever leave the town, but once or twice he has talked of moving to even wilder country in the north. As for the inconveniences of country life, they mean nothing to him. He doesn't mind fighting with snow and mud; in fact he rather likes to do it, as he likes to do anything at which he excels. He admits that things like running water and central heat are pleasant, but they are not essential. He wouldn't say, as I would, that he hates city noise and city dirt and the sense of people pressing upon him, but I am sure he does. One day early in the war, when we were talking about transportation problems and the difficulties of getting supplies, I said, "Let's give Roxborough back to the Indians and move to the city." In an instant Stan said, "Let's give Roxborough back to the Indians and *not* move to the city."

But Stan doesn't cling to Roxborough merely because he likes the scenery. Roxborough is to him a way of life. It means independence. It is a place where he can talk and dress as he pleases, where people know and accept him, where his quick hand is praised and his witty speech laughed at. So long as he keeps a foothold in Roxborough, he feels, he needn't worry too much about losing his job, for he is confident that here he can always make out somehow. He is willing to work in the city, so long as he is paid well for work he likes and doesn't have to give up too much of his independence, but he won't live in the city. He knows there are other ways of life, but he isn't having any.

And perhaps there is another side. I wonder if he isn't avoiding complexities that he is a little afraid of, dodging situations to which he might not prove adequate. Once, a year or so before he went to work in the chain shop, a friend told him of an excellent opening in a large industrial plant some thirty miles away. Stan applied for the job, but instead of being given a chance to show whether he could do the work or not, he was confronted with a long questionnaire. "Hell," he said, "I couldn't even read some of the questions, and if I'd started answering them, they'd have thought a hen walked over the paper." So he put the questionnaire down, picked up his cap, walked out, and went home. There have been other occasions, some Stan has talked about, some we have guessed at.

If Stan is conscious of inadequacies, what of the scores of other men in town, men no better educated than he and less skillful, less poised, less experienced in city ways? Roxborough is people they know and have known from childhood, people who know them, who know their faults and have got used to them, know their virtues and appreciate them. Every contact with Roxborough people falls into a familiar pattern, the disagreements and even the fist fights as well as the business relationships and the occasions of social intercourse. To leave Roxborough would be to abandon all this certainty for a world that could not be grasped. It would be not merely a change from the familiar to the unfamiliar but also a change from the manageable to the unmanageable. In Roxborough life's problems seem—one cannot possibly say more than that—life's problems *seem* to be cut down to human size.

All this is connected, both as cause and effect, with the process by which the population of the town has been selected. One has only to walk through the cemeteries to see how many once numerous families have vanished from Roxborough, and there are not a few families that are removed from extinction only by so much of life as is left to an old-timer or two. On the other hand, certain families have thrived. There are nineteen Westerns, for example, and twenty-five Carters listed as registered voters. Western is an old name in the town, and it appears that most, if not all, of those who bear the name are related, but the relationships are for the most part not close and not much attention is paid to them. The Carters, on the contrary, are a clan, almost all of them, descendants or wives of descendants of one Solomon Carter. What is more, virtually every living Carter in four generations is still in Roxborough. And other families, though less conspicuously loyal to the town, are well represented.

It is clear that economic factors, at least in recent years, have not played an important part in the process of selection. Jobs do not bring people to Roxborough and only in some rather special sense keep them here. If you ask a resident of Troy how he happens to be living in the city, he usually says, "Well, I got a job at such-and-such a plant, and I moved here," or, "I went to work for so-and-so after I got through school, and I stayed on." If you ask a Roxborough resident why he lives in the town, he begins by saying, "Why, I was born here," and often as not that is where he stops.

Most residents, whether natives or outsiders, are here because they would rather be here than somewhere else. (Of course this is less true of the women than it is of the men.) It would be easy to say that the more ambitious and more venturesome have left the town, while the shiftless and the timid have remained. To a certain extent that is true, but not all the people are either lazy or frightened, not by any means, and I am sure that there is a positive as well as negative principle at work. Why do the outsiders come to Roxborough? Some of them come for cheap rents, and leave as soon as possible. More of them come, as we did, for the scenery and the air and the space around them, for the chance to have a garden and maybe raise a few hens. But if they stay a while, they find themselves, as we found ourselves, thinking less of the scenery and more of the town. Even if they do not become involved in political or social activities—and many of them do, as I have pointed out—they get the feel of small-town life, and they learn to like it.

That is the crux of the matter. I think of Joe Macy, who doesn't live here at all but has been spending summers here since he was a child. He has a good business in the city and a substantial residence, but I know that he regards Roxborough as his home. If Joe can have that kind of feeling for the town, what about men and women who have lived here all or most of their lives? There are people, in other words, who prefer the small-town way of life. Most of them, no doubt, prefer it because it is what they are used to, but there are those who choose it deliberately.

It is generally recognized, even in Roxborough, that the small town is not what it was. In the blackest days of the depression, when the people of Roxborough did seem to survive by taking in each other's washings, the appearance of self-sufficiency was an illusion, and in wartime, with half the wage-earning civilians employed in the city, even the illusion vanished. Most people realize that independence is lost, and I have heard frank enough admissions in debates on the school question. "If it wasn't for Troy," one outspoken old-timer said, "Roxborough would vanish from the face of the earth." Yet these various debates indicated how tenaciously the townspeople are fighting to retain such independence as they have. "I may be wrong," one unrepresentative iconoclast said, "but I don't believe that in the future the State Education Department will pay any more attention to town lines than the power companies do now." The question most people ask, however, is a bitter one: "If we lose our schools, what will we have left?"

—⁓—

The question that might well be asked is, "What is left to us now?" Well, something. First of all, as I have tried to say, a memory. The fact that Roxborough was an isolated and partly self-sufficient community only thirty years ago is not important in itself, but it becomes important because there are so many people still in the town who remember that period and are constantly looking back to it. Secondly, the town still has a remarkably homogeneous population. More outsiders have come to Roxborough in the past twenty years, but not enough to make a strong impression on the character of the town. More natives have been working in the city, but they have been resisting its influence with singular success. In spite of the drastic change in its whole economic situation, Roxborough, so far as its people are concerned, is still Roxborough.

The character of the place displays itself in its social relationships. In cities and larger towns, according to Lloyd Warner, one can distinguish six social classes. I can find only two in Roxborough, and it is not easy to define the differences between them. Speaking of her three brothers and their families, a woman once said to us, "I suppose I belong to the poorer class of relatives.

What I hear, they all have beautiful homes. Of course I've never been in them." Certainly this woman's house is small, over-crowded, unattractive, with no conveniences at all, and her brothers' homes, though scarcely beautiful, are larger, are furnished with something more than the bare essentials, have running water and electric light. But one cannot depend absolutely on the criterion of household equipment. Some upper-class families, for instance, do not have electricity simply because they live too far from the power lines, whereas most lower-class families that live near enough to get minimum rates do have electric lights. Running water can be easily installed in some places, but in others the expense is practically prohibitive. It is true that some lower-class families live in absolute squalor and that most of the others have small and meagerly furnished homes. It is also true that most upper-class families have at least a few urban con-veniences, and almost invariably their houses contain an extra room—modern living room or old-fashioned parlor—in which visitors can be entertained. Even at this level, however, one has to recognize exceptions. I can think of a house that is very near-ly as poor and as dirty as any in town, and yet the people who live in it manage—by the skin of their teeth, to be sure—to hold an upper-class position. On the other hand, the son of the woman who described herself as belonging to the poorer class of relatives lives in a neat, well-equipped house but seems to have accepted his parents' lower-class status. Clearly the character of a person's living quarters does not rigidly determine and does not always ac-curately reflect his social status.

Income is an even less reliable criterion. In general, people in the upper class make more money than people in the lower class, but—at least in wartime—lower-class earnings sometimes reach up to and perhaps surpass the average of upper-class earnings, and one can always point to some particular lower-class individ-ual who has a much larger income than a given upper-class indi-vidual. Almost anyone with a regular job, I think, can qualify for the upper-class, and if some farmers and some skilled mechanics are in the lower class, that is in spite of their employment. The lower class includes a number of families whose men work irregularly, but I know of a dozen odd-job men who are regarded as uppers. The upper class even has to be stretched to take in three or four men who are poor, lazy, and given to heavy drinking.

Family cannot count for much in a town whose people are so interrelated, for even the best people are likely to have poor relations. On the other hand, it does seem to be true that if a man has relatives in the upper class, and if these relatives continue to treat him as one of themselves, he is likely to be accepted by the rest of the town, even though his economic status and personal habits would seem to relegate him to the lower group. Almost all the families that are treated as exceptions are families with good connections, and I conclude that good connections are a help but no guarantee. Several of the town's once eminent names survive chiefly in lower-class households.

Outsiders can belong to either class, and apparently their status, much more than that of the natives, is regularly determined by their economic position. The town always has a few transient families, whose men, as a rule, either cut wood or pick up odd jobs. They mix well enough with lower-class natives, but are looked down on by the upper class as lower-class natives are not. There are also one or two lower-class families that have been in the town for some years, and they appear to have been assimilated by the lower class but not by the town as a whole. Outsiders of foreign birth usually keep themselves so much aloof that it is impossible to assign them to a class, but, as I have said, the more prosperous ones are respected and probably belong in a vague way to the upper class. The other outsiders are almost without exception persons who have bought property in the town, and, since their incomes are or are supposed to be well above the native upper-class level, they are automatically accorded upper-class status.

Although I still find it hard to believe, I am pretty well convinced that class divisions in Roxborough are largely subjective. That is, a person by and large belongs to the class he wants to belong to. The interesting question is why some people want to belong to the lower class. I can detect a certain group of people who have been embittered by a long series of economic frustrations. They are the under-privileged, and they know it. Out of pride, and perhaps with some confused idea of punishing both themselves and others, they remain aloof. Another and larger group seem to be quite satisfied with their lower-class status and are not sorry to be free from the responsibilities a higher rank might entail. They range from squalid ne'er-do-wells to rather picturesque ruffians, men who enjoy their drink and their fights and their women. In so far as the class criterion is moral, and to a certain extent it is, members of the lower class are exempt from most of the burdens of respectability, and they take advantage of their privileges. A city social worker might be shocked by what can be seen in some of the homes on Button Road, and I myself shudder when I think of the children who are growing up there, but I know it is pure sentimentality to suggest that the residents are any less happy than the average.

Although I have had so much difficulty in stating what divides the upper from the lower class, the reader will have observed that I have no trouble in determining the status of a particular family. Neither has anybody else in town. An upper-class outsider was talking to me the other day about the conduct of some children at a public entertainment. "We all criticize certain people," she said, "but I couldn't help noticing that we didn't have any trouble with the Mitchell youngsters or any of Mary Bacon's children. They were perfectly behaved, while the children of some of the best families in town were acting like hoodlums." She might have said it in so many words: the lower-class children behaved well, and the upper-class children behaved badly. She knew exactly what she meant, and so did I, and anyone in town would have known. Yet by any economic criterion all the families in question belong to the lower class.

Class divisions are clearly recognized, and they are important. There is not an organization in the town, including the churches,

in which the upper class does not constitute a majority and mo-
nopolize the offices. (There are, on the other hand, few organizations that do not include some lower-class members.) Social
gatherings follow class lines, and even when lower-class persons
are invited to a shower—showers are the largest and most heterogeneous parties held in the town—they rarely attend. The
lower class, so far as I can make out, seldom has parties; the men
meet in the drinking places, and that suffices. The upper class
doesn't have many formal gatherings, but such as it does have are
class affairs, and some groups within the upper class lead a moderately active social life.

When all is said and done, however, the situations in which
class lines matter are less numerous than those in which they
don't count. People meet more often in the stores, the drinking
joints, and the barber shop than anywhere else. They meet and
they talk, and class lines, so far as I can see, make little difference.
People of the lower class come to square dances as well as people
of the upper class, and often they dance in the same sets. (There
may be some persons in town who don't attend square dances for
just that reason, but they are not a majority of their class.) Perhaps some lower-class persons deliberately avoid church suppers,
but others come and eat without embarrassment. Once in a long
time a political contest seems to align one class against the other,
but in general class has little to do with politics. Perhaps some
lower-class voters support the Democrats because they are always
the "outs," but the majority of the lower class, like the majority
of the upper class, is Republican, and on election day, when the
whole town turns out, the classes seem to fraternize with no
sense of a barrier between them.

The truth is that in nine situations out of ten the class structure is overshadowed by a basic social equality that results from
the smallness of the community and the sense of a common past.
People who are thrown in constant contact over a long period of
time learn to ignore distinctions that would make their relations
difficult. In Roxborough almost everyone dresses alike, at least

on ordinary occasions, and, except for some of the outsiders, everyone talks alike. Everyone knows everyone else and speaks to everyone else. My guess is that the upper class embraces nearly two-thirds of the population, and includes families that would be sorted out in a city into the upper lower, the lower middle, and the upper middle. The lower class has a few rather disreputable characters, but for the greater part it is made up of people not strikingly different in outward appearance or in income from the bulk of the upper class. It is no wonder that for all the more important affairs of life Roxborough is a classless society.

What Toynbee calls "the link of locality" is still important in Roxborough, and it is my guess that this is a far more significant tie than any other. Let us think, for example, of a group of men working in the same department of a factory. They see each other daily, perhaps eat lunch together, listen to each other's opinions and hear about each other's families. They have their work in common, their relation to the boss, and no doubt a wealth of daily incidents. Yet, living in different parts of the city, they rarely see one another outside of working hours. Perhaps a couple of them grow friendly enough so that they and their wives exchange visits or go dancing together. But outside of the factory they meet only by prearrangement. Some of them in all probability have friendly relations with neighbors, and, if they have lived in one section of the city long enough, they may have geographical ties of some strength. But the geographical relationships and the occupational relationships are quite different and often pull against each other. In the self-sufficient small town of the past, on the other hand, occupational ties strengthened geographical ties, and even in the Roxborough of today the link of locality not only remains strong but also, as I have shown in the case of the chain factory, determines the character of the occupational link.

I am well aware that strong loyalties to a geographical area can be developed in much larger towns than Roxborough and even in sprawling suburbs and great cities. There is something blatantly factitious, however, in such phenomena as the renowned devotion of Brooklynites to their borough. It is something that somebody thought up, not something that grew. I do not doubt that a man can be deeply loyal to a city of fifty or a hundred thousand, perhaps to a larger city, but it is not the same thing as the feeling of the townsman for his town. I suspect, indeed, that much of the trumped-up enthusiasm of the service club boosters is a wistful substitute for the small-towner's simple acceptance of his community as a given fact.

Many of the characteristics I have been trying to describe Roxborough seems to share with most small towns. If it has its peculiarities, or if it exhibits some characteristics in a peculiar degree, that may be because it is closer than most small towns to the nineteenth century type of community. We are dealing with a hang-over, a memory, an echo, but it is something to reckon with just the same. As may have been made clear already, and as certainly will become obvious later on, I realize that the influence of the ghost of Roxborough's past is not always benevolent. There is intense clannishness, suspicion of outsiders, hostility to new ideas, resistance to change. Indeed, when Harvey Dakin says this is the damnedest town—and he says it almost every time we are together—I am tempted to agree. Yet if one sees only too clearly what the small town is, one also achieves some understanding of what it was and catches a glimpse of what it could be in the future.

VI

The Mind of Roxborough

Public opinion polls contrive to give the impression that as a nation we are in a constant state of agitation over all sorts of domestic and foreign problems. Eighty or ninety or sometimes ninety-nine per cent of the people interviewed are able to say that they are for or against a particular man or a particular measure, and that is what the investigators want. Some experts, however, have begun to admit that people often have opinions on subjects about which they are less than adequately informed. The man in the street, they confess, may strongly support or bitterly oppose a bill that is before Congress without being able to describe one of its provisions. This admission is healthy, but the experts need to take another step. A man may turn up an opinion on demand, even a fairly well-informed opinion, and yet have only the slightest interest in the subject about which he is being interviewed. How much does the individual in question think about the subject? Does he feel that it has any real relevance to his own life? How do his thoughts and emotions on this subject compare with his thoughts and emotions on other subjects?

The problem that I wish the experts would investigate is not what people think about this or that but what they think about. Both psychologists and novelists suggest that people think mostly about themselves. The stream of ideas—call it interior monologue or what you will—that passes through the average human mind is concerned with *me:* my health, my state of mind, what people think about me and what I think about them, my problems, my children, my job, what I said to Joe and what he said to me, mostly what I said to him. Even the most public-minded citizen, I suspect, devotes only a fraction of his attention to the affairs of city, state, and nation, and any conception of democracy that postulates the constant and alert interest of the citizenry is purely romantic.

If, then, we are to be concerned with the ideas that circulate in Roxborough, we had better keep in mind that these ideas are not constantly seething about in the consciousness of the people. Not being a psychoanalyst, I cannot say exactly what ideas and feelings do seethe about. I am limited to the material that finds expression in ordinary conversation, and I am not even sure that the conversations I have engaged in or listened to are fully representative. Even a casual listener, however, knows that the opinions that can be formally organized and set down have their existence in a vast and chaotic world of thought and emotion.

To help us to keep the point in mind, we might begin by examining the ideas that are directly derived from Roxborough itself, before we turn to outside influences. Farming, for instance, though it has become a marginal activity, provides much of the material of conversation. Among the old-timers there is endless talk about crops and the weather, and I can imagine a period when these topics were of first importance, though today, they seem a little off-center. Where farming is more profitable, interest in agriculture often leads to an interest in science, but Roxborough's farmers pay little attention to the mass of scientific information that reaches them through bulletins, farm magazines, and radio programs. There is not even much interest shown in the handful of scientifically managed farms to be found in neighboring towns. Talk about farming is divisible into two parts: practical lore and superstition.

Listening to such talk, one may not learn much about agriculture, but one can learn something about the role of conversation. The constant repetition of the same facts or theories suggests at the very outset that communication in the ordinary sense of the term cannot be the major purpose of these exchanges. An old-timer makes a statement about the soil of Roxborough, for instance, a statement he has made a hundred times to the same listeners, and the listeners respond with the comments they have invariably offered. The old-timer, it seems to me, is talking for the sake of talking—that is, for the sake of establishing a relationship with the group. He is also reaffirming a basic truth, and to him the truth does not have to be novel. Of course, people in other walks of life do the same thing, but lawyers and teachers and business men sooner or later become aware of the boredom of their audiences. The old-timers are troubled by no such self-consciousness, and so long as they keep to themselves they do not need to be. Their attitude is the exact opposite of the intellectuals', for they are as skeptical of novelty as the intellectuals are devoted to it. Among the intellectuals an idea tends to wear itself out in a relatively short time: if an idea is not novel, it cannot be talked about, and if it cannot be talked about, it may as well be abandoned. This ridiculous faddishness, however, is merely the reverse side of a healthy and necessary receptivity. The imperviousness of the old-timers, on the other hand, though it has its admirable aspects, is obviously disadvantageous in a situation of change, and it is no wonder that agriculture in Roxborough is decades behind the time.

As for superstitions, it is hard to make out whether Roxborough people are more superstitious than the majority of city-dwellers or merely less embarrassed about mentioning their foibles. So far as I know, no one believes in devils, witches, ghosts, or other supernatural beings, but the widest variety of old wives' tales is accepted. Most farmers plant and butcher according to the phases of the moon, and they defend the practice by the pseudo-scientific argument that the moon governs crops as it governs the tides. Most women believe in birth-marking, and I recall the indignation with which an old-timer said, "You'll never convince me, and you needn't try." Young women with high school diplomas refuse to handle meat when they are menstruating, and can cite examples of meat that spoiled because this rule was broken. Bad and good luck signs, weather signs, and the like are numberless: an enterprise begun on a Friday will be beset with difficulty and may well end in disaster; the weather on the last two days of one month governs the weather for the whole of the next; a green Christmas will be followed by a winter of sickness and death.

What puzzles me is the way some of the natives talk about this mass of folklore. Mark Cutter, for example, will quote sayings by the hour, and discuss them in all seriousness, but I never know whether he believes them or not. One day, for instance, he referred to "the old whim that if you have fog in February you'll have frost in May," and he can be very condescending toward these old whims. My guess is that basically the superstitions he cites are something for him to think and talk about. Probably he observes them when it is convenient for him to do so, and disregards them when he sees fit. In a curious way his attitude toward political issues seems much the same. In New York City one of his close friends was a socialist, and Mr. Cutter can still talk socialist theories, but they have nothing to do with the way he casts his vote. Sometimes he says to me, "Did you listen to the Town Meeting of the Air last night? It was a wonderful argument." I will ask what they were arguing about. "I don't just remember. Something to do with the war."

Now and then I have wondered whether the old-timers, living close to the soil as they do, have any of the quasi-religious feeling for nature that writers have found in some peasant peoples. For a long time I would have said not. But there was the solitary, dirty, and rather mean-minded old farmer who said one day, "You know, I have a good life here." Looking into the alert, wonderfully expressive eyes, I was as surprised by what lay behind the words as I was by the words themselves. After that, I noticed that he always contrived to get a rather special, a rather personal note into his remarks about the weather. "Turned out to be a nice day after all," I said to him once. The old man shook his head in a pantomime of surprise and joy: "Certainly fooled me. I thought it was going to be a bad one." "Seems great to see the sun," he would say after a stormy spell, and I wish I could reproduce the glow in the eyes and the lift in the voice. One cold morning I happened to observe that the wind had changed about midnight. "That's what tied it up," he exclaimed, striking his leg. "Yes, sir, that was a hairy one," he would say, speaking of a storm. Good or bad, the weather excited him as a kind of drama and perhaps also as a manifestation of a force.

Finding so clear and strong an emotion where one would least expect to find it, I have come to believe that something of the same feeling lies behind much of the talk about storms and heat and cold. One hard-working farmer was a skilled mechanic for many years, and turned to farming because of a distaste for cities. "God didn't intend people to live that way," he has told me. He talks a great deal about his animals, often amusingly: "Pigs are clean by nature. I like pigs. I like 'em better than I do some people." When war time was adopted, Charlie stood out against it for a fortnight or so and then gave in. The morning he fed the stock for the first time on the new schedule his wife asked him as usual how the cows were. He said, "They wanted to know who that damned fool was who was waking 'em up in the middle of the night." Once he said to me of that day's sunrise, "You just want to go out and hold it in your arms. I may be foolish, but I'm glad I am."

Weather, crops, and animals, both domestic and wild, furnish material for thought and themes for conversation, but the great source is experience with people. For one thing, most ideas, whatever their ultimate origin, circulate through personal rather than impersonal channels. I know this is not peculiar to Roxborough. Some of the public opinion experts have concluded that even in this day of universal literacy and twenty-four hour radio service opinions are still transmitted chiefly by direct word of mouth. One study has indicated that in almost every neighborhood, every factory, every group of any kind, there is likely to be an individual whose word carries particular weight. Often this individual has no political position, and his social status may be low, but somehow authority attaches itself to his words, and this personal authority is more persuasive than the prestige of any radio commentator or newspaper columnist.

The power of the personal word, I suspect, is a hangover from a time when the majority of people lived in small communities more or less like Roxborough. Talk between neighbors used to be almost the only means for the transmission of news and opinions, and it is still an important means wherever neighborly contacts exist. They do exist in Roxborough. At a church supper the outsiders usually leave as soon as they have finished eating, but the natives sit around and talk until the dishes are washed and someone hints that the lights had better be put out. It is the rarest thing in the world for a native to leave the store as soon as he has made a purchase. At the least he will talk for a few minutes with the storekeeper, and if there are other customers, he will talk with them. A man, indeed, is likely to take a seat and stay for an hour or for an evening. Women, traditionally, do not sit around the stove, but a group may stand in some out-of-the-way corner for half or three-quarters of an. hour.

Many of the conversations in the store and the barber shop are desultory enough and, as I have noted, frequently repetitious. However, no local event—birth, illness, change of job, real estate transaction—is likely to go unremarked. If many persons are involved, political discussions are usually restrained, for it is an unwritten law that brawls are to be avoided in all public places of the town except those that sell alcohol. In fact, in so small and interrelated a community political controversy cannot be conducted in public with acrimony or even with candor, though there is a vast amount of whispered slander and adroit back-stabbing. A man can make his views clear, however, even though he says nothing at which political opponents and their relatives can take offense, and if he is a man of influence, his views are repeated, probably without benefit of his qualifications, in many homes. In the old days, I imagine, political destinies were commonly settled around the stove in the store. Today the talk in public places is probably more important in the circulation of news than it is in the formation of opinions, but its surviving influence on what people think should not be underestimated.

Personal contact not only passes ideas along; in itself it provides material for thought. If people think most of the time about themselves, a good deal of the rest of the time they spend in thinking about other people. It seems to be true that the more one knows about other people, the more interesting one finds them, and in a small town there are opportunities to know a lot. Moreover, a small town offers few of the impersonal spectacles with which urban life is so rich. A great city provides not only theaters, museums, restaurants, baseball games, boxing matches, and the like, but also stores, subway trains, the streets themselves. Roxborough has almost no impersonal spectacles, except those furnished by nature, and radio is the only modern means of mass diversion to be found. There is every chance for a person in Roxborough to learn about his neighbors, and few distractions to keep him from doing so.

As is natural in a group of homes so closely associated and, by and large, so nakedly exposed to each other, there is immediate and intense interest in any event that interrupts the daily routine. Illness is the commonest kind of interruption, and perhaps that is why it is so much talked about, though I sometimes feel that there is a special and almost morbid excitement over ill health. (The subject of health, I am sure, figures prominently in interior monologues, and I suspect that the individual's interest in the health of others is often an extension of anxiety over his own health.) Scandal is second in importance to illness, in spite of the fact that Roxborough in practice is a tolerant community, making no great touse about couples that live together out of wedlock or carry on more or less public affairs. The note of moral censure is only occasionally struck, but gossip is detailed, sustained, and widespread, As in sophisticated milieus that I have known, the practice of tolerance goes hand in hand with rapt interest. Births, marriages, deaths, fights, arrests, new jobs, and similar events receive appropriate attention.

I am not surprised by the interest that is shown in crises of one sort or another, for that has been displayed, in varying degrees of intensity, wherever I have lived. No, the striking thing is the simple interest in simple facts. If A digs his potatoes, if B goes shopping in Troy, if C fails to attend church, notice is taken. At one end of the scale is mere recognition of what is going on—a friendly acknowledgment of the familiar, comparable to the attention paid the weather on a seasonable day. At the other end there is passionate curiosity. I know persons who spend hours each day listening in on party lines, no doubt hoping for juicy bits but quite satisfied if they keep tabs on their neighbors. To such persons bare facts appear to be intensely interesting, and they assume the same interest on the part of others, for one woman may call another three or four times a day merely to report what she has been doing and what she has seen or heard of the doings of others. Curiosity on this level is more outspoken among the women than among the men, who usually find more objective subjects—politics, machinery, hunting—to discuss, but a casual inquiry quickly shows how much personal detail the masculine mind can accumulate.

It is significant that interest so often centers in the human fact for its own sake, but one would have to be very innocent to assume that the attention paid to other persons is always free from emotional overtones. Like most compact neighborhoods, Roxborough is frequently rent by quarrels, sometimes amounting to feuds. Often these quarrels have political, religious, or social implications, but even a political or a religious quarrel reduces itself to personalities. One year the assessors raised the valuation of our farm, and the chairman of the board boasted that this was done because I was a communist. I disapproved, but I was not surprised, for I had had some experience with political persecution. Some of my neighbors, however, brushed this explanation away. In what way, they speculated, could I have offended the chairman? Had I ever taken business away from him? Was it known that I had voted against him? To them it seemed obvious that the motivation must be personal rather than political. And when, years later, I hired this man in my capacity as school trustee to do a piece of work, simply because he was the best workman available, there was general agreement that we must have patched up our difficulties, and I was asked, as probably he was, what had happened.

At a session of the town board that I attended the question came up of the purchase of a tract of land for civic purposes. There was general opposition, not only among the board members but also among the citizens who had bothered to attend. One citizen, however, was not content to let the matter rest there but made a long speech on the subject of the price at which the land had been offered to the town. This was immediately interpreted as a personal attack on the owner of the land, and a dozen times in the next week I heard someone say, "I wonder what Bill's got against Mark. I always thought they were pretty close."

A few more incidents—and I could cite many—may serve to establish the emotional background of Roxborough's gossip. One time when Dorothy was running a dance as president of the PTA, the orchestra failed to appear. "Well," said a member, apparently without malice, "it makes a difference who asks them." In Red Cross and National War Fund campaigns there are always women who say, "Oh, he'll give me a contribution," or, "She can't get anything out of him." Needless to say, a vote against a candidate is generally regarded as a personal affront, and a vote for a candidate is both an acknowledgment of past favors and a bid for favors to come. Politics is very largely personalized, although in the last analysis the majority vote for the Republican candidates no matter who they may be. As for the churches, they have had so many quarrels that the wisecrackers will tell you that the Baptist congregation is entirely made up of angry ex-Methodists and vice versa. A feud may start in one of the churches, spread to the PTA, involve a whole section of town, and ultimately emerge as a political factor.

In such a situation it can hardly be supposed that the interest in personalities is always dispassionate or that the reporting is

always unbiased. On the contrary, though the talk about neighbors may be either friendly or neutral, it is likely to be tinged with
jealousy, distrust, irritation, or downright hostility. Intellectual
circles, I have observed, are also given to talk about personalities,
and though the terminology is often psychological and thus
achieves a semblance of objectivity, the note of malice is not always absent. ("If that's the way they talk about their friends,"
cried the new wife of an old acquaintance of ours, "how do they
talk about people they don't like?") Being used to what is called
plain speaking, I am not particularly shocked by Roxborough's
sharp tongues, and in fact I rather enjoy the sharpness, even
when it is turned against me. I have learned, however, to discount much that I hear, though I have the impression that stories are embellished not only out of malice but also—and quite
as often—for the sake of making them more interesting.

It must be said in defense of the urban intellectuals that,
much as they love gossip, they are usually less influenced by personalities than are my Roxborough neighbors. On the other
hand, I am quite convinced, as I have already intimated, that the
more perceptive and thoughtful of my neighbors have a better
grasp of human realities than most of the intellectuals have.
They know so many more kinds of people, and they know them
in so many more ways! They are, to be sure, much less articulate,
but they are acutely interested in motives, in the formation of
character, and even in human nature itself as a theme for gener-
alization. How could this fail to be so? The speculative mind—
and certainly there are speculative minds in Roxborough—has a
vast amount of human data to consider and not too much else.
Inevitably it takes its material and makes something of it. The
tradition of rural shrewdness is not a myth.

—∞—

When we come to the question of Roxborough conceptions of
what is going on in the world and how those conceptions are
formed, the facts are more difficult to interpret. Here again one

must start with personal experience. For instance, what about the old-timers who worked for a time in New York City? On first acquaintance one might easily conclude either that their urban experiences had had little effect or that the effect had long since been obliterated. More intimate knowledge, however, reveals that they are less provincial than their contemporaries whose whole lives have been spent in a country town. They are conscious of the existence of the great cities, and know that the cities determine the shape of American life. They have chosen to live in Roxborough, and their re-acceptance of Roxborough ways is complete, but they do know that Roxborough is not the hub of the universe.

Far more important for the town as it now is, of course, is the experience of so many Roxborough men and not a few women in the war industries of Troy and the vicinity. The impact of this experience manifests itself in surprising ways. I shall always remember the slow-spoken young woman who said, "I may look green, but I'm not green inside. You learn a thing or two working in a factory." And there was another, older woman, a woman whose speech was thick with country phrases. "In our union," she remarked one day, apropos of a delegation that was to interview a state official, "we've found that the more people go along, the more likely we are to get what we want."

Sitting in our kitchen one evening, Stan Cutter told a story. He and a friend had made talk that noon with a Negro who worked in their factory. There was a question: "Why are colored folks always so happy?" And an answer: "It doesn't take much to make us happy. We've learned not to ask for much." More talk, and then the Negro said, "I could be a better friend to you than any white man, but I can't be your friend at all unless you let me." "And," Stan added, "there were tears in his eyes when he said it." The Negro told how he had grown up with white boys and never had any trouble until one day a man called him a God-damned nigger. He talked about prejudice against Jews, too, and Stan, who has done his share of talking about kikes and coons and harps and wops, saw prejudice, perhaps for the first time in his life, from the point of view of the victim. "There are men in this shop who threatened to quit when I was given a job," the Negro said. "I bet they weren't from my part of the country," Stan answered. "Those same guys would stick a knife in my back quick as a wink."

Not always, of course, are experiences on the job so clearly on the side of enlightenment. Even in the matter of other nationalities and races, the prejudices of the town are sometimes intensified by the prejudices of the city. Stan Cutter has recited obscene anti-Semitic verses that circulated in his factory, and a worker in one of the largest defense plants in the area has picked up a large and sickening collection of stories directed against the Jews. Long before the war anti-Semitism was widespread in Roxborough, but it was of a rather mild kind and seldom operated against particular Jews. It was, in short, a special form of the general feeling against outsiders. Now prejudice has been fed by the bitterer, more specific hatreds of the city and by organized propaganda.

In general the contacts of Roxborough men and women with the various races and nationalities to be found in city factories work both ways. They may reveal a common humanity beneath superficial differences, but they are quite as likely to make the differences seem more important. The immediate response, I am afraid, is usually an intensification of prejudice. On the other hand, the hitherto unfamiliar is brought into the realm of the commonplace, and there may ultimately be an increase of understanding.

On many levels the influence of city jobs has been less than one might have anticipated, simply because of the positive resistance that has already been described. Roxborough men not only have sought jobs that would give them a maximum of independence; they have preserved a detachment from management and labor alike. They join unions only when they have to, and they rarely become active union members. Their friends in the factories are usually men from Roxborough or from nearby towns, and I have been told that the older employees look on them and all the other wartime workers from the small towns as a race apart.

Psychologically speaking, their detachment serves to prevent conflict. This becomes clear when one observes a white collar worker such as Newton Walker. He and his wife settled in Roxborough because they liked the country, and they became active here, as they would have become active in any community in which they happened to live. If they had stayed in the city, their friends would have been drawn from the lower middle class and perhaps in time from the upper middle class. They would have played bridge and gone on parties with other office workers until such time as Newt moved into the junior executive class. As it is, their closest friends are a couple of skilled workmen and their wives, and their favorite amusement is square dancing. Newt leads the kind of life he likes, but doing so is more of a problem for him than it is for Stan Cutter. For one thing, he has carried over certain middle-class standards with which Stan isn't in the least bothered, and, beyond that, there is the pressure of his job. A year or so ago he was persuaded by the hope of promotion to attend night school, and his Roxborough friends didn't understand. Occasionally he has to choose between Roxborough engagements that he would enjoy and city engagements that would be to his advantage. In short, he lives in two worlds. He gets away with it all right, but not without some sense of strain.

If most Roxborough men don't feel this strain, if they have successfully kept themselves detached from the social groupings that industrialism has created, that doesn't, of course, mean that they are unaffected by industrialism itself. Inventions, as many students have observed, are accepted much more easily than new ideas. In the world of the machine my Roxborough acquaintances are far more at home than most of the intellectuals I have known, myself included. Even in the early days, as we have seen, Roxborough took to machinery with some alacrity, and if it did not become an industrial community, that was not because of any

theoretical objection to machinery. Although the factories vanished one by one, the machine—in the form of the internal
combustion engine—was firmly established in Roxborough
before the last factory closed.

In the mythology of contemporary America the automobile is
a potent symbol. In 1943, I am told, a high OPA official said that
there would be little difficulty with rationing if people could have
all the gasoline and tires they wanted. The automobile has become the symbol of a very important and very American kind of
freedom—the freedom to go somewhere. Of course it is a symbol of power, too, but mostly of freedom. It means that city people don't have to put up with the city and that country people
don't have to put up with the country. In Roxborough its economic importance can hardly be exaggerated, but during gasoline rationing one had only to listen to the gripes to realize how
highly people valued the opportunity to get to city stores and city
movies. Even in the town itself the automobile means freedom to
go to church and to dances and to the store. A few old-timers get
along without cars—two or three have buggies and the rest go
on foot—but for the average resident an automobile is more important than anything except the barest shelter and a sufficiency
of the cheapest kind of food. When Stan Cutter went in debt
during the depression to buy a car, he didn't have to have one,
but he wanted one, just so he wouldn't be tied down at home,
so he could go shacking around, as he would put it.

The internal combustion engine, however, is more than a con-
venience that comes close to being a necessity; it is a focus of interest and an absorbing topic of conversation. Virtually all
Roxborough males are authorities, and this is not a phenomenon
of recent years. Forty or fifty years ago a native of the town made
inventions that played a part, however minor, in the development
of the automotive industry. Mark Cutter, to me the perfect old-
timer, bought a Stanley Steamer in 1904, and since then he has
always had a car, whatever else he may have gone without. He is
a pretty fair tinkerer, and his son is a first-rate mechanic. Stan,

who was brought up on a farm, doesn't understand horses and doesn't like them, but he loves machinery and drives his father's old tractor with a recklessness and a certainty of control that smacks of horsemanship. Stan has worked in garages at one time or another, and so have a dozen other men in town, while at least a dozen more could have garage jobs if they wanted them.

Hunting and machinery—those are the two great topics of conversation when men get together. Sam Josephs loves to talk about both, and he is usually the central figure in any discussion. Being currently employed in a garage, he is regarded as an authority, and the session is likely to open with a question directed to him, but once the topic is launched, everyone—everyone but me—joins in. The talk grows more and more technical, but human interest is never excluded, for Sam is always being reminded of what some stupid customer said or what some incompetent mechanic did, and his anecdotes evoke others. Some of the men in our group are closely confined to things they have actually worked with, but others are interested in general principles and capable of dealing with them. Stan Cutter, for instance, though he was unable or at any rate unwilling to finish the sixth grade, has a genuinely speculative mind, and has worked out certain theories of mechanics for himself, just from handling machinery, even as he has acquired some knowledge of physiology from the butchering of domestic and game animals. For all these men machinery is, among other things, a field of competence, and it is obvious that they enjoy talking about the subject simply because it is one on which they have something significant to say.

It is the interest in machinery that brings them into closest contact with the contemporary world. In that world the machine is central, and I have to admit that in this respect my neighbors are closer to the center than I am. I am not surprised to discover, however, that knowledge of mechanical technics does not automatically bring knowledge of social technics. When I read James Harvey Robinson's *Mind in the Making* in my early twenties, I was impressed by his suggestion that our social problems could all be solved if they were tackled by engineers rather than politicians. Six years' teaching in an engineering school, however, convinced me that there is no transfer of understanding from one field to another. In Roxborough it is equally evident that a man who has fathomed the mysteries of a differential can be reduced to befuddled helplessness when confronted by the kind of procedural tangle. that occurs regularly in the meetings of every organization.

I realize that I am dealing with two different and only partly related phenomena: experiences in modern, large-scale industry and contact with machinery. Both phenomena, however, do belong to the modern world, and the point I have tried to make is that one has a considerable effect on the minds of Roxborough men and women, whereas the other has very little. The further point must be made that the machine has been accepted because, in a manner of speaking, it can be domesticated. In the spring of 1945 I was told in the Tennessee Valley of the extraordinary skills developed by the backward people of the hill country when they went to work in war plants and of the inventiveness shown by farm boys as soon as power lines reached the isolated hollows in which they lived. "And yet they're the same old hill-billies," one of my informants said. Of course they are and in all probability will be for a long time to come. The mechanical devices and technics of western society are readily taken over by other civilizations, but that does not mean that our culture is accepted. So it is within western society itself: the machine makes many converts but merely to the machine, not to the culture out of which the machine has grown. We speak easily of this "lag," the word suggesting that people are pretty dumb but doubtless will catch up in due season. If I have learned anything in Roxborough, it is that resistances are not the product of stupidity. People take what they can use without surrendering their way of life.

It may be observed in passing that the effect of travel is limited in much the same way as is the effect of contact with machinery.

There are a few Roxborough men who have worked in the South and the West, and there are several families—not rich people but skilled mechanics and their wives—who have spent many winters in Florida. Except in wartime, trips to New York City, western New York State, the New England mountains and coast are common. These travels are geographically broadening, but not much more can be said about them, for people find what they want to find. One year two young couples went to New York City simply to see the rodeo. For the men at least the attraction was quite obviously the American adolescent's dream about cowboys and Indians. They went, in other words, from the relative primitivism of Roxborough to the relative sophistication of New York for the sake of being shown what they believed to be the simon pure primitivism of the western past.

—⚬⚬⚬—

In the summer of 1945 a group of students from Antioch College spent a month in making a study, more or less under my direction, of currents of public opinion in Roxborough, and their findings have enabled me to correct personal impressions of the reading habits of my fellow-citizens. Although it is fairly obvious that not many people are great readers, I have always realized that most of the people in town have access to sources of information about what is going on in the world. My most optimistic estimate, however, was much too low. The students interviewed 116 women, entering approximately half of Roxborough's homes, and discovered that only nine of these homes were without a daily paper. The great majority take the paper that is published in the county seat, but three out of every four see another paper as well, on Sundays if not on weekdays. I found that I had underestimated the number of New York City newspapers that are read in the town, chiefly because I did not realize how many men bring home tabloids from work. I had also underestimated the number of magazines that are read. In all, seventy-four different magazines were named in the course of the interviews. Of these the *Farm Journal* and the *Rural New Yorker* are the most popular, with *Woman's Day* and the *Woman's Home Companion* next, but the *Reader's Digest, Better Homes and Gardens,* and *Life* are well represented. Moreover, all but eleven of the homes have radios, and approximately half of the women interviewed specifically mentioned commentators whom they are in the habit of listening to.

All this suggests that few families are without means of learning what is happening. The paper that is most widely read is a fairly respectable daily for a city of less than a hundred thousand. It has both AP and UP service, and its reporting of national and international events is as good as that of all but a handful of newspapers published outside New York City. It is violently Republican, especially in the weeks before an election, and its editorial policy can only be described as conservative, but its news is reasonably impartial. It subscribes to the columns of Westbrook Pegler, David Lawrence, and Drew Pearson, prints some of the best known comics, and carries a miscellany of syndicated articles on housekeeping, science, education, and the like. In short, a careful reader can pick up a good deal of information from it, as well as some misinformation. Furthermore, as we have noticed, the majority of families see other papers with other policies more or less regularly.

Many of the women interviewed stated that they read the whole paper, but a few admitted that they turned to the local news and the obituary column after a glance at the headlines. Approximately a third said they read Pegler's column, and less than a third read Pearson, whereas nearly half said they read the editorials. Further questioning, however, suggested that very few read either the columns or the editorials with any care. Many women admitted that they read the advertisements more attentively than they did the news.

In addition to investigating the sources of information, the students asked for the expression of opinion on various subjects of current interest. The detailed findings do not concern us here, but one or two points are worth observing. To certain simple and specific questions the response was strong and clear-cut. For example, ninety-seven women expressed approval, qualified or unqualified, of President Truman, and only five expressed disapproval. (This was in July, 1945.) Seventy-nine favored peacetime conscription, and twenty-two opposed it, both sides giving clearly formulated reasons. On rationing the replies, by and large, were both more favorable and more discriminating than I would have anticipated. On the other hand, a question about the United Nations Organization bewildered most of those interviewed. Obviously they knew little about the San Francisco conference, and they were forced to fall back on generalities, with a few referring to the Bible to prove that war cannot be abolished. With regard to the possibility of a post-war depression, the pessimists, the optimists, and the undecided were almost equally divided, and most of the answers suggested that there was a deep fear but little attempt at understanding.

There is nothing in all this to surprise me or anyone else. I have no doubt, however, that these women could be better informed if they wanted to be, for I know two or three careful readers of the Troy paper who show a remarkable familiarity with world events. The women—and the men too—get from the paper and from the radio what they want. One intelligent, high-school educated young woman told me that she always paid attention to the beginning of a news broadcast but stopped listening if there were no big news—"like the invasion of Europe." In this particular instance I am sure there was deliberate rejection rather than mere lack of interest: like so many others, this woman had personal reasons for not wanting to think about the war, and though she could not suppress her desire to learn about major developments, she found it painful to concentrate on the details of the fighting.

Mr. Cutter is an inveterate listener to news broadcasts. (He once said to me, "I listen to all the news I can get, and she [his wife] listens to the comic serials.") During the war he seemed to have a clearer picture than most of what was happening, and yet he remained much more acutely interested in railroad accidents, the death of celebrities, and domestic calamities of various kinds than he was in even the major military events. Unlike the millions of readers of the metropolitan dailies, he pays almost no attention to notorious crimes and trials, but he refers to a first-class fire as soon as I enter the house, asks every time he sees me if I have heard the latest broadcast, and alludes to the fire for days to come. A fire or a railroad accident is a phenomenon his imagination can deal with, whereas the war was not.

Years ago Mr. Cutter heard a program broadcast from the Philadelphia mint. It led him to wonder how new money was put into circulation, and he worried the question for a long time thereafter. It is impressive that a radio program can stimulate speculation on so abstract a subject, and yet Mr. Cutter's interest in monetary transactions remained wholly unrelated to the rest of his thinking. So it is, I suspect, with most of odd bits of information that may be derived from educational programs. And for the most part such programs are not heard. Radio sets are kept on from rising time to bed time in many homes, but the women in these homes—and the menfolk and children when they are present—have a great capacity for not hearing. The women follow the comic serials, as Mr. Cutter called them with conscious or unconscious humor, but I doubt if they are much influenced by them. A few persons listen to serious programs, but in Roxborough, as elsewhere, these are men and women who do more or less serious reading.

No account of Roxborough's reading habits would be complete that failed to speak of the Montgomery Ward and Sears Roebuck catalogs. The former is the more common in our town, presumably because there is a large retail store and warehouse in the vicinity, but many families have both. The catalogs are not only consulted when purchases are to be made; they are standard reference works, and are frequently used to settle arguments over prices and designs. Stan Cutter has even constructed a few simple household devices by studying the pictures in the Monkey Ward catalog. These volumes bring to Roxborough, as to every rural community in the nation, a panorama of all that urban civilization has to offer, everything that the family needs and a great deal that the average Roxborough family has never thought of needing. With what emotions are these handsomely illustrated pages scrutinized? Do Roxborough people feel a great passion to possess the luxuries and refinements they see displayed? Not as a rule, I think. I doubt if they are much interested in the $238 fur coats and the $1500 watches. Their reading of the mail order catalogs, like their reading of newspapers and magazines, is highly selective, and they pay attention chiefly to what seems relevant to their situation. I do suppose, however, that the catalogs—and the newspapers and magazines, too—serve to suggest that there is something almost within reach that might be desirable. On the typical Roxborough mind the pull is slight but steady, and even the old-timers change.

No one can guess what the influence of the printed word is in a town like Roxborough, but experienced politicians do not place much confidence in it. When we were making plans for interesting people in the establishment of a fire district, a politician said, "That's all printed matter, y'unnerstan' what I mean? All printed matter. That won't get you anything. You got to talk to 'em. Either you got to get 'em together and talk to 'em in a body, or you got to go to their houses and talk to 'em separately. But you got to talk to 'em." Since our library came into existence, a number of men and women have said that it was a nice thing for the kids, and as a matter of fact even the librarian has been surprised at the number of adults who patronize it. Old Wilbur North used to thank me for bringing his paper to him, saying, "I'd go crazy if I didn't have it. I'm a pretty good sleeper, but I can't go to bed soon as it gets dark, not in the winter at any rate."

I do not know how unrepresentative small towns like Roxborough are. The gossip columns, the society pages, and the reports of murder trials in metropolitan papers show the eagerness of city-dwellers for news that is or is made to seem personal. Public opinion experts, as I have said, are beginning to admit that most people take only a casual interest in many issues that crucially affect the general welfare. Plenty of studies have shown how highly selective the reading of a newspaper usually is. I would be willing to grant that city people on the average are more aware of what is going on than country people, but I am not sure that the difference is very great.

—ww—

What do Roxborough people know? Neither I nor anyone else, can possibly say. When I think of the vast diversity there is in this little town, I realize that the most cautious statement would have to be qualified a hundred times. Moreover, I cannot trust such evidence as I have. Harvey Dakin, for instance, though he did not go beyond grammar school and though he is by temperament a man of action, lets his mind function freely in every conceivable field and holds carefully considered and always defensible opinions on a great number of subjects. It took me a long time to discover how rich Dakin's interests are, and I have no doubt that there are other men whose range I have failed to explore. I can do no more than offer a series of guesses.

In the fields of religion and philosophy I suspect that there has been a marked deterioration in the past fifty years. The number of churches has dwindled, church attendance has fallen off, and it seems likely that the intellectual and moral quality of the regular church attendants has fallen off too. This is a manifestation of a general tendency, but perhaps the tendency has gone faster and farther in Roxborough than in most places. At an earlier period, I feel sure, most people in the town must have been familiar with at least one set of Christian dogmas. Their adherence may have been a matter of inheritance, prejudice, or blind faith, but up to a point they knew what they believed. I have no illusions about the profundity with which the farmers of the mid-nineteenth century discussed the nature of God and the destiny of man, but

I suppose they did discuss them. In contemporary Roxborough there are some devout believers, and with persons they know and trust, as they don't trust me, they probably talk about their beliefs, but they have grown defensive, feeling themselves in the minority. As nearly as I can make out, the larger number of church-going Protestants in town are fundamentalists, believers, as they would say, in "Bible religion." A smaller number are in some sense modernists. Taken together, fundamentalists and modernists do not represent more than a fifth of the nominally Protestant population. Many of the others consider themselves good Christians, but a surprising number make no bones of their indifference to religious dogmas and institutions. "I'm no more religious than you are," an official said indignantly one day. He would have been equally indignant, I am sure, if anyone had called him an atheist. He meant simply that he wasn't interested in religion one way or the other, and it was the element of conscious neutrality that made his attitude so representative. George Holcomb, as we have seen, was open-minded enough to attend all available churches, and I imagine that many of his neighbors frowned upon this eclecticism. Yet Holcomb devoted a portion of his tiny supply of cash to the purchase of theological studies. Almost no one in Roxborough today has that kind of interest in theology, and yet there are only the rarest and faintest hints that any other body of ideas has taken the place of the dogmas that were current in an earlier generation. "When you're dead," Stan Cutter says, "you're dead." That is not merely boisterous defiance; it is a conclusion drawn from the rudimentary but honest thinking that Stan does with regard to the natural phenomena with which he is familiar. Almost certainly there is other speculation, but it is private, and it doesn't seem to occupy much time.

So far as practical morality is concerned, there has been a similar deterioration. I am not sure to what extent principles of conduct were ever a subject of intellectual consideration and discourse, but I am sure that in the nineteenth century there was general agreement as to what was right and wrong. Today the prevailing attitude is a bewildered latitudinarianism. The narrowness that is supposed to prevail in small towns does exist, but it is not common nor influential. In some ways the new tolerance is a good thing, but I am afraid it is a mark of growing confusion, not evidence of clear thinking. People are increasingly tolerant, it seems to me, not only of deviations from strict monogamy but also of falsehood, malicious scandal, political chicanery, law-breaking, and sharp practice. The development of new situations, for which the old standards prove inadequate, seems to have undermined those standards, so that they are not applied even where they are relevant. I feel that my more thoughtful Roxborough friends, like my sophisticated acquaintances elsewhere, have developed a far-reaching relativism. The only standard they are sure of is consistency. "I wouldn't care how many men she slept with," one woman said of another, "if she'd only keep her mouth off other people." "I can put up with drunkards," a man said, "but I can't stomach them in church." Among some of my close associates, men and women active in community affairs, there is a sense of responsibility to the community as a moral principle, but I can find no such feeling in the majority. The old controls have disintegrated, and no new controls, whether operating from within the individual or imposed from outside, have been developed.

Political thinking also has deteriorated. Republicanism meant something in the past, or, rather, a series of things. At first it meant the preservation of the union and the freedom of the slaves. Then it meant high tariffs, the full dinner pail, and American prosperity. And in the twenties it meant the leadership of business interests. Most recently, however, it has meant merely opposition to Roosevelt. Three-quarters of Roxborough's voters have remained staunchly Republican through the four Roosevelt elections, and it seems clear that the shifting of national issues has resulted in confusion. To be sure, there is confusion everywhere, but in urban communities the clash over Roosevelt policies has brought about some degree of clarification. In Roxborough traditional Republicanism has prevailed, but it has been progressively shorn of any intellectual content. The more than three hundred Republicans voted as willingly for Landon as for Hoover, as willingly for Dewey as for Willkie. I do not assume that there was ever a time when all Roxborough Republicans were well informed, but I doubt if political feeling ever had so slight a connection with political issues as it has now. The situation, moreover, is complicated by the fact that candidates run for local offices as Republicans or Democrats and party loyalties are almost as strong in local as in national elections. Since the differences between the national parties, obscure enough at best, have no relevance in town contests, distinctions are hopelessly blurred.

On the other hand, I can see some progress in the general area of political awareness. It is almost certain, for example, that there is an increasing realization of the size and complexity of the United States. It is true that Mrs. Cutter speaks vaguely of Boston as "over east," and that I was once asked in all seriousness and by a grammar school graduate whether the Hudson River flows into the Atlantic or the Pacific, but it is also true that Mark Betterton visited the TVA some years ago and, Republican that he is, approved of it, and that some of the younger men— moved by the appeal of the last frontier—have talked of going to Alaska. New York City is real to almost everyone, and many citizens have visited it. New York and Washington and Chicago, Florida and Texas and California—all these are located on the average person's map of the United States.

Many far countries became real during the course of the war, if only because Roxborough boys wrote home to tell about them. The war also caused people to think about our enemies and our allies. Japan was easy: the Japs weren't human, and that was that. China and India were large and mysterious, and it was not necessary to think much about them. Germany was, a puzzle: German people seemed to be all right in this country but all wrong at home; the main thing was to give Germany a thorough beating and hope that she would behave herself. England was a fine country, but if some skeptic said that England would bear watching, almost everyone agreed. On Russia sentiment was fairly clear: the Russians were good fighters, but that was one more reason why they were to be looked on with suspicion. Some rudimentary conception of the United States as a world power with world responsibilities did emerge during the war. (I lent my copy of *One World* to several Republicans, but I am not sure any of them read it.) Even while the war was going on, however, most persons were content with a set of rough-and-ready stereotypes, and interest in foreign affairs diminished with the coming of peace.

Whether economic views have been modified or not is hard to say. In the little group of citizens that can be described as respectable and ambitious, the business man is still the ideal. "He's a business man," Mark Betterton will say, as I might say, "He's a great novelist," or, "He's a fine musician." Rodney Brothers has the same attitude, although it is likely to reveal itself, because of his wry humor, in a deprecatory comment: "And he's a business man. You'd think he'd know better than that." On the other hand, the less respectable tend to distrust business men, and so do some of the older farmers. In general, even among those who accept the ideal of the business man, "Big Business" is a term of abuse, though a very vague one. A man can admire Henry Ford and Henry Kaiser and Tom Girdler and still dislike "Big Business."

The depression, so far as I can make out, changed no one's views about private enterprise. Even so small a town as Roxborough has a couple of crackpots who attack not only Big Business but even capitalism. In the next breath, however, they are likely to blame all our national difficulties on the fact that aliens are allowed to take jobs away from good Americans or on the fact that women are not forbidden to work outside the home. The town also has a handful of reflective men and women who wonder what can be done to avoid depressions in the future. To the majority, however, the depression was a natural catastrophe, in no wise different from a drought or a hurricane. During the depression relief was handled as it always had been, and there were people who could see no need for the large-scale plans that were adopted for the nation. Perhaps, deep down, the depression did create doubts about individual self-reliance, but that is as far as change went.

With regard to trade unionism, Roxborough remains hostile or at least unsympathetic. The opposition rests primarily on old-fashioned individualism, bolstered by some feeling that union organizers are (a) city slickers and (b) racketeers. Mr. Cutter, after one of his sessions with the radio, announced that the veterans would have to come home and shoot John L. Lewis and the rest of those crooks. Stan Cutter, who had many just complaints against the management of the factory in which he worked, talked now and then of the possibility of a union, but it was an independent union he wanted, and when the CIO attempted to organize the factory, he and most of the other Roxborough men refused to join. The men and women who do belong to unions are usually willing to admit that their unions have helped them, but, as has been said, they are seldom active members, and some of them are as opposed to unions in general as any of their non-union friends. Perhaps it should be pointed out that these individuals have for the most part seen unions in operation only under the abnormal circumstances of war-time, but at any rate it is true that for them membership has had little educational value. The blame may in part be attributed to a union leadership that is satisfied if dues are regularly paid, but we have already observed that there is a resistance to be overcome. The whole industrial experience, including union membership, tends to be marginal.

Presumably that is why the majority of persons in Roxborough remain indifferent to the broader issues that have been raised by the development of industry. I suppose there aren't a dozen persons in the entire town who could offer passable definitions of capitalism, socialism, fascism, or communism. Communism and fascism, of course, are bad words, but they are almost as bare of specific content as the curse words that circulate so freely. Only the crackpots—and they are crackpots from my point of view as well as Roxborough's—ever talk about capitalism. Other people assume that the current system of production always has existed and always will exist. (It should be remembered that "capitalism" did not become part of the vocabulary of *New York Times* editorials until 1931 or 1932.) As for social planning, I imagine that most people would be more interested in *a* plan to control the weather and would think it more feasible than any plan to regulate production and distribution.

Many realms of thought that are important for me and for all intellectuals do not exist for the people of the town. Though there are some persons who read novels, and occasionally good novels, there is no interest in criticism and certainly none in esthetics. Music, aside from current dance tunes, ballads, and folk songs, is something to be ignored when it comes over the radio. (Stan Cutter has a positive aversion to any form of orchestral music, and when an orchestra is playing he becomes sufficiently aware of the radio to turn it off.) As for the graphic arts, a truck driver said to me one fall day, "No artist could paint a prettier picture than that." This and similar remarks suggest that the function of art, in the view of Roxborough, is to portray the ideal, which the real sometimes measures up to and even surpasses. On the walls of the majority of homes one sees only calendars and family photographs.

Applied science affects Roxborough in many ways. Machinery, as we have seen, is of absorbing interest in itself and in some minds stimulates free speculation. A little is known about the sciences that bear on agriculture, but less than might be. The radio carries news about discoveries in medicine, and Roxborough, preoccupied as it is with sickness and death, is interested, but advertising so garbles the facts about vitamins and the new drugs that what purports to be scientific information descends to the level of superstition. Indeed, the apparent fickleness of medical science is often mentioned in defense of folklore, and not without some justification.

Of pure science there is naturally little knowledge, but I cannot say that there is no interest. Once, for instance, I was present when an unusual rock formation brought forth an hour's discussion of geology. It was a rather desultory, ill-informed discussion, but I think that if a geologist had been present, he would have had an audience. Again and again problems have arisen in biology, chemistry, and physics, and in almost every instance, I believe, a clear exposition of first principles would have been listened to. On the other hand, I admit that interest in the sciences seems to be limited to the younger men, especially those who work with machines. The more widespread attitude is probably that of Mr. Cutter in the matter of the mushrooms. There is a summer visitor who every year sets himself a task in nature study. One year mushrooms occupied his attention, and sometimes Mr. Cutter accompanied him on long trips to gather specimens. An account of these expeditions became part of Mr. Cutter's long saga on the eccentricities of the visitor, and one day I heard it at the store. It was a good story, too, with gestures of poking here and there, a back bent under a heavy load, expressions of chagrin and triumph as the specimens were examined. It came to a climax: "He doesn't eat 'em; he doesn't even like 'em."

If there is one topic on which sentiment does get itself organized and expressed, it is education. Minor issues are raised at every annual school meeting, but the basic and persistent issue is that of centralization. Mark Betterton has often said to me that he wants the kids to have the best there is—"within our means, of course"—but he usually goes on to say that he doesn't know whether all these frills are good for anything. He went to the school in the center when the teacher was only paid a dollar a day, but he learned penmanship—he is justly proud of his handwriting—and he learned how to figure and he learned how to spell, and that's more than a lot of the kids seem to learn today. Betterton, I imagine, will vote for centralization when the issue is

Oil-on-canvas portrait of Granville Hicks painted in the 1940s
by George Cole.
(Courtesy Corporation of Yaddo)

Granville Hicks (center) enjoying coffee with two of his neighbors at his home in the winter of 1946–1947, and (below) splitting wood that same winter. Both photographs by Kosti Rouhomaa for potential inclusion in a *Life* magazine article.
(Courtesy Craib family)

Grafton's main street (State Route 2) in the 1930s.
(Courtesy Grafton Historical society)

The Hicks home on Shaver Pond Road in Grafton in the
winter of 1946–1947, photographed by Kosti Rouhomaa for
potential inclusion in a *Life* magazine article.
(Courtesy Craib family)

Granville Hicks walking down a country road (known as "The Beltway")
near his home in the winter of 1946–1947, photographed by
Kosti Rouhomaa for potential inclusion in a *Life* magazine article.
(Courtesy Craib family)

squarely raised, but the doubts that he voices are more dogmat-
ically held by most of the old-timers. I imagine they will be out-
voted, as they were out-voted not so many years ago in the
matter of electric lights for the school, but they will not be convinced. And it may be that they can convince enough of the
younger natives to delay centralization. "This is a funny town,"
an outsider in politics said to me. "If you can get the old people
on your side, you've as good as won." Not many of the old people will be on the side of centralization.

Yet the demand for something better than the one-room
schools does exist, and it is the clearest expression I have found
of a recognition of change in the world. People say it again and
again and in a variety of ways: our children are going to have to
face different conditions, and they must be educated to deal with
them. There are even a few old-timers who like to tell how they
have fought for progress for the past forty or fifty years and who
say that centralization has got to come. Most of the women in
town, according to the researches of the Antioch College students, expect their children to find employment in the cities and
want them to have the kind of education that will fit them for city
jobs.

If, however, most parents realize that their children must be
prepared for a kind of life that is different from their own, that
does not mean that they feel a sense of personal responsibility for
that preparation. The job is left to the schools. Whatever the parents may say, those of native stock are engaged in inculcating all
the old Roxborough attitudes. To some extent, of course, this is
inevitable: the parents are what they are, and the children take
after them. But that is not quite the whole story, for there are
both conscious and unconscious influences. The average male
parent, I suspect, wants his son to have all the Roxborough qualities plus just enough of city slickness to make good money. As a
result, the boy who goes to a city high school may find that family and town pull one way and school the other. Often enough
family and town win.

What education does do and what it should do are subjects that will be discussed later, but it must be said here that the schools are not performing with notable success the task that has been thrust upon them. I am sure that a centralized school would be better than the one-room schools we now have, but I cannot be too cheerful about even the best schools in this area. I know something about all of them, and I have seen some of their products. Once Harvey Dakin produced a quiz book at a party. "Anything across the pond is out," said Stan Cutter. So, I decided, was anything earlier than memory. Stan never finished sixth grade, but half of those present were high school graduates, and I couldn't help wondering what high school had done for them. More and more Roxborough boys and girls are finishing high school, but it would be hard to demonstrate that the general level of knowledge, to say nothing of intelligence, has risen correspondingly. Whatever education may do, it does not provide a background for ideas or create a medium in which ideas can thrive.

VII

HUMAN NATURE, ROXBOROUGH STYLE

As I have said, nothing gives Roxborough greater satisfaction than a first-class scandal. Some five winters ago we kept hearing that various summer places had been broken into and pillaged. To begin with, gossip was chiefly occupied with the failure of the state police to halt this rural crime wave, but one snowy morning a neighbor phoned in great excitement to say that three boys, two of them local boys, had been arrested. That noon I heard talk of nothing else in the post office and the store. "I don't know that I'm sorry for the boys," an old-timer said, "but I'm sorry for their parents." "Maybe their folks is some to blame, too," the store-keeper put in. Another old-timer, one of the oldest, nodded his head: "We know one of 'em's spilt." And in the post office an old woman said, "It was on the radio—what a disgrace for Roxborough!"

Such things happen, of course, in any kind of community. The very next spring I heard in a medium-sized New England city of an exactly comparable case. A house in which no one was living had been gutted: pipes had been ripped out and sold for junk, furniture had been smashed, and the walls had been covered with obscenities. The Roxborough boys had committed just such acts of vandalism, and so far as thefts were concerned, they had taken only what could be easily disposed of to junk dealers. In the New England city it was the vandalism that convinced the authorities that the offenders should not be treated as criminals. In Roxborough, however, wanton destruction clearly seemed worse than burglary, and led to demands for severe punishment.

It was the boys' hard luck that some of the more flamboyant acts of vandalism had been committed in the pretentious summer homes of wealthy and influential residents of a nearby city. At least one of the victims proceeded to bring pressure upon the district attorney, and he was a person whom even a courageous district attorney could not have ignored. (The victim's wife, it was reported, said that if the boys were not given heavy sentences, she would turn the place over to Father Divine. We felt that the town might be the gainer, but of course we were in the minority.) The district attorney, though not anxious to risk his political future, was not vindictive, and perhaps he treated the boys as mercifully as he dared.

We knew one of the boys well, Steve Wilson, and were fond of his parents. To the Wilsons' acute sorrow and shame was added an agonizing sense of helplessness. Mr. Wilson, a sick man even before Steve's arrest, brooded miserably, saying at one moment that he would not lift a finger to save the boy from just punishment, then striking out bitterly against the corruption and favoritism of the courts. His wife, meanwhile, desperately sought for some remedy, grasping at all the straws the professional politicians threw her way. They could fix it, they assured her, and afterwards they said that they would have fixed it if she had done as they said. But it wasn't fixed, and talking with Steve's lawyer and the district attorney, I knew it couldn't be fixed. The lawyer, one of the city's most vociferous liberals, told me to mind my own business, while the district attorney politely heaped evasion upon evasion. I came to feel, as certainly the Wilsons felt, that we were facing not the impersonal majesty of the law but the whims, stupidities, and especially the fears of highly fallible individuals. The case was settled long before it was tried. The boys were given sentences that, if served successively, would have kept them in prison for more than a century, but the judge, with due emphasis on his leniency, sent them to reform school.

To this point, the affair had been Roxborough's only in so far as the town was the scene of the boys' offenses. The townspeople, that is, had played no role except that of chorus. A new phase began, however, when the boys had served their first six months in the school and were about to come before the parole board. The parents of one of the boys based all their hopes on the influence of a friend, but the Wilsons, encouraged by certain officials, decided to try a petition. It may as well be said now that neither the friend nor the petition did any good: the two boys were not released until later,. and they were released at the same time. The hearings, in other words, were a legal formality, the reality being an agreement between the officials and the vengeful householders.

Our campaign for signatures began badly enough. The first man we showed the petition to signed without argument: "I did just as bad things when I was young; only I was lucky and didn't get caught." But the second said, "No need of boys acting that way. If my boys cut up, I give them a good whaling." And the third happened to be a politician who had had ideas of his own about fixing the case and was peeved because his advice wasn't taken.

The next day, however, we called on a town official, who talked for a long time about the case. "When you get to thinking about it," he said, "it just doesn't seem right for people to be shut up like wild beasts." He not only signed the petition but agreed to accompany us on a tour of the town. Our own efforts in the next day or two proved fruitful, for we limited ourselves to the plain, solid people of the town, people with no political ambitions and no political obligations. By the time we went out with the official, we had a respectable number of names on the petition, and three out of four of those we encountered agreed to sign. In the end, when there were more than a hundred names, some of the politicians climbed on the band wagon.

Most of those who refused to sign the petition were either embarrassed or belligerent. That is, they ran true to form, and, regarding it as a personal matter, expected us to hold a grudge. Harvey Dakin was almost alone in assuming that the question could be reasonably discussed, and even he had to make it clear that, although he hoped we wouldn't be sore, it wouldn't change his mind if we were. Dakin took the position of the stern disciplinarian. No great respecter of the courts and the agencies of law enforcement, he pointed out that the boys had certainly committed the crimes for which they were being punished, and held that they had only themselves to blame if they were caught in the unfair and arbitrary entanglements of the law.

Although no one else stated the argument as well as Dakin, there were others who took his position, and of course it was a position that we could respect even though we disagreed with it. However, most of those who refused to sign did so out of prejudice or timidity, and timidity was the more common motive. "The camp owners are taxpayers, and they wouldn't like this." "I never sign petitions." Or, more typically, "Well . . . " and once or twice, with complete frankness, "I'm not sticking my neck out." Disapproval of the Hickses, on political or other grounds, operated in some instances, and there were other personal factors. As for the men who thought of themselves as big shots, they exhibited their characteristic distrust of anything so open and aboveboard as a petition.

Among those who signed, there was a good deal of simple friendliness. The boys had done wrong, but they had been punished at least as severely as they deserved, and they ought to have another chance. There was also, perhaps, a certain amount of inertia: it was easier to sign than to refuse. And some of the politicians were thinking of the coming election. On the whole, however, I was struck by the readiness with which the majority set down their names. We found what Mr. Willkie was later to call a reservoir of good will, and it was broader and deeper than I had dared hope. Yet I know and knew that the reservoir would never have been tapped if we had not taken the initiative. Even the town official, whose forthright assistance was as surprising as it was valuable, would never have undertaken such a venture.

—◊◊◊—

Most people, in any time and place, dodge responsibility, and the inefficacy of good intentions is proverbial, but I wonder if it is common for inaction to be so directly traceable to fear of criticism. In the PTA, the Defense Council, and the fire company, when a decision had to be made, I have again and again studied the doubtful faces as everyone waited for someone else to take the lead. At town board meetings I have seen the justices and the councilmen glancing shiftily about the table. Invariably people have opinions, and invariably the opinions are privately expressed, with more or less conviction; but a clear, unqualified public statement is rare.

"I'm not sticking my neck out." That, we have sometimes felt, might be the motto of the town. An apparent corollary of the refusal to take responsibility is sharp criticism of the people who do. This criticism merges into an intense suspiciousness of motives, which may in part serve as a defensive rationalization of inaction. A town official once told me that after he had done several favors for an old woman, she said to a neighbor, "I'll never vote for Vincent again. He didn't charge me a cent. He must be making plenty out of the town." Suspiciousness is sometimes part of a more general cynicism. It was one of the least savory of the town's politicians who said to us when we were first active in civilian protection, "I don't see why you do all this work for nothing. I bet the higher-ups are getting plenty of money." And on one of the many occasions when Dorothy was sweeping the town hall in preparation for a PTA meeting, a political hanger-on said, "Why do you have to do all the work? You don't get any more out of it than anybody else, do you?"

All this explains why organizational leadership is usually left to outsiders. The native, when asked to take an *office*, is immediately aware of the kind and quantity of criticism to which he will be subjected. Far better than the outsider he knows how his actions will be scrutinized and how they will be misrepresented. He knows that his failures will be jeered at and his successes belittled. He knows, too, that he can scarcely avoid giving offense to persons he has to associate with daily. On the other hand, if he accepts no responsibility, he will not only be safe from criticism himself; he will have all the pleasures of criticizing others. If the outsiders are fools enough to stick their necks out, let them do it.

If, however, natives are seldom found in positions of leadership, one can almost always discover some of them among the hard workers. These, however, must be divided into two groups. There are those who do their work conscientiously and quietly, whether it is preparing for a supper, canvassing for the Red Cross, or managing a dance. But there are also those who will work only if they are praised for everything they do. I have never seen such an appetite for flattery as some of the natives exhibit, so naive and naked a yearning for assurance and recognition. And it is coupled, as of course it would be, with a touchiness that makes the smallest enterprise a diplomatic feat. "You have to butter them up," the experienced say. Harvey Dakin, however, expounds a doctrine that seems to work equally well: "Just treat 'em rough and they'll respect you all the more for it." As a matter of fact, whether they are buttered up or treated rough, sooner or later they get their feelings hurt, and sooner or later they can be lured back for more work, more praise, and more quarrels.

These are some of the elements that enter into the life of the community, and whenever there is a job to be clone, one sees them in operation. In the autumn of 1945 the board of fire commissioners of the newly established Roxborough Fire District presented to the voters two propositions calling for the issuing of bonds to buy a fire truck and build a fire house. Although we had prepared a statement that seemed to us clear and comprehensive, we heard plenty of rumors of growing opposition, and we were not surprised when the propositions were defeated. What made our position almost hopeless was the fact that we were never able to meet the objections squarely. One opponent, possibly piqued because he was not a member of the board, left behind him a trail of rumors and charges in the barber shop, the beer joints, and the stores, but it was as impossible to involve him in direct debate as it was to catch up with all his stories. While we were convincing one individual that we hadn't made a deal to purchase a certain expensive tract of land, and hadn't the power to make such a deal if we wanted to, a dozen individuals were being told that their taxes would be doubled or that the money would be used to pay the commissioners exorbitant salaries. While we dealt with the few concrete objections that were mentioned to us, a great body of vague but damaging charges circulated in the untouchable region of private whispers.

Possibly the propositions would have won if we had conducted our campaign more energetically and more realistically, relying less on what seemed to us to be the obvious and overwhelming merits of our case. At best, however, there were four powerful factors working against us. In the first place, most of the commissioners were outsiders who had been active in community affairs of one kind or another and had thereby invited criticism and made enemies. In the second place, the prevailing suspiciousness of motives led to ready acceptance of the most fantastic and most discreditable stories. In the third place, the old-timers' perpetual resistance to change made most of them easy victims of the active opponents of the measures, a fact that the opponents were quick to take advantage of. Finally, and most important of all, the habit of avoiding direct public discussion did us irreparable damage. If the people who didn't want fire-fighting equipment had had to come out publicly and say so, I think we should have won. That this is true may be indicated by the fact that no opposition slate of commissioners was nominated, though the existing board had not been popular. To nominate candidates it was necessary to secure only twenty-five signatures, and more than twenty-five blank ballots were deposited in sign of disapproval, but the ballots could be deposited secretly, whereas a signature on a petition was a public matter.

It is not to be supposed that the natives never commit themselves publicly. I can think of a few public meetings in which natives took an active and even violent part. One could hardly call their participation constructive, however. If a native feels sure that he is speaking for a majority of his kind, he is likely to be cocky and even bullying. Even with his feeling that the majority are behind him, he has to work himself up to the point of self-expression, and he usually talks wildly. If, on the other hand, he thinks he is in the minority, a still greater emotional pressure is necessary to bring him to his feet, and when he gets there, he usually explodes.

One cannot say that these people are in any literal sense inarticulate, for in private they can express their grievances eloquently if not logically, but there is a kind of unwillingness to confront issues squarely. This unwillingness exhibits itself in domestic as well as social relationships. Because of the upbringing I had and the career I have followed, it seems to me only natural that any kind of grievance or criticism should be immediately articulated and fully discussed. This does not mean, of course, that my grievances are always rational or that my expression of them is invariably calm and considered, and it may well be that I sometimes speak out when silence would be better, but it is true that almost anything I think or feel gets itself into words. The contrary is the rule in Roxborough. Indeed, the typical resident will go to almost any lengths to avoid a situation in which an issue has to be clearly stated. One day an old-timer told me about the house he had bought in New York City when he worked there. "It was a two-family house, and after we come back here, we let half of it to a sort of cousin. He was supposed to collect the rent for the other half and take care of the repairs, and he got his rent free. Well, he didn't send me any money, and after a while I found that he hadn't even paid the taxes." "I bet you made it hot for him," I said. The old-timer smiled slyly. "I made up my mind I wasn't going to put up with that, so I sold the house, and he didn't know a thing about it till he got his orders to get out."

I know a father and son who live in adjacent homes, each being enough dependent on the other in a variety of ways to make the arrangement an advantageous one. There are, however, the inevitable conflicts between the two families. We and all their other friends can measure the mounting pressure of resentment, and we know when the steam is about to blow off. Again and again we have been sure that a crisis could be avoided if there were a session of frank talk, but there never is. Each family grumbles to its acquaintances, and of course the complaints come back, more or less distorted, to nourish the ill temper in the other house. Soon, as half the town knows, each family is planning some sort of demonstration against the other. Perhaps the younger woman goes away for the day, expecting her mother-in-law to look out for the children when they return from school. Immediately the mother-in-law sets out for a visit, and the children find both houses empty. They don't suffer, of course, for the neighbors take them in, but their mother is outraged, demands that her husband move to the city, and forbids the children to enter their grandparents' home. The grandparents, on the other hand, having made their gesture, become more conciliatory, and in time the crisis is dissipated. The younger family, when it takes the offensive, behaves in the same fashion. The father may return from the city late some evening to discover that the cows are unmilked. It is true, of course, that he didn't ask his son to milk them, but in ordinary circumstances the son would have milked them without being asked. Their not being milked, therefore, is a kind of declaration of war, initiating the familiar process of retaliation and reconciliation. So far as I can see, arrangements are never made in advance, disagreements are never articulated and discussed, and. reconciliations are never explicit.

Of course such behavior can be found everywhere, but in a small town people are constantly aware of what is going on, and the most innocent bystander is likely to find himself involved. The small-towner, indeed, has to learn to accommodate himself to a world of mysterious grudges and unspoken grievances. One of the most intelligent women in town lives in semi-isolation rather than risk unpleasant contacts with the quarrels of others. Naturally forthright and personally incapable of petty jealousy and indirect assault, she will not attack others, and she is pained when they attack her. The bystander's position is particularly dangerous because, here as elsewhere, a family will forget its own quarrels and unite against an attack from without on any of its members. Articulate agreement, however, is as rare in moments of unity as articulate disagreement is in moments of dissension.

The question of articulateness is not a simple one. What I have been talking about, as I have been trying to make clear, is an attitude of mind rather than a mere lack of facility with words. In point of fact, most of the natives are fluent and picturesque talkers, but their gift is for narrative and description rather than argumentation. I have sat through far too many meetings, from Sunday school conventions to Communist Party conferences, to assume that any group of human beings can be expected to deal with its business in a businesslike way, but it does seem to me that no meeting I have ever attended elsewhere, even a college faculty meeting, has wandered along such irrelevant bypaths as almost any meeting in Roxborough follows. The bypaths always seem interesting, and persons who have nothing to say on the topic at hand discover that they are full of ideas on unrelated topics that are somehow suggested to them. Since the purpose of any meeting is felt to be largely or wholly social, those present cannot see why they should deny themselves the pleasure of saying whatever they feel like saying. The ability to focus the mind is a skill that many people fail to acquire, and they find the discipline of logic too arduous to be borne.

I have observed that I am almost—but not quite—the only person to be disturbed by the irrelevancies, and I have reached the point of admitting that the attitude of the majority is natural. I will even go so far as to grant that there is a certain value in the circumlocutory approach. Logic is a fallible instrument, and insistence on keeping to the formal point can sometimes lead one to miss the real point. When Harvey Dakin conducts a meeting, he is endlessly tolerant of digression, and there is no herring too red for him to follow with alacrity and thoroughness. I usually grow impatient, but now and then Dakin's least logical sallies bring forth facts in the light of which I find myself changing my opinions. His method is perhaps a more natural way of attacking a problem than mine. I move or try to move in a straight line. He draws a circle and then explores the area inside it until he feels that he knows where he is. Furthermore, he wants other people to know where they are, and he believes that conviction takes time—even if the time is apparently misspent.

But though there may be some efficacy in Roxborough's methods of conducting an argument, I am certain that they work only for certain purposes and in certain situations. Even in Roxborough the articulate individual has marked advantages, and though others may distrust him, they are likely to turn to him in any situation that is out of the ordinary. Outside of Roxborough, the inarticulate person is clearly handicapped. One of our town officials can make his influence strongly felt when he is with his own kind and can proceed at his own pace. I have seen him with city politicians, however, and he seems tongue-tied. Too self-conscious to talk as he would at home, he knows that he cannot talk the language of the city slickers, and he says nothing.

All this raises the question of the connection between articulateness and a sense of adequacy. In any given instance it is hard to tell what is cause and what is effect, but it seems to me that most men are articulate when they feel adequate to a situation and that most men feel adequate to a situation in which they can find the right words. One thing I have noticed and that is that in general the old-timers seem to be more articulate than their sons. I do not mean that they are any more forthright about the kind of community issue I have been discussing but merely that one rarely finds them ill at ease. The explanation seems to be simple: they are still living in a world to which they have proven themselves adequate, and they are seldom called upon to discuss topics with which they feel incompetent to deal. Political issues are apparently as simple to these men as they were in the days when they cast their first votes for Garfield or Harrison. They

have no businesses to acquaint them with the complexities of
government regulations or the power of monopolies, and they
have never seen the inside of a modern factory. In general the
things they talk about are the things they know well, and the
many things they do not know well infrequently impinge upon
their consciousness.

If this analysis is sound, it would seem to follow that the relative inarticulateness of the middle-aged and younger men must
have something to do with their exposure to a more complicated life. One can call them only relatively inarticulate, of course,
for they can talk eloquently enough on such topics as automobiles and hunting, and some of them are admirable story-tellers
and amusing mimics. Stan Cutter, for instance, is a first-class
raconteur, and everything he says has a kind of style—a crispness
of rhythm and deliberate picturesqueness in expression. He loves
a good phrase, indeed, as much as any writer I have ever known.
As I have said, he has a genuinely speculative mind, and with us
he will talk about war, birth control, science or any other topic
that happens to interest him. Yet it is particularly in our home
that the contrast between Stan and his father reveals itself most
vividly. Mr. Cutter is never in the least abashed by any of our
friends, never betrays the slightest awareness of differences in status or income or manners. Always pleased to meet strangers, he
assumes that they are as interested in him as he is in them, and as
a matter of fact they almost invariably are. If he happens to be
present when there is a conversation on literary matters, he listens without surprise or embarrassment or apparent boredom,
and then, when the right moment comes, throws out a topic of
his own. Stan, on the other hand, though his outward manner is
as easy as his father's, grows uncomfortable in comparable situations. His humor becomes defensive, or perhaps he grows silent,
not quite in his father's courteous way but with a touch of
malaise. Mr. Cutter's manner, when he looks at the long shelves
of books in my study, suggests that he could read them all if he
wanted to, but of course he doesn't want to. He never refers, as

Stan often does in a half-humorous way, to his inability to read a book through, and apparently he has never been embarrassed by the lack of formal education as Stan was the time he applied for a job and was handed a questionnaire. Mr. Cutter's poise may be, as we sometimes feel, an almost unique triumph of character, but there are other old-timers who come close to it, whereas Stan, who is so much like his father in a variety of ways, has been jolted by his contacts with the world outside Roxborough into a sense of differences that could become, in the right circumstances, a sense of inferiority.

There is a story that goes a long way toward proving my point. Some years ago, after long deliberations, Mr. Cutter embarked on a rather ambitious business deal. Hesitant as he had been before the decision was made, he became increasingly ebullient in the days after his name was signed to the document. Suddenly his partner broke off the deal, availing himself of a technical excuse that was legally valid but was certainly not the real cause of his action. For a moment Mr. Cutter seemed to be relieved, but almost at once he began to brood, and within a day or so he had evolved a dozen explanations, most of them assuming that the partner had lacked confidence in Mr. Cutter. The hypothetical insult hurt Mr. Cutter's feelings, and the legal technicalities bewildered and embittered him. And beyond all that, the disruption of plans he had so carefully formulated left him with a sense that his life had lost its purpose. He was not, of course, a young man, and his lack of resiliency was not surprising, but it was amazing and distressing to watch the sheer physical deterioration that took place. He lost weight; his mild, amiable face grew lined; his walk became slow and uncertain. When he was arrested for a traffic violation and fined, he spoke and acted as if society were conspiring to undo him. In time—it was a matter of months—he returned to normal, but I have noticed that, fond as he is of talking about his past, he never alludes to this disappointment.

A guest of ours, after attending a square dance in Roxborough, said that there were just two expressions: apathy and resentment.

This is much too simple—perhaps too literary—an account. What looks like apathy is often enough a kind of mask, and one has to guess what is behind it by catching a twist of the mouth or a brightness in the eye. But conscious as I am of the complexity of Roxborough characters, I cannot gainsay that apathy and resentment are common expressions—and common attitudes, too. What I do maintain, however, is that apathy and resentment are also common expressions on the streets of Troy and the streets of New York City. A great many people, in other words, seem to feel that they are being pushed around, and either they have grown used to it and expect nothing else, or they are perpetually sore about it.

What interests me is that in Roxborough I can see some of the forms that the pushing around takes. In the first place, the economic factor is smaller than I would have supposed and probably smaller than it is in the cities. That is to say, the people as a rule are not worrying about losing jobs or feeling sore because they are underpaid. They were pleased to be making good wages during the war, and there has been some griping as wages have fallen off, but they got along with very little in the early thirties, and they can do it again if they have to. I do not doubt that my fellow citizens would be different, and might very possibly be better and happier, if they had had nothing but healthy food in childhood, if they had been given adequate medical care, and if they had received the best possible education, but to say this is not quite the same thing as saying that their problems are primarily economic. In the second place, I do not think my neighbors are suffering chiefly from the blows of fate or fortune or providence or whatever it is they believe in—physical disasters, that is, ill health, the death of relatives. It has always seemed to me that the lower classes take such blows more philosophically than the upper classes do, and people in Roxborough are certainly philosophical. Most of my neighbors regard death as a natural—or a divine—phenomenon, not as a personal affront. No, if people in Roxborough feel that they are being pushed around, and many of them do, the forces that are doing the pushing are social forces. These are in part the very forces that hold the community together: it is a strain to live constantly in the face and eyes of your neighbors, and I suppose it always has been. For the rest, they are the large and certainly mysterious forces that lie outside the community and are more and more strongly impinging upon it.

It is easy enough to ask who is adequate to the life he has to lead. A whole school of *New Yorker* short story writers thrives on exposing the inadequacies of middle-class and upper-class persons, and in particular the inadequacies of intellectuals. So far as the intellectuals are concerned, however, the stories merely prove that words aren't enough, and that is something I have learned for myself—in Roxborough and elsewhere. If, however, Roxborough has taught me the importance of non-intellectual traits, it has also, in a curious way, led me to respect the equipment of the intellectual as a weapon in the warfare of contemporary life. There are, to be sure, plenty of situations in which the intellectual is helpless, but he has the gift of words, and he has at least some understanding of the world he lives in. Nobody understands that world very well, but the intellectual is not often exposed to the shock of the unfamiliar.

—∿—

While I am on the subject of inadequacy, something ought to be said briefly about neuroticism. In the magazines I sometimes encounter an assumption that only intellectuals develop neuroses, but friends of mine, nursing their mental ailments in various sanatoria, report that these institutions are filled with business men who appear to be as extraverted as George F. Babbitt and considerably duller. Roxborough, backward little town that it is, has its share of neurotics. Naturally I do not know the causes, and I cannot be absolutely sure that in any particular instance the condition is related, one way or another, to small-town life. The chief point is that even a small town has its instances of nervous disorder.

Beyond that, there are some plausible guesses. I can think, for example, of two women, neither of whom was born in the town, though both have lived here for many years. For one of them small-town life seems to have been beneficial. She has had plenty of opportunity to dominate various groups of less aggressive women, and she revels in the petty intrigues and the secret campaigns of slander. The other has grown steadily more suspicious and morose, so that, although she is city-born and city-educated, her attitude toward life seems like a caricature of one aspect of the native mentality. Very possibly her disease would have followed this course wherever she happened to live, but from the outside it appears that the small-town atmosphere has aggravated her neurosis, just as it appears that the other woman has made an easier accommodation here than would have been likely in a city. Incidentally it might be pointed out that the small town provides wonderful opportunities for observing the damage that neurotics can do.

There are also neuroses that can in some sense be called Roxborough's own. Guy and Mary Chester, for example, both members of old families, displayed nervous disorders in childhood, and though both of them managed to get along reasonably well in adult life, one could easily guess that their home was not the healthiest environment in the world. Their several children, however, seemed to be as stable as the average, though I remember them as rather intense and apprehensive boys and girls. Lucy had the best disposition of the lot, and we were all pleased when she married a young man we liked. If everything had gone well for Lucy, I suspect she would have got through life as well as most. Soon after their marriage, however, her husband was drafted, and, more or less against her will, she went to live in a city near the camp where he was stationed. I knew at the time that she was afraid of what this new kind of life might hold for her, but her first letters, telling of the job she had taken, seemed buoyant. Suddenly she came back to Roxborough, lived with her parents, and refused to see anyone. At first people said she was going to have a baby, and then they said she had had a nervous break-down. The sequel is reasonably happy, for she has made a sur-prising recovery, at least on the surface, since her husband's discharge, and is living a normal life. If, however, one catches a glimpse of her face when she does not know she is being watched, one can see evidence enough of persisting tension.

A good many years ago a successful farmer named Bill Fairlee, a man who was then about fifty, suddenly began to say that he didn't feel well and to sit around the house instead of doing his work. I suspect that he was going through the male menopause, but, whether that is true or not, his difficulties seemed to be magnified by the lack of privacy. Lack of privacy, indeed, is gross understatement; his relatives and friends simply concentrated their attention upon him, begging to hear his symptoms, offer-ing him remedies, proposing doctors. Yet I must say that when the crisis was past, all this attention seemed to do him good. People were genuinely sympathetic and as helpful as they knew how to be, and their telling him how much better he looked proved encouraging, just as their lugubrious advice had proved depress-ing. I am only guessing, but it does seem to me that the small-town situation speeded his decline and speeded his recovery.

Then there are the drinkers. Once again I have to remind my-self that one is conscious of the amount of drinking in Roxbor-ough because one is conscious of everything that goes on. Certainly there does appear to be a good deal of it, and it does manage to loom larger than the drinking I have known of else-where—say in New York literary circles—if only because it has less competition as a subject of conversation. A town official, himself a total abstainer, once said to me, naming three upper-class citizens, "They're three of a kind, always talking about the last time they got drunk or the next time they're going to get drunk." These are escape drinkers, I surmise, and they have a good deal to escape from. But there is Art Dibble, a young fel-low with a chest like a barrel, easy-going, a good mixer, good company drunk or sober—why does he get soused every night?

And there is Les Godfrey, a pillar of the church, who is pickled by noontime six days a week, a gentle, good-natured old man, whose wits are probably none too good even when they aren't befuddled. There are others, plenty of them, as there are people who drink in moderation and people who don't drink at all. Perhaps a psychiatrist could make something of this; I can only point out that we do have our alcoholics.

Perhaps something ought to be said about the lower class in connection with this whole problem of maladjustment. I have pointed out that membership in the lower class is, at least in part, a matter of choice. I might add that the choice sometimes seems to be made on what can be called healthy grounds and sometimes on unhealthy. That is, some lower-class men and women seem to be well adjusted to the kind of life they are living and some don't. Perhaps I am romanticizing, but I believe that the well adjusted ones are quite willing to put up with a low standard of living for the sake of the freedom they have. A steady job is a kind of slavery for them, and they would rather hunt and fish and loaf and drink as they please than have expensive homes and dressy clothes. Inevitably this is a type that drifts to the small towns, and though such people contribute little to the community, I do not know that they do it any harm. On the other hand, one has only to look at the hangdog expression on some lower-class faces to realize how much unhappiness can be found in this group. There are more unhappy women than men, I should say, but there are plenty of men who have been beaten down and who know it. Resentment, I think, is less common than apathy.

"We have all kinds of people in Roxborough," Harvey Dakin once said to me, "except maybe downright idiots. I guess they've all been put in institutions." As I have already confessed, I am not qualified to discuss the relationship between small-town life and various types of maladjustment. I can only observe that we have our neurotics, our drunkards, our lawbreakers, our "bums." And what is more, we know we have them. For the average city-dweller, the various types of maladjustment are elements in a problem that he is able and willing to leave to the proper authorities. Of the misfits themselves he knows little or nothing. In Roxborough, on the other hand, one has to reckon not only with adultery but also—and face to face—with adulterers, not only with drunkenness but also with drunkards, not only with violations of the law but also with violators, not only with poverty but also with the poor.

—⁓—

Thus far I have defined human nature as it manifests itself in Roxborough largely in negative terms. What is important, however, is what people are, not what they are not. The problem of values can perhaps be best approached by asking, "Who are the good guys?" It is not a hard question to answer, at least at the outset. Vernon Eldridge is a good guy: a hard-working, self-respecting old-timer, living very much to himself but neighborly and hospitable, and generally admired for the day's work he can do at the age of eighty. Stan Cutter is a good guy. He was a hellion, everyone says, in his younger days, but since he did nothing vicious, the reputation is an asset rather than a liability. He is admired for his physical strength, his wit, his good nature, and his independence of spirit. Independence is the key word: for certain younger men it makes him not merely a good guy but something of a hero. Mark Betterton is a good guy, a storekeeper who has managed to make money without being mean. He does not embody the characteristic Roxborough virtues in the way that Vernon Eldridge and Stan Cutter do, but his shrewdness and soundness are thought of as good qualities, and in him they fit into the Roxborough pattern.

There are other men over whom one has to hesitate a little. Carl Billings, for example, is generally liked, and I have almost never heard a word against him, but he is regarded as a little too much withdrawn to be one of the good guys. The same thing is true of Art Winslow, who minds his own business, slanders no one, fears no one. He is respected, but nobody feels any great warmth toward him. Steve Porter, on the other hand, is remarkably popular for an outsider, but I would say that he is not admired. People like him, but they do not feel quite sure of him, perhaps because it takes a long time for anyone to be fully accepted, perhaps because he retains too many of his city ways.

The case of Jim Morris is illuminating. Probably he is the one man in town who is criticized more frequently and more vigorously than I am, and yet he is looked up to by a great many people. Although he has maintained a summer home in town for many years, he was for a long time engaged in business in the city, and business men, as a rule, are both admired and distrusted. After he settled in Roxborough, Jim went into politics, and, as so often happens with glib-tongued outsiders, he was immediately given a chance to show what he could do. He managed to make himself a power in the Republican party, not only in the town but also in the county, and, what is more remarkable, he has been able to hold his position. He is a typical politician, a born manipulator, a man who worships influence, works hard to acquire it, and does his best to convince other people that he has it. Because so many of his promises have not been kept, he has made countless enemies, but his ability to deliver the goods once in a while keeps a certain group hanging in attendance, like suckers around a con man at the county fair. In general he is regarded as a shrewd man but an untrustworthy one, and though his untrustworthiness is recognized, his shrewdness wins him a respect that is by no means limited to his hangers-on. Furthermore, he performs the task of political leadership, if not with brilliance, then with a certain competence, and in a community in which the qualities of leadership are strikingly rare this is not to be sneezed at.

More dubious is the case of Joe Briggs, who has had a number of small businesses in the town. Most people, I believe, would tell you that Joe isn't in the least a good guy, but there is a certain group that looks up to him. He appears to combine something of Stan Cutter's boisterous independence with the ability to make money. Actually, if my friends are to be believed, he is a coward—and a self-pitying coward at that. As for his financial acumen, that seems to be a matter of cheating, lying, and on occasion stealing. But he has a manner, and so far he has got away with his crimes, and at least a few people are taken in.

I mention Joe Briggs, not because any large number of persons look on him as a good guy, but because it is remarkable that anyone at all regards him as admirable. No one, so far as I can make out, has ever thought of Wallace Burt or Carl Morse as a good guy, and if Harold Bates once had his admirers, he has lost them by now. All three men are better citizens than Joe Briggs, but Wallace is regarded as unbearably bossy, a know-it-all who has to have the last word on any subject, and Morse is a little too coldly opportunistic and greedy. As for Harold Bates, he once made quite an impression on the town, but he talked so loudly and so extravagantly that people have come to think of him as a bull-thrower and nothing, else. As a matter of fact, though he is scarcely the kind of all-round genius he makes himself out to be, he is in many ways an able man, but few persons in Roxborough are likely to believe it.

If my neighbors were asked what virtues they believe in and admire, many of them, I have no doubt, would say honesty, generosity, sobriety, and so on. But it is mostly the women who would list the conventional virtues, and I am not sure how many of them believe what they think they believe. The majority of men would put first such qualities as Stan Cutter displays: physical strength, courage, and independence. Harvey Dakin, for instance, who has all these qualities, is almost universally respected, though he is disliked by some who are rubbed the wrong way by his outspokenness. Next in importance would come shrewdness in the management of one's own affairs, and this might mean a relatively scrupulous efficiency such as Betterton has or a rather dubious skill in manipulation such as Jim Morris counts on or even petty crookedness of the kind Joe Briggs engages in. Last on the list would be the social virtues. Of these, pure sociability would rank highest—the gifts that make Stan Cutter good company, the gifts that lead people to forget for a time that Steve Parker is an outsider. Qualities that might prove directly useful to the community probably would not be mentioned at all, but if you were to suggest that so-and-so had done a good deal for Roxborough, so-and-so would be praised—unless he had happened to offend the person with whom you were talking.

The absence of any very acute sense of social responsibility is sufficiently demonstrated by the attitude most Roxborough men take toward the law. I can understand their indifference to game laws, their feeling that these apply only to city slickers. I can also understand their disregard for traffic laws and similar regulations, since in this respect their attitude is merely that of the majority of Americans. What bothers me is a more general cynicism. I am not naive enough to be unaware that this kind of cynicism is wide-spread, and I would expect to find it in such a metropolitan area as William H. Whyte describes in his *Street Corner Society,* but I am a little surprised to discover how easily it has naturalized itself in a community that might be expected to have some defenses against it. It is, of course, good American doctrine that every man should look after himself with the devil taking the hindmost. In many relationships this doctrine is less thoroughly applied in Roxborough than in most of the cities I have known: self-seeking is at least curbed by the obligations of neighborliness. But every predatory pioneer instinct goes into operation when the average native is confronted with his government—town, state, or federal. Governmental bodies apparently exist to be cheated, and regulations were made to be evaded. It is no wonder that during the war the black market had its Roxborough customers. Many of those who bought in the black market were intensely patriotic, and not merely in words, but they followed their deepest convictions and got theirs when and where the getting was good. The fact that in getting theirs they were putting something over on the government did not diminish their pleasure.

I have occasionally discussed these matters with Harvey
Dakin, who insists that, far from maligning the people of the
town, I hold much too generous views of their ethics, I always
reply that there is Harvey Dakin. And there he is. He has standards all right, and not much tempered with tolerance or mercy
either. The drunks, the incompetent hangers-on, and the shiftless
are bums to him, and though he can be pleasant to them—"Hell,
I'll speak to anybody"—he has never been known to flinch when
plain talking was called for. For the subservient and cowardly he
has less regard than he has for the bums, and for hypocrites he
has no use at all. Physical courage he holds as highly as Stan Cutter does, and he is even more genuinely independent, for he has
a subtler mind and cannot be swayed by mere affability, and, on
the other hand, his independence rarely lapses into irrational
stubbornness. His attitude towards the law, as has been suggested, is somewhat ambiguous: he has little respect for the men who
make laws and he knows all the tricks of the men who enforce
them; yet he has a deep-seated regard for the idea of the law. In
practice he trusts his own acute sense of justice rather than the
statutes, and he tends to rely on the sharpness of his tongue and
the power of his arm for the enforcement of fair play, but he is a
long way from the lawlessness of a Joe Briggs. At bottom he has
strong feelings of social responsibility. No busybody, no would-
be big shot, he never thrusts himself forward, but his support is
forthcoming whenever it is needed. Fond as he is of denouncing
the backwardness of Roxborough and the spinelessness of its
citizens, I am sure he has some unconfessed hope of change.
Whether that is true or not, he stands ready to do what he can.

To our way of thinking, Dakin is the best that Roxborough
can offer, and a best that the town need not be ashamed of. I
have known few persons anywhere who were clearer about their
values or more loyal to them. There are other men and women,
scattered through the town, who also have standards of their
own and do their best to live up to them, and in praising Dakin
I would not want to seem to disparage them. But there is not

much to be said for the values of the majority. They are purely personal or at most can be stretched to include a family or a small clique. Measured by whatever principle one chooses—the ethical teachings of Christianity, the public school conception of the good citizen, even the utilitarian doctrine of rational self-interest—they stand hopelessly low. I once would have said that these people have no values, but I know that is wrong. What I can say is that their values are almost entirely unformulated and are never subjected to rational examination. I can say, furthermore, that they are not values on which a civilization of any very notable quality is likely to be founded.

The proof of the pudding is in the bringing up of children. I have seen a good deal of the children of Roxborough over a period of ten years, and I am prepared to make certain generalizations. First, I would say that there are a few homes in which a conscious attempt is made to instill a positive code of ethical values through indoctrination and example. Second, there are rather more homes in which the parents try to impose their views of right and wrong by sporadic scoldings and an occasional beating. Finally, there are many homes in which the only curb on the children's behavior is the bad temper of the parents. In the homes of the second as well as in those of the third group, children naturally acquire their parents' disregard for the welfare of others, their habits of evasiveness and deception, their lax views of law. I might quote Harvey Dakin again. He says, "Nobody likes kids any better than I do, and nobody is any more anxious than I am to see them get ahead. But they haven't got a chance in this town unless a lot of the old folks die off before they've had time to ruin them." I omit the profanity.

—⚶—

Whatever I say about values in Roxborough is of necessity extremely tentative, but I can speak with some certainty on one point, namely, the effect of our years in Roxborough on my own scale of values. In general I have acquired a greater respect for the qualities my neighbors admire—for physical strength, physical courage, manual dexterity. On the other hand, as I have intimated, I place a higher estimate on sheer intelligence than ever before in my life. Knowledge—to say nothing of erudition or sophistication—seems less important, but intelligence seems more so. Most of my neighbors are more or less handicapped by lack of knowledge, but some of them can grasp a set of facts and some can't, and I am constantly struck by the vast difference between the former and the latter.

Loyalty—to the town, to an organization, even to friends—I have come to appreciate in proportion as I have discovered its rarity. I was brought up on Galsworthy's "it's not enough," and of course I know that loyalty isn't enough. But it is something. In the rarefied world of the intellectuals loyalty may not be greatly missed. The best of the intellectuals are loyal to ideas, and that is a kind of loyalty for which I have great respect. But even the simple human loyalty to be found in Roxborough has come to seem admirable, for it is. the chief corrective to greed and malice. By contrast with all the selfish, the two-faced, the weak-willed, the people who can be counted on are fine people.

Efficiency I have always valued; it is one of the allegedly American virtues for which I have great respect. And I have found it considerably less common than it is supposed to be—in the academic world, in political organizations, and certainly in business itself. In Roxborough it is not common at all. Even in those areas in which Roxborough men have solid skills, one does not often find a man who knows what he can do, who does what he promises, and who does it on time. Not only is it hard to find men who will accept responsibility; it can be counted the greatest good fortune if, once a man has agreed to do a job, he actually does it. In this respect if in no other, I am convinced, Roxborough is representative: the world's affairs are almost certainly conducted by persons who are habitually late for appointments, who always do less than they promise to do, and who constantly keep their associates in the dark. Running head on against this kind of slackness, as one is bound to do in a small town, I give periodic thanks for the few men and women who can and will make a decent job of whatever they undertake.

Finally, I have a new respect for what is unquestionably the small town's transcendent virtue—neighborliness. To many of the older people it is a whole code in itself, and few of the younger ones will fail to inconvenience themselves if a neighbor is in trouble. You may gossip about your neighbor, and you may even quarrel with him openly, if you and he are the quarreling kind, but you help him when he or any of his family falls sick, you tow his car if he can't get it started, look after his stock when he goes away, rush to his aid if his house gets on fire, and put on your best clothes to go to his funeral. Behind all this is the simple fact of interdependence: you need your neighbor and he needs you. And there is also the effect of proximity: you have to be tough to ignore the misfortunes of a person you are going to keep on seeing day after day. But whatever its origins, neighborliness has gone deep into the grain. More than once, on thanking a man for a favor, I have been told, "We've got to be neighborly." Mr. Cutter has often said, "If I couldn't be neighborly, I'd feel pretty small." I can see the limits of neighborliness—the vices that are compatible with that virtue—but it is a candle that throws a considerable beam and gives off heat as well as light.

What I come back to, whenever I consider Roxborough's values, is the difficulty of getting at the vital principle of any human life. Habitually we think of other people in negative terms, and that habit is in itself an assertion of our vital principle. In Roxborough men talk of niggers, kikes, and wops, trying to push certain people out into some limbo where they don't have to be dealt with. Why are they to be pushed out? Simply because it makes it easier for the person who does the pushing to assert himself—the sacred, positive self—with less fear of challenge. I have seen the phenomenon at every level: the snobs disdaining the lower classes; the intellectuals with their scorn for the booboisie; the communists ruling out the capitalists and (at certain stages) the reactionary middle class and the un-class-conscious proletariat. I know all the words that shut people out: intelligentsia, liberal, progressive, right-thinking, Nordic, Gentile, 100 percent American. What is dangerous in these words is not that they imply, "I am right and you are wrong," for that can be argued about and should be. No, the danger lies in the assumption, "I exist and you don't."

All of this I might have learned from psychology—to say nothing of literature—and of course in a way I had learned it. But I have learned the lesson in a more concrete and practical fashion by being confronted with a diversity of temperaments in a situation that eliminates the easy possibility of evasion. Most of us have energy enough to know only a few persons, and the persons one chooses to know, in this sense of the word, are naturally persons more or less like oneself, while persons not like oneself, it is convenient to believe, are not worth knowing and perhaps really aren't persons at all. In having to deal with persons quite different from myself and my earlier associates, I have been forced to break down some of the old habits of exclusion. I have always thought that it was unintelligent and evil to throw racial or religious or national groups into the discard, but it is just as wrong-headed to think one has said something significant about a man when one has called him immoral or shiftless or stupid as it is to assume that one can dispose of an individual by naming the color of his skin. It may be more meaningful to say that some members of Roxborough's lower class are stupid than it is to say that Marian Anderson is a Negro, but anybody who supposes that their lives can be defined solely in terms of stupidity is almost as wide of the mark as the most bigoted fascist. For certain purposes it is convenient to classify certain individuals as capitalists, but for other purposes the classification is simply a barrier to understanding—as anyone who has listened to radicals talking about "They" ought to know.

Furthermore, I have come to realize—again not for the first time but in a more practical way—that every individual not only is a positive personality but has an idea of himself as a positive personality. Everyone creates a picture of himself, and everyone tries to sell that picture—and not merely to others. A writer is fortunate, for he has talents that enable him to develop his picture with a richness of convincing detail, but if he is good for anything, he knows better than other people what he is doing, or is at any rate more fully aware of the existence of a reality that is infinitely more complex than the created image. Moreover, as Dostoyevsky discovered when he wrote *Notes from the Underground,* no matter how hard the writer tries to strip his self-image of conventionally admirable ornaments, no matter how rigorously he seeks to avoid flattering interpretations, no matter how mercilessly he denounces himself as a miserable sinner, he knows that the result is simply another picture—more interesting, perhaps a little nearer the truth, but still an image and not the reality.

This, too, is a lesson I learned from the psychology textbooks, but it is somehow a different matter to see the principle expressing itself in Roxborough. The swing of octogenarian Vernon Eldridge's shoulders as he strides down the highway—does it not say beyond the eloquence of words, "I'm Vernon Eldridge, eighty years old, still hale and hearty, still able to do a day's work that would send most of you weaklings to bed?" Is Jim Morris really a politician, or is he merely an actor of indifferent talents who has assumed for a decade or two the politician's role? And Stan Cutter, so magnificently spontaneous, so careless of public opinion—he is an actor, too, though he would be indignant if I said so to his face. Stan knows his part and loves it, but others aren't so sure. Joe Briggs wants to be smart and virile and domineering, but he also wants to be a pathetic child, mistreated by fate and in need of mothering. Mark Betterton the American Business Man yields the stage now and then to Mark Betterton the Misunderstood Husband. The study of the *imago* is as complicated as it is interesting.

Economic equalitarianism, it has been pointed out, would eliminate the existence of people living in different ways and therefore incapable of understanding or feeling each other's problems. Roxborough, as we have seen, is not quite class-less, but it comes fairly close to it, and within its narrow boundaries people do pretty well understand and feel each other's problems. I do not pretend that I like everyone in the town. There are a few persons I like very much indeed, some I strongly dislike, some of whom I disapprove, and many toward whom I have no particular feeling. But there is no one in the town—well, to be honest, almost no one—who is a blank, who exists for me merely as a function or a type. Good, bad, or indifferent, they are there— forces, dynamos, or, more accurately, entities, organisms, or, to he quite clear, human beings.

VIII

INSTITUTIONS AND PEOPLE

People who live together create or adopt or have forced upon them institutions that more or less adequately serve their common needs. On the surface the institutional life of Roxborough is easy to describe. What lies below the surface is a different matter.

The most important institution is the machinery of town government. This would always be true, I think, in a New England town, but it is not necessarily true in New York. The township in New York seldom counts for so little as it does in the South and West, but it can be relatively unimportant. Roxborough, however, has no sub-divisions to which residents feel prior loyalties. Sectional feeling does exist here and there, but there is little for it to feed on, for the stores and the churches and the town hall are all in the center of town. Not everybody feels that he belongs to Roxborough, but most people do, and after all there is nothing else to which one can belong.

Roxborough is what New York State law calls a third-class town. Every two years it elects a member of the county board of supervisors, who is also the leading official of the town, with control over most of its financial affairs. The governing body is the town board, composed of the supervisor, two justices of the peace, and two councilmen. The justices and the councilmen serve four-year terms, one justice and one councilman being elected biennially. The justices, as their title indicates, have judicial duties, misdemeanors coming within their jurisdiction and also damage suits involving less than $100. The supervisor presides at board meetings, and the town clerk, along with his other duties, serves as the board's secretary, though he has no vote. Other elected officials are the road superintendent, the tax collector, and three assessors. A welfare officer is appointed by the board.

The school system is entirely independent of the town government. Roxborough has seven common school districts, six of which are currently operating one-room schools. (The seventh school was closed in 1943 because there were so few children that the state withdrew its aid, but the district continues to function as a legal entity, contracting with other schools for the education of its children and levying taxes to pay for this.) Each district elects a trustee and a collector-treasurer at its annual meeting and votes upon a budget. The trustee calculates the tax rate on the basis of the budget, and the collector takes in the money. Theoretically the trustee has almost unlimited power, but in fact, if his district is to obtain state aid, he has to observe a multitude of regulations. The district superintendent, whose territory in this instance embraces four towns, keeps the trustees in line, straightens out the messes they get into, and does a considerable part of the work they are supposed to do.

The fire district also is legally independent of the town government. A fire district ordinarily embraces only part of a township, but ours was established to include the whole of Roxborough. When the district was created, the town board appointed five commissioners and a treasurer to serve until the first annual election, but after the election in December the district was on its own. The commissioners are authorized to spend up to $1000 a year for the purposes of fire protection, taxes being levied to pay for these expenses. Larger sums can be expended only with the approval of the resident property owners of the district.

Roxborough has three churches—Methodist, Baptist, and Catholic. The Baptist and Methodist churches have considerable histories, whereas the Catholic church is relatively a newcomer. It is open only during the summer months, when there are people from the lakes to attend mass, and it is served by a priest whose principal charge is a parish some miles distant. The Methodist church also has a non-resident pastor. Both the Methodist church

and the Baptist maintain Sunday morning services and Sunday
school throughout the year. The Baptist church has a Thursday
evening prayer meeting, and the Methodists have sometimes
held Sunday evening or midweek services.

Other organizations come and go. Roxborough once had a
lodge of a fraternal order, and the Ku-Klux Klan flourished
briefly in the town. A few years ago a Community Benevolent
Association was formed, but it lasted only for a season. Of the
current organizations, the oldest is the Parent-Teacher Association, which was founded in 1936. The Defense Council, as has
been noted, came into existence soon after Pearl Harbor, and
transformed itself into the Community League in the summer of
1944. The volunteer fire company was organized in the spring
of 1944. There have been 4-H clubs in various parts of the town,
and for a time there was a youth group sponsored by the Community League and the PTA. In the winter of 1945–46 a branch
of the Veterans of Foreign Wars was organized.

This is the framework. The list of institutions seems meager
enough, and an outsider might feel that there was little to be said
about them. That is not the way one feels when one has lived
with them for a few years.

—∞—

Of the religious life of the town I can speak only at second hand.
The Catholic church is loyally supported by certain residents, including a few old-timers, but the fact that it is open for only part
of the year and has no resident priest limits its effectiveness in the
community. Its chief contribution to the social life of the town is
its annual carnival, and though some old-timers object to the sale
of beer and the use of gambling devices, many Protestants turn
out for it. Individual Catholics, so far as I can perceive, are no
more and no less likely to participate in community activities than
individual Protestants. Although Roxborough was once a Klan
town, Catholics are now prominent in both political parties, and
Republican Catholics have frequently been elected to office.

Theoretically the Baptist and Methodist churches divide between them a great section of Roxborough's population. Much of the time, however, either church is lucky to have a score of worshippers at a service. The Baptist church is made up largely of old-timers, and is fundamentalist in theology, its ministers usually being graduates of Moody Bible Institute or some similar Bible school. One of its ministers took an active part in community affairs and was friendly with non-Baptists, and he was dismissed though theologically he was orthodox. The present pastor is a young man who prides himself on preaching nothing but the Bible, and he has succeeded in attracting larger congregations than have been common in recent years. As a rule the church holds only a single public function, an annual donation supper for the benefit of the pastor, and even this is frowned upon by some ministers, who can find no scriptural authority for it. The members oppose the use of church property for any secular purpose, and in general keep the church aloof from the community. Certain individual Baptists, however, participate in the work of the Community League and the PTA.

Protestant outsiders, who are not welcomed into the Baptist fold unless they are bona fide Baptists, naturally turn to the Methodist church, but the core of that institution is a group of old-timers. The Methodist ministers who have served the church in our time have all come under liberal influences, and the members put up with a certain amount of preaching on social issues, though not always without complaint. The present pastor has made notable contributions to the community in which he has his home and the larger of his parishes, and we cannot help wishing that he lived in Roxborough. The Methodist church, more willing to serve the community than the Baptist, has lent its hall to the PTA for clinics, and in. the days of blackouts the hall was headquarters for civilian protection and a meeting place for first-aid classes. The Community League meets there, and so on occasion does the board of fire commissioners. In view of the town hall's limitations, Roxborough is lucky that the Methodists are so hospitable. As a body the Methodists do not contribute much to the town's social life except occasional suppers. There are more Methodists than Baptists, however, in the community's various organizations.

When a town has so few institutional resources as Roxborough, it seems a duty to support those that there are, and, in view of the part that the church has traditionally played in community life, I have often felt that it was illogical for me not to associate myself with one of Roxborough's churches—which could only mean in practice with the Methodist church. Of course there is some question whether I am not doing the church a favor by remaining aloof from it, since it is one institution that people cannot say I am trying to run, but, aside from that, I have never been able to convince myself that dogmas should be lightly ignored. Some years ago there was a minister who suggested, in a rather offhand manner, that good intentions were all that mattered. I could not and cannot agree. What I don't believe is as important to me as what I do believe, and the right to disbelieve seems to me one of the fundamental freedoms. I know that disbelief appears to be getting on well enough in the world as it is, but there are still plenty of people who are being bulldozed into pretending to accept dogmas of which they would like to be skeptical. There are compromises the intellectual in a small community has to make and can make with a clear conscience, but adherence to orthodoxy does not seem to me to be one of them.

Furthermore, I find a certain doubt arising as to whether work in the churches is an effective way of helping the community. In some communities it would be, but perhaps not in Roxborough or in the towns that are like it. Decay has gone too far. The Catholic church, here as elsewhere, continues to exert influence over virtually all persons who consider themselves Catholics, but the two Protestant churches reach only a small proportion of the nominal Protestants. When I think of the revivals that shook the town all through the nineteenth century, and when I remember that as recently as the eighteen-eighties two new sects were established, I marvel at the progress indifference has made.

Is there anything the churches could do to restore their standing in the community? The Baptists, of course, profess to believe
that the old-time religion is the only way to regain the old-time
prestige, but mostly, I think, they have little faith in this, and live
in the past because they like to. They set their teeth and say,
"This is ours; this we shall keep no matter how the world goes."
Certain Methodists feel the same way, but they have less control
over their ministers and have had to listen to a different doctrine.
Small doses of modernism and the social gospel, however, seem
only to irritate the old-timers without capturing the imaginations
of the younger members. If the change had begun earlier or had
been more drastic, the results might be better, but I am by no
means sure of that.

So far as the practical problems of both churches are concerned, they might be solved by a merger, but this is not likely to
happen until a generation—and perhaps it will have to be two
generations of Baptists—have died.

—⁓—

The other organizations of the town I know better. They have
developed in our time, and we have had a share in their growth.
The Parent-Teacher Association, as I have said, is the oldest, and
it has been in existence for less than a decade.

No native has ever been president of the PTA, and in 1944-45
its president, both its vice-presidents, and its secretary were outsiders. A goodly number of natives pay their annual dues, but
only three or four can be found among the active members.

Even more striking is the poor representation of parents of
children in the Roxborough schools, Even in normal times winter travel is difficult in Roxborough, and the outlying districts are
bound to be poorly represented, but the district in the center and
a neighboring district that also lies on the highway do not do
very well. Studying these two districts in 1944–45, we found that
only six mothers out of a possible twenty-six attended PTA
meetings. Most of the active members are not parents of children
in the schools, and some are not parents at all.

The problem can be understood partly in terms of class divisions. In District 1, for example, seven or eight of the families with children in school belong to the lower class, and, like most members of that class, rarely participate in any organized activity. Some of them are perhaps timid and a little ashamed; some are resentful, feeling that the PTA is an upper-class organization and the upper class can have it; some are indifferent. Almost certainly the PTA could do more than it has done to reach these people, but at bottom the problem is one that involves the whole community. Of course the PTA everywhere tends to be a middle-class organization. The trouble in Roxborough is that so many of our children do not have middle-class parents.

There have been various attempts to reform the PTA, but they have come to little. By and large the organization is dominated by a small group of women who are willing to work hard so long as they can have the power and the glory. They are more interested in a large membership list than in reaching the parents of schoolchildren, and they are more concerned about the approval of the district office than about education in Roxborough. Under their leadership, the PTA has done one job well—medical services for the children. It has held clinics, bought glasses for children whose parents could not afford them, and arranged for tonsillectomies. What it hasn't done is to help Roxborough parents and teachers to understand what is happening to education in the world today and why it fails to take with so many Roxborough children.

I myself have had little to do with the PTA, but Dorothy has been its president and has served in other offices, and I think she would not disclaim her share of responsibility for its shortcomings. One must always wonder what one could have done with any organization if one had had a little more tact or a little more energy. Aside from this question of personal inadequacy, she feels that blame is to be attributed to the particular Roxborough situation but also to the ideals and theories that guide the work of the PTA on the national scale. The self-expression of middle-

aged, middle-class women is doubtless important, but it doesn't
have much to do with the problems of Roxborough's schools.

—∿—

Civilian protection in Roxborough was largely Harvey Dakin's
creation. At first he was simply chief of the auxiliary police, but
later he became deputy director of civilian protection for the
town. From the beginning he insisted on complete freedom from
political interference and careful selection of personnel. Most of
the nearby towns enrolled large numbers of volunteers. Dakin
was satisfied with less than thirty men, but he saw to it that they
were good men to begin with and were given proper training.
The number dwindled, of course, as the younger men went into
the army and navy, and interest declined as the danger of raids
diminished. Meetings were weekly, then bi-weekly, then monthly. But Dakin made sure that he had an adequate force until civilian protection was officially abandoned.

The Defense Council, as it was organized soon after Pearl
Harbor, was composed of the heads of the protective forces, the
chairman of the Red Cross, the town supervisor, and the chairman of the salvage committee. In the spring of 1942, when New
York State clarified its system of civilian protection, the council
ceased to have an official status, but by then it had proven too
convenient an arrangement to be abandoned. It continued to coordinate protective activities and also supported Red Cross, National War Fund, and bond campaigns. It held dances and
suppers, and in the winter of 1943-44 ran weekly square dances,
not so much to raise money as to provide recreation for the people of the town. It set up the town honor roll, and each year it
raised a fund to send Christmas presents to Roxborough men
and women in the services. From the spring of 1942 to the autumn of 1944, it issued a bi-weekly bulletin, which carried news
of the protective agencies, reports of blackouts, appeals for the
various wartime drives, notes about Roxborough service men,
and a certain amount of miscellaneous community news.

So far as civilian protection was concerned, most people were thoroughly cooperative. Even at the outset there were a few haters of Roosevelt who seemed to believe that he had invented blackouts especially to torment them, and of course people became bored with the whole business as the war proceeded, but from first to last the majority scrupulously observed blackout regulations. That did not mean, however, that the Defense Council was universally popular. Dakin's outspokenness had offended a certain number of individuals at the outset, and my participation bothered others. There came to be an anti-council faction, whose members asserted that we were trying to run the town, and on occasion public opinion was sharply divided. When we first raised the question of an honor roll, certain members of the town board opposed us, presumably because they wanted to show us who was boss. They and their supporters were naturally irritated when we refused to be beaten, and feeling was high for and against us. There are few persons now, I imagine, who are sorry that Roxborough has an honor roll, and there cannot be many who suppose that the town would have had one if it had not been for the Defense Council.

At first it was easy to keep the Defense Council and the civilian protection forces distinct, but as the one expanded and the other dwindled, they tended to become identified. Most of the wardens and policemen supported all Defense Council activities, and we began to forget who was formally a member of the council and who wasn't. In the end we were all meeting together, and our work was done in an atmosphere of good feeling.

It seemed a pity that that kind of esprit de corps should be lost, and as the end of the war came in sight, we transformed the Defense Council into the Community League. When we decided to incorporate, a lawyer friend of mine drew up the papers, and he composed a handsome statement of purposes, including a reference to "the highest ideals of Americanism." Actually our aims were perfectly simple. In the first place, we had enjoyed meeting together and we wanted to continue. In the second place, we thought we had shown those people who said that nothing could be done to change Roxborough, and we wanted to show them some more. Naturally the league hasn't the spirit that the Defense Council had in the days of war excitement, but its record isn't bad.

One thing the league has done is to continue the bi-weekly bulletin. When this was abandoned in the autumn of 1944, there was an outburst of lamentation, some of them from the unlikeliest sources. All through the winter people spoke sorrowfully of the bulletin's passing, and we on our part found that our activities were handicapped by the lack of effective publicity. In the spring I announced that I would revive the bulletin if I could be given some help and if contributions were forthcoming to pay for postage and paper. Thus far the contributions have been adequate and the assistance dependable. Whatever people think of me, whatever they think about the Community League, they read the bulletin and are glad it exists. I overheard a man say in the store, "I do like that little paper. That's one thing this town's got that no other town round here has got anything like it."

The library also has been a success, and the town board, which was so indifferent to our original proposal, has actually agreed to contribute to its support. The success of the library has surprised many people, and I confess that I never thought we should have fifty borrowers within the first month. We have a thousand books now, and there are always fifty to a hundred out on loan. The library is open two afternoons and two evenings a week, and sometimes the volunteer worker sits and shivers while nobody comes, but at other times the two little rooms are crowded and gay and neighborly. There have been plenty of problems, particularly the problem of shelf space and the problem of heat, but we have managed to get along, not so well as we should like but better than we dared hope. Although there is always more work than we can find time to do, the essential jobs are done and the books do circulate.

Everyone in the league knows what the next task is: we need a community center that will give the library a permanent home and provide recreational facilities for the young people, and such a center could be an appropriate war memorial. As I write this, the league is still hesitating, more than a little staggered by the dimensions of the undertaking. Skepticism has been strengthened by the defeat of the propositions at the fire district election. Will a town that refuses to finance a fire house contribute enough money to build a community center? The fire house could have been paid for over a long period, and the annual increase in taxes would have been imperceptible. The community center can be built only if large numbers of people are willing to make considerable contributions. I imagine we shall have a try at it, but at this point I will not predict success. Much depends on what happens to the economic life of the town, and this in turn depends on the economic situation of the region. That is uncertain, and the temper of the townspeople, I am afraid, is equally so.

Whether we succeed in our ultimate ambitions or not, I think it is clear that the Defense Council and the Community League have made an impression on the town. Our numbers have never been large, and we have had steady opposition, but we did our wartime jobs reasonably well, and we have some solid peacetime accomplishments to our credit. When I try to define the spirit of the league, I always think of the sort of thing Dakin used to say to a new member of the protective forces: "We get along together all right. Maybe some of us make mistakes. Maybe we all do. Who doesn't? But we do the best we can. And if anybody does make a mistake, you can tell him about it and he won't get sore. I don't care whether it's me or Mrs. Hicks here or who it is. If anybody's got any peeves, he can spit 'em out. We don't go round talking behind each other's backs. We don't have to, because anything we want to say we can say right here. You'll hear people saying we're a bunch of damn fools. Maybe we are. But we've got along pretty good so far."

No doubt it is obvious that I have a special affection for the league, and some Roxborough people might say that this is natural enough in as much as the organization is a Hicks show. In a way it is a Hicks show, for it was our idea that the Defense Council should be given a permanent form, and we have suggested many of the projects that the league has sponsored. On the other hand, we have never put forward a plan that we had not discussed in detail with Dakin and others. Plans are sometimes so well discussed in advance that they can be voted on without discussion at the meetings, but when there are disagreements, they are unhesitatingly expressed. A friend of mine who attended one of the meetings said that I did too much of the talking. I pointed out that in the league I could talk whereas in other organizations I couldn't. In other organizations any moderately articulate individual—Jim Morris or myself or anyone else—can talk his head off without opposition and secure the passage of almost any motion he wants to present, but disagreement will be expressed privately, and the proposal, whatever it may be, will be effectively sabotaged. In the league I can be reasonably sure that someone will tell me if I get too far off the track.

The situation within the league seems to me to be perfectly healthy. I am not so happy about the league's relationship with the community as a whole. We have been careful about adding new members, for a rapid expansion, as Dakin is always pointing out, could destroy the good fellowship and mutual confidence that are our great assets. Inevitably, however, we have alienated persons who might have worked with us if they had been coaxed to join. From the earliest days of the Defense Council, as I have indicated, we have had two types of opposition to contend with: the opposition of certain politicians, who want nothing in town that they cannot control, and the opposition of certain old-timers, who are resentful whenever outsiders participate in town affairs. When we were doing the specific job of civilian protection, we could not worry too much about criticism, and no doubt Dakin is right in saying that we shall get nowhere if we pay attention to the critics now. But it is an anomalous situation, for

I am sure we are looked on in many quarters as a little band of conspirators against the peace and well-being of Roxborough. I keep wondering whether, at some point, there was something we could have done that would have lessened hostility without impairing our effectiveness, but I don't know what it could have been, and now our only course seems to be to move straight ahead in the hope that misunderstanding will eventually be cleared up and that prejudices will fade away. We have made mistakes, and probably we shall go on making them, but we have made mistakes because we were trying to get something done, and perhaps some day people will give us credit for trying.

—m—

The council and the league may have been too exclusive, as some of our more moderate critics charge, but the story of the fire company does not offer much support for the policy of going into the highways and byways.

For a long time I thought I knew the exact process by which the fire company was created, but, nearly two years after the first meeting, one of the members and I began to exchange confidences, and I discovered that I had been mistaken. The details are unimportant, but the incident itself should be noted, if only as a reminder of the need for caution. For no reason that I can now perceive, I believed a man whose words I ordinarily take with a good many grains of salt. As a result I set down in an earlier version of this book an account of the origins of the fire company that was essentially incorrect. What is more important, my false impression was shared by other members of the company, and the consequent misunderstanding nearly wrecked the company in the first year of its existence.

It had always been a scandal that Roxborough had no fire protection, and in the spring of 1944 two bad fires started the talk going again. Suddenly Jim Morris, the Republican boss, called a meeting of all men interested in forming a volunteer fire company. Forty men turned out, and Jim—in his best big-shot manner—told them that if they would organize immediately he might be able to get them a piece of equipment. Irritated by Jim's secretiveness and his demands for haste, the men grumbled, but they were bullied into action, and they elected the slate of officers Jim proposed. The next morning one of the town trucks went to the city and brought back an OCD pumping unit mounted on a trailer.

There was not the slightest need for secrecy, and, so far as I can make out, it did not even serve Jim's purposes except in so far as it made him feel more important. He did manage, it is true, to give the impression that only a man with his political influence could have got the pumper for Roxborough, but he must have known that in a very short time these pumpers would be spread all over the county.

As Jim and his admirers will go on saying to the end of time, it was Jim Morris who started the volunteer fire company, and I do not suppose Jim and his admirers will ever understand the harm that was done by his coup. After the first meeting, Jim said to me, "You didn't think I could put over my slate. Why, I could put over a Chinaman on those guys." It was true enough. But the putting over of the slate antagonized nearly half of the men who were present, and they quietly dropped out. The remainder were evenly divided between those who wanted fire protection at any cost and those who were in the habit of taking Jim's orders.

The resulting deadlock virtually paralyzed the fire company during the first year of its existence, and it was our good luck that Roxborough had no serious fires in that time. Most of the more active members, as was bound to happen, were also members of the Defense Council. They took the initiative in raising funds and working on the apparatus, and the Morris faction gave its support, sometimes in good measure, sometimes grudgingly. Political control, however, rested with Morris, who could always swing his men into line.

When Morris drew up his slate of officers, he included Republicans, Democrats, and, as he said, Defense Council members, but he made sure that the Republicans had the majority. His greatest finesse was shown in his selection of Sam Josephs as chief. Sam was a Republican and therefore the Republicans could not kick, but he had never been active in politics and was in no sense a Morris man. He was treasurer of the Defense Council, and Jim knew he would have the support of the council group, but he had never been so closely identified as Dakin and I with the activities for which the council had been criticized. Except for his work in civilian protection, he had lived very much to himself ever since moving to the town a dozen years earlier, and if he had only a few friends, he had almost no enemies. Finally, he was a first-rate mechanic, and had belonged to a volunteer fire company in another town.

Anyone could see why Jim chose Sam Josephs, but the fact remained that he was a good choice, for he was ingenious in improving our meager equipment, and he gave unsparingly of his time. When, after a few months, the situation seemed to be hopeless, we managed to create an emergency committee, with Sam as its chairman, and work on the apparatus went ahead. But if Sam could do almost anything with machinery, he was not so good with people. The fire company was not a hand-picked group as were the protective forces, and it would have taken more talent for leadership than Sam had to get the most out of this mixed and by no means harmonious aggregation. What complicated the situation was the fact that the Defense Council faction, misled by the story to which I have already referred; believed that the president had made a deal with Jim Morris. The resulting distrust put the president in a most uncomfortable position, since he had the confidence of neither faction, and could not give the leadership that Sam failed to provide.

In the spring of 1945 the president showed no eagerness for reelection, and Harvey Dakin was chosen in his place. I hoped that he and Sam Josephs, who had worked together so well in the protective forces, would create an efficient organization, but Dakin is inflexible, and could not work with so heterogeneous a group of men. Instead of helping the fire company, he hurt it, and I think he must have realized this, for he resigned in the fall.

However, one by-product of his administration may in the long run turn out to be the salvation of the fire company. No sooner had he taken office than he insisted that we must find out exactly what we were doing, and he and the chief and I went to Albany to talk with various officials. We were quickly convinced that our only hope lay in forming a fire district, and we set about it. There were only a few of us, as usual, who would take the time to circulate petitions, and it turned out to be no small job, but the response from the people was better than we had hoped, and in the end we satisfied the legal requirements. There was a little political jockeying after that, but the town board ultimately appointed a satisfactory board of fire commissioners, and the five commissioners and the treasurer were unopposed at the first annual election. It was at this same election, however, that our two propositions were defeated, and we found ourselves at the beginning of 1946 with makeshift equipment garaged in a shed that was barely big enough for it. Some members of the company, incidentally, were among the active opponents of the propositions.

Because of the lack of equipment, the future is uncertain, but the fire company itself seems somehow to have outgrown the worst of its difficulties. Factional issues have not intruded themselves for some time, and we are gradually adding new members to whom the old fights have no meaning. In the winter of 1945-46 we were at least prepared to use what we had, and even though the taxpayers refused to authorize the purchase of a new truck and the building of a fire house; the existence of the fire district guaranteed some improvement, however slow.

For my own part, I have found membership in the fire company a rather chastening experience. The mechanical skill that so many of the men have and that some of them are willing to expend so freely is the very basis of the fire company's existence. On the other hand, I see clearly that this skill is not enough;

there must also be a talent for leadership. I am no more a leader than I am a mechanic. I am an idea man, and my talents are effective only in combination with others that I do not possess.

—⁓—

This question of leadership is the great question for Roxborough. The shortage cannot be easily exaggerated. Of the nine men most active in the Community League, all are members of the fire company, and six are or have been officers. Three of the six most active women in the league hold office or have held office in the PTA. Two of the men and three of the women are leading church members. If six families left town, the league would almost certainly collapse and probably the fire company would too. The removal of another two families would finish the PTA and would leave one of the churches in a bad way.

I am not suggesting that there are no other persons who are capable of leadership; I know there are; but they refuse to step forward. Some of them are natives, and have all the apathy and suspiciousness of which I have spoken. I know one young native who is active in a fraternal organization in the city but will have nothing to do with Roxborough affairs. "I'd always be stepping on somebody's toes," he says. Then there are the outsiders who have been discouraged by the criticisms that were directed at them when they did take office and have made up their minds not to expose themselves again. And of course there are the people whose interests really lie elsewhere, as ours did for so long, so that they are almost totally unaware of what goes on in the town.

Is the situation worse here than it is in most communities? I do not know. Almost all small towns have suffered, as Roxborough has, through the draining off of the more energetic stock, and many are caught, as Roxborough is, between the old and the new. The point about Roxborough is that the question of leadership is so crucial at just this time. The town has not slumped into a hopeless decline, and there is material here on which a decent future could be built. But it is a town in which many of the characteristic virtues are in a sense anachronistic, and in which many of the urban influences are destructive. It is a town in conflict, and only effective leadership can save it.

I am not thinking of the totalitarian kind of leadership or of anything but the common, ordinary, American brand. I am thinking of the man who knows what he can do and is willing to do it. At a fire company meeting, for instance, someone may say that the heating system in the shed must be overhauled before cold weather sets in. All those present know this is true, all of them want to have the job done, and most of them are willing to contribute a reasonable amount of labor, but nobody says a word. Finally the chief says, "Well, we'll have to get together some evening and take care of that." And of course nothing happens until the thermometer hits zero. A leader would say, "I can come at such and such a time, and I will do so and so if you will do this, that, and the other thing." He would see that the necessary materials were available at the appointed time, and he would do a little more than his share, but not too much.

Intellectuals rarely make good leaders, perhaps because they are usually individualists by temperament and habit, whatever their theories may be. An intellectual in the Roxborough situation is particularly at a disadvantage for the reason I have already given—that is, because of the barrier that exists between him and the farmers and mechanics with whom, in Roxborough enterprises, he is necessarily associated. In so far, however, as he has a moderately systematic mind, he can at least clarify the problems that arise, and that is a help. I am not very good at persuading people to do things, but sometimes I can show them what has to be done.

What Roxborough needs is a kind of all-round leadership. We need men and women who have foresight and energy and courage and at the same time enjoy the confidence of their associates. Harvey Dakin has most of these qualities, and he did a first-rate job with the protective forces, but, as I have pointed out, he is inflexible. He will not work with men and women he does not respect, and he would rather see a job left undone than lower his standards. Sometimes I wonder what a younger, less embittered, more resilient Harvey Dakin would do for Roxborough.

We struggle along with what we have. I have seen all the existing organizations pass through crises and slumps, and I have learned that a state of coma is not necessarily fatal. The winter of 1944-45 was a difficult time for all three, partly because of the severity of the weather, partly because of a general weariness that seemed to be the product of wartime strains. The years since Pearl Harbor had been an uncommonly active period for Roxborough, with more social affairs than usual and more demands on people's time and attention. The leaders were tired, and so were the followers. For a time I was afraid that one or more of the organizations might be buried under the winter's snows, but all three revived with spring. Then I began to hope, with the end of the war, that there might be a kind of renaissance. That did not happen either. At the end of 1945 the PTA, the fire company, and the league were all better off than they had been a year before, but the improvement could be seen only by a careful and sanguine observer.

—⁂—

Volunteer organizations come and go, but politics remains. The weeks before the biennial election of local officials are always full of excitement, and the election itself brings every recluse out of his hiding place, summons the sick from their beds, and sometimes, according to rumor, resurrects the dead from their graves. Political interest may not always be of the most searching and discriminating variety, but it is certainly intense.

The town is overwhelmingly Republican. So far as national and state elections are concerned, that is understandable, for it is the tradition in rural sections of the entire Northeast. What I cannot understand is why the town officers have to be Republicans. Perhaps there is some excuse for partisanship in the choice of a supervisor, since he is a member of the county board, and the control of the county is as much a matter of party politics as the control of the state. But is there any real reason for selecting a road superintendent or a tax collector or a town clerk on a party basis? In most New England towns and in many incorporated villages of New York State, candidates for local offices do not run as Republicans or Democrats, but in Roxborough party affiliation is what counts.

The Republican party is controlled by a triumvirate: Jim Morris, Mark Betterton, and Josiah Prescott. Morris I have already described as a fairly common kind of politician, a man who loves power and all the arts of manipulation. Betterton also enjoys the political game, but I think his principal satisfaction is in the prestige that party leadership gives him. This means that he is in a weaker position than Morris and can usually be controlled by him. Prescott's attitude is the hardest to understand. His father was long the political boss of the town, and Josiah seems to have inherited his influence. Although he spends only his summers in Roxborough, and most of the time seems indifferent to the town, he comes to life just before the caucus and stays alive until the election is over. He holds a position in the state government, which I suppose was originally given him as a reward for his own or his father's political services, but the position has long been secure, and I cannot see that he has anything to gain in a material way through political influence. Nevertheless, he plays the game as if his life depended on it. He may seem remote from the town, but he has minutely detailed information on the voting habits and personal lives of most of its inhabitants, and can marshal his forces with the precision of a Tammany lieutenant. Morris and Betterton ordinarily work together, though they have had their disagreements. Prescott goes through the gestures of cooperating with them, but he is his own master, and it is obvious that he and Morris have no affection for each other.

The Democrats make a respectable showing on the voting lists, having approximately one-third of the enrolled voters. But the party has been demoralized by the habit of defeat, and each of the six or eight persons who aspire to leadership is more interested in knifing his rivals than in beating the Republicans. The situation is made worse by the general incompetence of the Democratic leadership in the county. Machine interference in the affairs of Roxborough Democrats has in recent years been almost invariably disastrous, and the machine has alienated some of the ablest Democrats in town. A Democratic caucus is likely to be a free-for-all, furnishing plenty of excitement and producing new feuds to guarantee defeat. In all the elections that I have watched there have been enrolled Democrats who worked against the Democratic candidates, and cynics say that certain individuals enroll as Democrats only because in that way they get more out of the Republicans.

Since the Republican nomination is equivalent to election, one would expect that the caucus would be the scene of the real battles. Ordinarily, however, Morris, Betterton, and Prescott have such perfect control that only a few malcontents enter their names and they are easily disposed of. It is only once in a decade or so that there are significant contests, the most recent caucus being one of these exceptions. The bitterest fight in this caucus was for the position of road superintendent. The Republican incumbent, who had come surprisingly close to defeat in the 1943 election, decided not to run again, and four men immediately entered their names as candidates. Morris and Betterton were backing one of these men, but he was not a strong candidate, and when Prescott gave his support to one of the other three, their man was doomed. Betterton was angered by Prescott's action, and threatened to resign as committeeman, but was persuaded by Morris to stay on. The man who won the nomination and election, incidentally, is almost certainly as good a man for the job as the town has.

There were others contests. Jess Berge, whose term as justice of the peace was expiring, did not live in Roxborough at all, though of course he maintained a legal residence there, and he had not always cooperated with the party leaders. Nevertheless,

Morris and Betterton hesitated to oppose him, for they knew he would fight back. At last they got up their courage to back a younger and more capable man, and they carried him through the primaries by a margin of two votes. Jess then entered the election as an independent candidate, but despite an active campaign came out a weak second. There was also a fight in the caucus for the nomination for councilman, with neither candidate being officially supported by the party leaders.

The election of 1945 raised the general level of town government several notches, simply because the Republican party leaders did not have things their own way and relatively able men got a chance to run for office. Yet it would be wrong to assume that no case can be made for such men as Morris, Betterton, and Prescott. Within their various limits and in their different ways they are leaders: they show foresight, they work hard, and they elect their men. If the Democratic party had leadership of that kind, its chances would be considerably better. Of course the Democrats are handicapped from the start, but there is always some weak spot in the Republican defenses, and in all the elections I have seen the Democrats could have won an office or two if they had been capably led.

Campaigning follows a peculiar ritual. In spite of the fact that Republicans are elected ninety-nine per cent of the time, Republican candidates usually worry about their chances, and there are always a few optimists in the Democratic camp who are sure they are going to win. Candidates for the more important offices go from house to house, each carrying a box of cigars and cigarettes and a box of candy bars. After every member of a family has had his pick, the candidate sits down and talks, usually about the weather and other neutral topics. If his host makes any comment on political affairs, he deals with it to the best of his ability, and he may bring up a political issue on his own initiative, but more often than not he leaves without directly mentioning the campaign. As a rule it is considered unwise for a candidate to ask for a vote, and if he refers to his rival, it is good form for him to say that he has nothing against the man. The war compelled some modifications in the ritual, but I think it will be revived when candy, tobacco, and gasoline are all available.

On election day itself there are more substantial inducements. One of the churches serves dinner and supper on that day, and the leaders of both parties distribute tickets to the voters. Moreover, it is general gossip that the Republicans always buy votes and that the Democrats do when they have the money. I find it hard to understand why a person should be paid for voting Republican when he wouldn't vote Democratic if his own brother headed the ticket but I am told that, though they wouldn't vote for a Democrat, some people might not vote at all if they were not bribed. At any rate the bribe has become the perquisite of a certain group. One of the leaders tells me that money is the only way to get the vote out, but I suspect that he enjoys the feeling of being a big shot as he slips a bill into this hand and that pocket.

Among other things, an election is the town's great social event. As I have said, everyone votes, and most of the old-timers make a day of it. If the weather is good, the politicians stand outside the town hall, joking with their rivals, handing cards to newcomers, sometimes capturing an individual and taking him aside for a final argument, financial or otherwise. Candidates in the same party compare their predictions: "I'm giving Carter 97 votes; I figure I've got 156 certain and 65 more possible." Inside the hall election officials sit at a long table with the voting machine behind them. Hour after hour good-natured Glen Wister guards the machine, his hand on the rope that controls it. Having voted, men and women cluster around the stove if the day is cold, along the walls if the temperature is comfortable. Old-timers visit with other old-timers, sometimes persons they have not seen since the last election. At noon little groups move down the road to the church hall. Some people go home after dinner, but those who have *nothing* better to do return to the hall for the afternoon. The political leaders check their lists, sending cars for voters who have no means of transportation or regard a free ride as an election prerogative. The men who work in the city begin to come in about six o'clock, and many of the voters return after supper to learn the results. The hall becomes crowded and noisy and smoky, and there is a last-minute flurry of voting before the polls close at seven. Results are known soon after the voting machine is opened, and within an hour or less the hall is dark and the victors have begun their celebrations.

The excitement is over almost as soon as the votes are counted, and for another two years, or slightly less, nobody pays much *attention* to town affairs. The monthly meetings of the town board are open to the public, but as a rule the only visitor is Jim Morris, who drops in, as he says, to keep the boys straight. A new state law requires an annual hearing on the town budget, but it is seldom that half a dozen citizens appear, and those who come say nothing.

It would be pleasant to conclude that citizens can afford to ignore the conduct of town government, but as a matter of fact town affairs have been wretchedly mishandled in the past decade or so. (As I have hinted, I hope for somewhat better things from the new officials, but Harvey Dakin tells me I'm going to be fooled again.) Certain office-holders have been essentially honest and eager to do their best for the town, but even these men have lacked initiative and courage, and though they have done their own work capably enough, they have made little headway against the petty corruption, the stupid partisanship, and the general incompetence of the majority. There have been periods, indeed, when the town was being governed by some of its least capable citizens.

How did such men happen to hold office? By and large they were put over on the town by the Republican leadership because they were believed to be manageable. Some fifteen or twenty years ago, I have been told, a supervisor boasted that he had secured the nomination and election as justices of the peace of two of the stupidest men in the town. "I've got it fixed up," he said.

"If I take a piece of paper out of my pocket and lay it on the table, they're to vote yes. If I pick up a piece of paper from the table and put it in my pocket, they're to vote no. It took them quite a while to get it straight, but they're doing all right now."

Partisanship is the root of the evil. An official who is personally honest admitted to me one day that for years he had covered up a shady transaction carried on by one of his colleagues, even to the extent of paying money out of his own pocket. When I asked him why he did it, he said, "If that had got out, it would have killed the Republican party in this town." Of course he is quite wrong, for the party has survived greater shocks than that and appears to be completely invulnerable, but the leaders have somehow convinced him and almost all of his associates that blind support of the party is not merely a solemn duty but an ever-present necessity. People who marvel at the docility with which communists accept the shifts in the party line might study the behavior of good Republicans and Democrats in their own communities. Communist partisanship covers more territory, but the principle is the same.

The domination of the Republican bosses might be tolerable, from the point of view of a majority of the voters, if the incompetent board members were so led that they served the voters' interests, but the truth is that the system consistently fails to deliver the goods. The powers of a town board are so restricted by state law that ineptitude seldom results in catastrophe, but that is the best one can say. Occasionally the bosses push the board this way or that in accordance with their designs, but they are politicians, not administrators, and often they are not in the least concerned with the matters that most affect the welfare of the town. Since the board does nothing it does not have to do, its sins of omission are without number. One of the officials I have described as competent is given to saying, "I've told the board every meeting for the past year that so-and-so ought to be done." No one ever heard him making a motion, however; that would be sticking his neck out.

Everyone knows that there has been a great deal of incompetence, and most persons believe that there has been corruption as well. For many years we heard that the road superintendent used the town's equipment and the town's men for the conduct of his private business. There was plenty of complaint, but the complainers voted for the man year after year. After all, he was a Republican, and he had done or might do favors for them and their relatives.

I am not surprised that there is corruption, but I could understand the situation better if I could discover a structure of political obligations. It is only in the maintenance of roads that the town spends any considerable sum of money, and therefore that is the natural field for graft. During the depression work on the roads was important, and even in prosperous times the road gang, as it is called, is regarded as a privileged group. Of course the road superintendent counts on the road gang to vote for him, but there the matter stops. The bosses not only do not make the members of the road gang pay for their right to graft; they are obviously afraid of the gang as a political force that might be turned against them. When I ask Dakin about this, he says, "That's what's wrong with this town; everybody's scared of everybody else." In a way it seems to be so. The bosses can manage an effective campaign—"Why, Tammany Hall could take lessons from these guys"—but they have never been able to give their political machine a firm financial basis. One of the bosses holds a minor county office, and another gets a little extra business because of his political connections, but neither is adequately paid in dollars and cents for the time and labor he puts in.

Analysis of the situation in terms of cold cash reduces it to an absurdity. The road superintendent, for example, is paid a pitifully small salary, and I doubt if even the maximum of graft can bring the total up to the level of factory pay for skilled labor. Yet four men were fighting for the job in the summer of 1945. Even taking town politics at its worst, there is so little money in it that one would expect to have to beg people to run for office.

As matters stand, the justices are being paid more than they earn, but the amount involved is small, and most other officials work like dogs for what they get.

Why do they do it? Well, there is glory of a sort, or at any rate the satisfaction of doing the other fellow out of something that he obviously wanted. Politics, in Roxborough or anywhere else, is an exciting game, and there are people who love to play it. But beyond that, I think, there is a misapprehension, which can only be a survival from the past. To a farmer on a subsistence basis the money he got in a political office was of real importance, and I know of one or two lesser officials, even today, who would be financially embarrassed without the small sums the town pays them. Many people, I believe, think of political income on that scale, not on the scale of the wages they or their sons or their neighbors are being paid in the city.

Values are slowly changing. At present all five members of the town board work in the city, and I am confident that at least two of them sought office because they were interested in the town's welfare. They have a passion for the game, of course, but I do not think they are much concerned with what little money may be in it for them. Their presence on the board may be a sign of things to come. In the old days the control of the town's affairs naturally came into the hands of those who had a major stake in the town's welfare, and though some of them no doubt sought to serve their own interests, they also served the interests of the majority, and in any case the voters were in a position to check up on them. As the character of the town changed, and as the state interfered more and more in town business, the relationship between officials and voters became less direct and intimate. The old intensity of feeling about politics remained, but, as people lost sight of their objective, it became mere partisanship. There are no people today who have so obvious and impressive a stake in the welfare of Roxborough as the Middletons had in the days of the shirt factory. Yet everyone has reason to desire the well-being of the community in which he lives, and the people who see that most clearly are the ones who ought to hold office. Because the money involved is so inconsiderable, by urban standards, community spirit ought to become the dominant political force. This has happened in many New England towns, in some of New York's incorporated villages, perhaps in some New York towns, and I believe, in spite of Dakin's pessimism, that it is slowly happening in Roxborough.

But the change is slow, and while it goes on volunteer organizations, which will always have their place, are critically important. The fire company, as I have told, found it necessary to acquire a legal status and tax support through the creation of a fire district, but we have learned that the fire company, because it is a voluntary association of interested individuals, can do certain things for itself that the board of fire commissioners cannot do for it. The Community League, like the Defense Council before it, has always stood outside politics and against politics—that is, against partisan politics. We put up the honor roll and we founded the library not only without the help of the politicians but actually in spite of the opposition of some of them. Furthermore, if the government of the town is improving, that may be in part because the league has helped to raise the standards of community life.

Obviously, however, the political issue cannot simply be dodged. As I began this chapter by saying, the political apparatus affects the lives of the people more deeply than any other institution. Scores of people participate in caucuses and hundreds in elections who have nothing to do with the churches or the societies of the town, and the persistent sense of Roxborough as a community makes itself felt on election day as on no other occasion. This interest in politics has to be used as a force for change or else, in the hands of the current breed of politicians, it will be used against change.

My position in the town is such that I couldn't get elected as dogcatcher, but the abstract question of the intellectual's participation in politics remains interesting. One thing I am pretty well

convinced of is that an intellectual is foolish to run for office unless he is willing to abide by the recognized rules of the great
American game. That is, he must be prepared to accept a lower
standard of morality than the one he personally lives by. He can
keep his conscience clear, by refusing to make any personal profit, but he cannot keep his hands clean. Furthermore, he can expect
to have to give up some measure of his precious right to criticize;
he need not become the slave of his party, but he cannot ignore
his obligations. Finally, he must think about the quid as well as
the quo, for the measures he wants will be passed only if he
supports measures he doesn't want.

I am not purist enough to feel that the price is necessarily too
high, and if there were some intellectual in town who was willing to run for office and who had a chance of being elected, I
should certainly urge him to go to it, for his own sake and the
town's. On the other hand, I can console myself for my own
unfortunate lot by thinking of the influence that an independent
individual, even an unpopular one, can exert. My guess is that
there can be no general rule, either for the Roxboroughs or for
larger political areas. There is good to be done either way, and
either way one has to count losses as well as gains.

New Englander that I am, I believe that New York State
would be better off if the town meeting system had persisted on
this side of the border. I know, however, that the town meeting
itself is an institution that is having to be reshaped to meet new
needs. Our institutions will suffice if we are wise enough to make
the most of them.

IX

The Future of the Town

The people of Roxborough frequently say—Stan Cutter with enthusiasm, most others with regret—that the town is going back to forest. It is one of the Roxborough stereotypes, this conviction that more and more houses will be abandoned and more and more land yielded to brush and woods. Yet most persons are planning their lives on the assumption that the town will remain unchanged, and there are even some optimists who predict a bright new era of prosperity.

Has Roxborough a future? Has any small town a future in this age of industrialism, urbanism, and specialization?

The problem of the American small town in general and the problem of Roxborough in particular cannot be precisely identified, for Roxborough is a rather special kind of small town. In the West or the South a town of Roxborough's size is likely to be the largest community in a considerable area—perhaps in a whole county. James West's Plainville, somewhere in the Ozarks, is the trading center of a region twenty miles long and eight miles wide, and it has four grocery stores, two restaurants, two drugstores, a hardware store, a produce house, a jeweler, a cobbler, two barbers, an undertaker, a blacksmith, and a number of filling stations. The village of Irwin, Iowa, has a large new school, a movie house (open once a week), and a bank.[1]

---

[1] See *Plainville, U.S.A.*, by James West (New York, 1945) and *Culture of a Contemporary Rural Community: Irwin, Iowa*, by Edward O. Moe and Carl Cr. Taylor (Rural Life Studies: #5, Bureau of Agricultural Economics, Washington, 1942). The population of Plainville is given as 275, that of Irwin as 345. However, Plainville and Irwin are villages, whereas Roxborough is a township. If Roxborough were regarded simply as the center of the town, or if Plainville and Irwin were given the same area as Roxborough, it is probable that the three towns would have much the same population.

Whereas Roxborough is only fifteen miles from Troy, Irwin is sixty miles from Omaha, and Plainville is seventy miles from the nearest city of any size. Plainville is the next to the largest town in the county, and Irwin is one of the major centers of trade in its area. Roxborough, on the other hand, is the smallest of fourteen towns in the county. None of the towns is more than twenty-five miles distant from a sizable city, and only one is a shopping center for people from other communities. The town of Warsaw, for instance, has a population of 1400, and, like Irwin, has a bank, a school, and a once-a-week movie. In preautomobile days it was even more isolated than Roxborough, but today its people look to Troy, and its institutions have taken on a semi-suburban aspect.

I became acutely conscious of the difference between a population of eight hundred in the Northeast and a population of eight hundred elsewhere when I visited the Tennessee Valley in the spring of 1945. In the 125 miles that I traveled by bus between Nashville and Clifton, I passed through only three towns that were recognizable as such. Clifton is forty miles from the nearest city of any size and more than a hundred miles from any metropolis. Although well-to-do persons in Clifton frequently visit Nashville and Memphis, many of Clifton's people have never been farther away than Waynesboro, the only slightly larger county seat.

Clifton is like Roxborough in never having had a railroad, but it does have the Tennessee River, and in earlier days it was a shipping center of some importance. At the turn of the century, the town's octogenarian banker told me, seven boats arrived each week, and people drove in for supplies from as much as forty miles away. Lumber was the region's principal resource, and the banker said he had seen 100,000 ties piled along the riverbank. Lumbering was still a major industry in 1945, but the best of the timberland had been cut off, and it was obvious that only a wise conservation policy could keep the industry going. The future of cotton appeared to be even more dubious, and the blight of tenant farming was apparent in the agriculture of the whole district.

At first glance Clifton seemed to me in a more advanced state of decay than Roxborough. There were a number of stores, but, with one exception, they were dingy, poorly stocked, and little patronized. A cellar hole showed where a business block had been burned and had not been replaced. The only hotel was closed, and the only restaurant might almost as well have been. In two vacant stores men were making brooms—tenant farmers who had decided, in view of the current demand for brooms, that they wouldn't bother to make a crop that year. At mail time there was a little flurry of activity, and on Saturday afternoon the farmers, black and white, came to town, but most of the time the loafers had the main street to themselves.

Yet just around the corner were larger, more expensive, better kept houses than Roxborough can display, and I soon learned that there had been and still was money in the town. Only the Middleton family ever made money out of Roxborough, but a dozen families, mostly intermarried, had grown prosperous and even rich out of Wayne County's lumber and cotton and shipping. Some of the money they had made was still invested in the county, but much of their capital was employed elsewhere. Members of the leading family owned the principal store, controlled the bank, had a major interest in the lumber industry, and rented many farms on shares.

So far as I could make out, there are three classes among the white people of Clifton. The lower class is made up of the tenant farmers, the broom makers, the workers in the button factory, and the woodchoppers. Above this line social relations are largely unrestricted, but the few rich families and some others, less wealthy but well-connected, are in certain respects set apart and constitute an upper class. As in Plainville—but not Roxborough—church affiliation follows class status, the Presbyterians being predominantly upper-class, the Methodists predominantly middle-class, and the members of the Holiness Church lower-class.

Because Clifton is so much more isolated than Roxborough, and because it retains some of the fruits of its earlier prosperity, as Roxborough does not, I was surprised to discover even fewer evidences of community spirit than I can find in my own town. It is true that Clifton became an incorporated city in 1944, but this step was taken chiefly because the inhabitants wanted a city water supply, and few persons seemed to be interested in the new form of government. (In the spring of 1945 the white people were still relying on cisterns, and the Negroes were still drinking river water.) There was a Masonic lodge in the town, and there were two or three women's organizations connected with the churches, but there was no service club nor any group, formal or informal, devoted to the welfare of the community. The local grammar and high school, which served the surrounding area as well as Clifton itself, appeared to play little part in local affairs. There was no library, and few citizens seemed to feel the need of one. In general I got the impression that the upper-class families had once taken care of the town but had fallen down on the job as their financial and social interests were spread over a wider area. There had been a revolt of sorts, and the "kinsfolk" had failed to win control of the new city government, but the leaders of the rebellion seemed to have no plans beyond vague dreams of attracting industries to Clifton.

In spite of the low level of organizational life, and in spite of class divisions, Clifton is more unified than Roxborough. Its isolation is partly responsible for this unity: people's interests center in Clifton, except for those who can make their periodic jaunts to Memphis and Nashville and, for that matter, to Palm Beach and New York. More important than this, however, is the almost universal acceptance of middle-class standards of morality. Members of the upper class conform to these standards in such matters as drinking and (so far as the women are concerned) smoking, at least while they are in Clifton, and most of them go regularly to church. As for the lower class, large sections of it are ostentatiously devout, and the young hellions who drink moonshine and get into fights are condemned by the community and know they are. Clifton is in the Bible Belt, and a visitor from the Northeast soon feels what a difference that makes.

The visit to Clifton was valuable rather because it helped me to see what Roxborough is not than because the two towns are easily comparable. Yet for all the dissimilarities, their problems are fundamentally the same. Either in eastern New York or in middle Tennessee it is unlikely that agriculture will ever again be what it was in the past, and it seems certain that both Roxborough and Clifton have seen their best days. On the other hand, Roxborough has already shown its potentialities as a summer resort, and Clifton, thanks to the TVA, has brand new possibilities for attracting vacationists. Clifton, of course, can never become a suburb, and if its young people want jobs elsewhere, they will have to leave town, but the lumber industry, which has been given intelligent guidance by the TVA, can help to sustain the present population. Each town has resources of which something can be made, and the problem for each is to do what it can with what it has.

—⁀—

I have learned what I could about other communities, if only because in this way I can define more accurately the particular elements of the Roxborough situation. There is Landaff, New Hampshire,[2] for instance. Landaff, in the northcountry between the White Mountains and the Connecticut River, was settled by the same wave of migration that climbed the Roxborough hills. It reached its population peak in 1860, declining in eighty years from one thousand to four hundred persons. It is not even so much of a trading center as Roxborough, for its people do their shopping in nearby Lisbon, which is on a railroad. Like Roxborough, Landaff was once a successful farming community on a subsistence basis, and, again like Roxburogh, it was unable to achieve the shift to a money economy without a sharp decline in population. It differs from Roxborough, however, not only in its remoteness from large cities but also in its failure to attract

---

[2] Rural Life Studies #3. By Kenneth MacLeish and Kimball Young.

summer visitors. It has become, therefore, a small community of independent, self-reliant farmers, each raising a large part of what his family needs and, in addition, some kind of cash crop, usually milk.

What has happened to Landaff is what might have happened to Roxborough if it had not been so close to Troy. It is only in the northern part of New England, however, that towns are likely to be so isolated as Landaff. The Berkshire towns I know are like Roxborough in that they are near enough to cities for easy contact and even for commuting. They are also, of course, resorts for summer visitors. If a younger generation should refuse to accept the hardships of mixed farming, Landaff would disappear, but in most of the towns in southern New England, as in Roxborough, there is a chance of survival as a marginal part of the urban world.

The obvious but nevertheless important fact is that the typical American small town is no longer economically independent. Landaff comes closer to independence than most, but even Landaff farmers are part of Boston's milkshed. Four possibilities seem to exist for a small town. First, it may be either the home or the shopping center of specialized farmers. As the residents of Clifton, Tennessee, or Irwin, Iowa, or Harmony, Georgia, or Sublette, Kansas,[3] can testify, specialized farming means complete dependence on the national or even the world market. Second, a small town may have a factory or some other industry, and if so, it is thoroughly enmeshed in a nationwide industrial network. Mineville,[4] for instance, isolated in the Rockies, has its share of small-town traits, but economically it is controlled by a great corporation that has made a whole state its domain. The little factories one finds in the town near Roxborough are less likely than hitherto to be locally owned, and in any case the goods they make and the wages they pay are, determined by forces outside

---

[3] For Irwin see Rural Life Studies #5; for Harmony see #6; for Sublette see #2.
[4] See *Small-town Stuff,* by Albert Blumenthal (Chicago, 1932).

the community. Third, a town may be a summer resort, and if it is lucky, it can live all year on what it takes from its visitors in a few months. Summer resorts, however, as the thirties proved, are as vulnerable to depression as the cities from which their paying guests come, and they seldom escape from some taint of parasitism. Finally, if a town is properly situated, it may become a suburb or, like Roxborough in wartime, a semi-suburb, and then, of course, its fortunes rise and fall with those of the city to which it is appended. Whatever course it chooses; or has forced upon it, the small town loses its independence and runs the risk of losing its identity.

Nothing is easier than to trace the process by which the small town has been forced into this situation. The first step was really the decisive one—the shift from a subsistence to a money economy. In Landaff, for instance, farmers began as early as 1840 to specialize in sheep raising because of the demands of the new textile industry. They thus exposed themselves to the risks of competition with farmers throughout the nation, and they were soon outdistanced by western rivals. Because of the shortage of cotton, sheep raising revived during the Civil War, but the market vanished when the war ended. In the closing decades of the nineteenth century the opportunities for subsistence farming in Landaff were as good as they had ever been, but the kind of life that had seemed so attractive to the pioneers had little appeal for their grandsons and great-grandsons. Having tasted the sweets of a money economy, most people decided that if they could not have them in Landaff, they would seek them elsewhere.

Reading the diary of George Holcomb, one can understand why the change took place so rapidly. Holcomb's great passion was for a cash income. He was only one generation removed from the pioneers, but subsistence farming was not good enough for him. Who could be surprised if his children decided they wanted the money that could be made in cities or moved to land that would yield a cash crop?

The small-towners threw themselves into the larger society
that industrialism was creating, but the towns themselves
seemed for a long time to remain much the same. So Landaff
today is much the kind of town it was a century ago, though
considerably smaller, and in the first and even the second
decade of the twentieth century Roxborough seemed to its inhabitants to be as self-sufficient as it had ever been. But the influence of the larger society is pervasive, and it works in many
ways, chief among them being the growing power of the state
and federal governments. This power, in so far as it directly affects such towns as Roxborough, has grown extravagantly in
the past two or three decades. Take, for example, the matter of
roads. Local pathmasters and road superintendents could not
build roads fit for fast touring cars and giant trucks, and so the
state and the county stepped in, providing employment for
some residents of Roxborough and altering the character of the
whole town.

Then there is education. From early in the nineteenth century
New York State exerted a mild degree of control over rural
schools, but it was only in the nineteen-twenties that a plan was
evolved for thoroughgoing reform. The plan was based on the
idea that the rich cities should subsidize rural education, a sound
principle in as much as the products of the rural schools had for
years been giving the cities the benefit of what they had learned.
But as the state increased its aid to the rural schools, it insisted
on supervising educational methods, physical equipment, and fi-
nances. It also undertook to abolish the one-room school as
rapidly as possible, setting up large central districts that could
provide for small-town children educational facilities comparable
to those found in the cities. I shall discuss later the educational
implications of all this. It is enough to point out now that we
share our control of education with the state and that the people
know it. They also know that more drastic changes may come.
"What will happen to us," people say, "if they take away our
schools?"

The process goes on everywhere. Attending a town meeting in the Berkshires a few years ago, I was amused to note how skillfully reports concealed the extent of state subsidies to schools and roads. The intransigent individualists of New England know that the state gives money and takes power, and they do not like to confess the decline of their independence. But of course they accept the money.

Federal intervention is more recent than state. Roxborough had no WPA projects, managing to get through the depression with the aid of the established county welfare agencies. But certainly the people were familiar with the WPA, and though most of them talked scornfully and frequently of boondoggling, all but a few admitted that the government had to do something to keep people from starving. Social security, old age assistance, deposit insurance, and other New Deal measures are accepted and perhaps admitted to be necessary.

The federal government looms larger in the agricultural communities of the West and South. The people of Sublette, in the Kansas Dust Bowl, know how much they owe to it, for WPA, NYA, and AAA (later the FSA) saved them from starvation. Less hard hit, the people of Irwin, Iowa, nevertheless approved of the Farm Security Administration and the Rural Electrification Administration. Plainville has a WPA library and a school built with WPA funds, and James West discovered that the county agent and the social security administrator, though often criticized, occupy crucial positions in the community. In many rural areas it appears that the federal government is needed not only as a bulwark in time of crisis but also as an organizing force for agricultural reform.

If the depression did not teach Roxborough a lesson, the war did. What everyone discovered was that the government is enormously powerful and can be a correspondingly enormous nuisance. That the government should be powerful for military purposes was generally admitted, and so far as I know, nobody in Roxborough objected on principle to the most drastic of all expressions of government power, the conscription of men. The regulation of wages and prices and other types of regulation were usually approved in the abstract, but there was much criticism of particular laws and their administration. By no means all of this criticism was unjustified, but a certain amount of it resulted from failure to understand the organizational problems of modern warfare. However, whether individuals approved or disapproved, the fact remained that the nation had reached into Roxborough, taken eighty of its men and women, established the rate of pay of most of the wage-earners, helped itself to a generous share of that pay, determined what people could buy and what they must pay, regulated the speed at which automobiles could be driven and the amount of gasoline that could be purchased for them, and stimulated a great number of optional activities such as civilian defense, the collection of salvage, and the purchase of war bonds.

Many people in Roxborough deeply though inarticulately distrust the federal government and fear the extension of its power. Self-styled liberal journalists often speak as if such fears were nothing but rationalizations by which the ruling class seeks to protect its privileges. It is true that the fear of regimentation is frequently played upon by selfish interests, but it is a real fear, and no one who has watched the way of the world in the past twenty-five years can say that it is baseless. What Roxborough's individualists and most of the theoretical defenders of free enterprise and laissez faire ignore is that totalitarianism is merely a symptom. The fundamental reality is the increased interdependence that has resulted from the progress of invention. Recently Sam Josephs was holding forth to some of us on the evils of monopoly in the automotive industry. He then went on to speak of conditions in the garage business, pointing out that the mechanics are underpaid but that the owners nevertheless seldom get rich because of the cutthroat competition. "There's no organization," he said, and immediately I had a vision of chain garages, far more efficient and profitable than existing garages but utterly destructive of the individualism Sam prizes. The larger society does exist, and it is constantly seeking for appropriate forms. Totalitarian government is one way of trying to cope with the problems of the larger society, and those problems cannot be solved by denunciations of totalitarianism.

—ᴡᴡ—

What is the place of the small town in the larger society? It is certain that the economic life of the individuals who live within the boundaries of Roxborough, or any other small town, will be increasingly shaped by forces that are operating throughout the entire nation and, many of them, throughout the entire world. It is equally certain that state and federal government will count for more and the town government for less in the political life. Can the town survive?

So far as Roxborough is concerned, this is not a rhetorical question. I can easily visualize a Roxborough without schools, without stores, without churches, without a post office. There would be houses along the highway, I suppose, but much of the town would be reforested, and the people who lived on the highway would work in the city, shop in the city, send their children to school in the city, and think in city terms. Under such conditions there would be little point in electing a town supervisor or a road superintendent or any of the other officials that Roxborough currently ballots for; their jobs could be taken care of by employees of the county or the state. There would be nothing left but a name on a map.

More isolated towns would take longer to die than Roxborough, and perhaps it is inconceivable that a Plainville or a Clifton or an Irwin should utterly vanish, for there will always have to be small shopping centers scattered through the farming regions. But it is not inconceivable that feeling for the community as such might dwindle even though a store or two, a church or two, a school, and a post office remained. The people of Irwin are not likely to become dependent on Omaha in the way in which the people of Roxborough are dependent on Troy, but Omaha could nevertheless become the real center of their lives. Obliteration is not the only or perhaps the worst danger, as anyone who has seen much of small-town decay can testify.

Some of my city friends are impatient when I talk this way. They insist that urban civilization is vastly superior to rural and that we all should hope and pray for its spread. Certainly a case can be made. If we and our neighbors do most of our shopping in city stores, that is because goods are cheaper and better and there is greater variety. Already the local stores are conveniences rather than necessities, not much more important than the neighborhood groceries one finds in residential sections of a city. As for the local office-holders, they are seldom models of efficiency, and it is conceivable that their jobs could be done better by impersonal outsiders. I am even willing to admit that city people are, as a rule, more alert, better informed, and less prejudiced than the small-towners. In Roxborough itself it is usually the men and women with urban experience who are willing to work for a better community.

And yet . . . I have learned to like trading in a store where I am known by name and can meet friends and swap gossip. I like knowing the storekeeper not only as a man behind a counter but also as a human being. I feel that I know what I am doing when I vote for or against men I have seen again and again and in a hundred different situations, men I have talked with, men I have heard talked about. I like the old-timers, too, though they don't always like me, and I know they are no fools. Their talk gives the town a past, and sometimes it makes the smart city folks seem shallow. I find it good, as I have said, that I am thrown with many types of men and not merely with intellectuals. In short, I like living in a small town.

The urbanites may say that this is sentimentality, but I refuse to let the word frighten me. I believe that small-town life has values that should be preserved if they possibly can be. After all, the human race has spent the greater part of its existence in small communities, and I doubt if we have outgrown the need for a comprehensible society. Most human beings want the support of some group that can be intimately known. They want not only friends—i.e., personally selected intimates—but also neighbors in the small-town sense. Harvey Dakin is always saying that the cities are full of farmers, and some sociological investigations suggest that he is right. For instance, Geoffrey Gorer[5] speaks of the loneliness of the urban middle classes, and suggests that the movies and the radio fill an urgent demand for comradeship. Kate Smith can persuade thousands of people to buy bonds because they think of her as a warm, generous, friendly person— a real neighbor, in short. And there are even cruder, if more concrete, substitutes in the "lonely hearts" clubs.

Then there is a political argument, but one that has to be stated carefully. I know that pure democracy does not flourish in Roxborough, and I am not prepared to find it in other small towns, even those of New England. Moreover, I am aware that local government, however well conducted, is bound to have less and less importance. Yet I am unwilling to surrender to the larger society any more power than it is absolutely necessary to yield, and I am impatient with theorists who are determined to go the whole hog. There is a good deal of talk these days about the common people and the grass roots, much of it being done by individuals who recommend measures that would inevitably concentrate power in the hands of a small minority. To me the problem of practical democracy in a large and complex society seems exceedingly difficult, and it is not going to be solved by slogans. The very difficulty of that problem, however, makes me all the more certain that people should have as much power as possible over the things that directly affect their lives. I hope I have made it clear that I have no illusions about the practice of politics in small towns, but I cannot assume that persons who act foolishly in a situation that is familiar to them would therefore

---

[5] Geoffrey Gorer, *Certain Hypotheses with Regard to Movies and Radio* (mimeographed, 1939).

make wise decisions on issues they did not understand. Small-town government is a school in practical democracy. If not all its graduates deserve high honors, that is no reason for abolishing it.

There is a third argument for the small town, and one that seems to me to be underscored by Roxborough's failures. If the people in Roxborough want a better community, they can work for it and they have to work for it. A great deal is done for people in cities, done by remote councils and commissions that work in mysterious ways. And if the individual happens to want something that isn't being done, his voice is not heard. In Roxborough even a single individual can initiate processes of change. He may get nowhere, as we have seen, but he knows that it is his responsibility and that the task is not necessarily beyond his powers. In better towns than Roxborough, and of course there are better towns as there are worse, the improvement has been wrought by individuals and small groups. As studies and experiments have shown, the difference between a community that is really alive and one that is just getting by can be tremendous. It does not take a mass movement, armed with all the paraphernalia of modern propaganda, to raise the quality of life in a small town. The individual can count if he wants to.

I have no idea of starting a crusade to abolish cities, although personally I do not want to live in a large city. I am not unappreciative of the good things that can be found in New York, and only in New York, but I am inclined to think that if New York didn't exist, the good things would manifest themselves elsewhere. A friend writes me, "The modern industrial city dominating our lives is a terrible defeat, a defeat morally, biologically, appreciatively, even economically." I think he is right, and if, under the threat of atomic warfare, we do away with our big cities, I believe that civilization will be the gainer. But I know that many persons like cities, and in any case I have no illusions about my ability to do away with them. What I am interested in doing is helping to prevent city people from abolishing the small towns. The old basis of the small town has been destroyed, and cannot be rebuilt, but I believe that new foundations can be established.

—⁓—

So far as Roxborough is concerned, there are three conditions that have to be satisfied if the community is to survive in any significant sense. The first essential, obviously, is an economic basis for the existence of the town, The second is the establishment of a standard of living comparable to that of the cities. And the third is the development of forms of activity that will bring the people of the town closer together—that will take the place of the network of personal and economic relationships that once linked the members of a self-sufficient community.

The economic problem is at once the easiest and the hardest to deal with. There is no reason to believe that Roxborough will ever be an area in which specialized farming can profitably be practiced, and it is unlikely that there will be a return to subsistence farming except perhaps in a time of acute depression. It is less impossible that small industries might locate in the town, but a factory could easily turn out to be a liability in the long run, and in any case there seems little chance of any industrial development that would fundamentally change the economic situation. But Roxborough does have mountains and lakes and good air, which have already proved considerable assets and have possibilities for future development. And it is near enough to a city so that people can drive to and from work. Commuting, it is true, is not always easy, but the difficulties are not great enough to deter either natives with a love of the town or city people with a taste for country living. Land is plentiful, and part-time farming can be productive. Roxborough, then, can survive as a summer resort and a rather special kind of suburb—other things being equal.

The trouble is likely to come with the other things. In so far as it is a suburb Roxborough is dependent on the economic condition of the region. The region was wonderfully prosperous during the war, and the outlook has seemed encouraging in the first months of peace, but I have heard gloomy predictions, and I am afraid they may prove true. If employment declines sharply in the area, of course Roxborough will be hard hit, and that will be the end, for the time being, of our hopes for a better community. The future of Roxborough, in short, cannot be planned without reference to the region and the nation—and, for that matter, the world. But that is a theme for another chapter.

If the region does remain at least moderately prosperous, what are Roxborough's chances? They depend, in part at least, on the satisfying of the second condition. What does the small-towner need to keep him happy?

In the first place, he needs an automobile. With a few stalwart exceptions, Roxborough families have come to place cars next to shelter and food. The shelter, moreover, may be a one-room tar-paper shack, and the food may be limited largely to potatoes and pork. In the forties an automobile means access to a job, but it also means—and long has meant—freedom of movement both within the community and without. City stores, city doctors, and city amusements become available, and most of the limitations of which the small-towner himself is most acutely conscious disappear.

The telephone also has a special meaning for small-towners. It is true that most lower-class families, although they will make almost any sacrifice to buy a car, do not have phones. Most other families, however, have them if they can get them, and there is bound to be a considerable increase in the number of subscribers whenever the company is able to build new lines. Convenient for a man, the telephone is almost a necessity for a woman. No matter how far she is removed from her neighbors, a woman is not truly isolated if she has a phone. Nothing would do so much to reduce feminine dissatisfaction with rural life as the extension of the telephone system.

A city-dweller might easily assume that electricity is more important than either automobile or telephone, but he would find that many people in Roxborough do not agree with him. Almost anyone who could not have both would prefer a car to electricity, and I am sure there are some people who would give up electricity rather than lose the telephone. In the nineteen-forties, as a hundred or fifty or twenty-five years ago, a family can be clean and well-fed and self-respecting and moderately comfortable without electricity. We tried it for several years, and we know it can be done. Yet most families do want electricity as soon as they can get it, and it does raise the standard of living. Families begin with lights and a radio, but a refrigerator and a washing machine are soon added, and then, if income is adequate, an automatic electric pump may be bought and running water installed, and maybe there will be talk about an oil burner and central heat.

Bathtubs and flush toilets also are likely to seem more essential to city-dwellers than they do to small-towners. The introduction of running water is one problem, and the installation of a system of sewage disposal is another. The difficulties of the two jobs, to say nothing of the expense, are likely to frighten persons who have always got along well enough with primitive devices. Indeed, the more rugged old-timers speak scornfully of the sissies who find an outdoor privy a hardship. Slowly, however, the number of bathrooms does increase.

The great fact is that "all the modern conveniences" can be made available to dwellers in a country town. What the Rural Electrification Administration is doing for the sparsely settled areas of the South and West will be done in due course by the public utilities of the Northeast. And once electricity is installed, the rest becomes merely a matter of time, money, and desire. Bathrooms, oil burners, electric ranges, quick-freezing units, and much else will more and more assume the aspect of necessities. There is a lag, but as the small town becomes more completely integrated with the larger society, its inhabitants do aspire to the benefits of that society. And if incomes stay up, there is no reason why they cannot have them.

But what of the less material aspects of city life at its best? "The 'decent' urban knowledge," writes James West, "upon which our industrial and 'money-conscious' civilization depends is beyond the reach of the majority who are born and die in cities. Plainvillers have virtually no contact with it. Since there are millions of 'Plainvillers' in America, the problem of Plainville is the problem of America." I will not say that Roxborough has virtually no contact with "decent" urban knowledge; mere proximity to cities counts for something; but the contacts are few and tenuous. What might be called a "decent" rural knowledge is clearly in decay, and urban knowledge has only begun to take its place.

A decent urban knowledge, I suppose, includes an awareness of the size and complexity and interdependence of the modern world, and a recognition of the differences among its people and their basic similarity. It includes a perception of the science of government, as opposed to mere shrewdness in politics, and of the possibilities and dangers of the human control of social processes. It is based in no small measure on a general understanding of the scientific method, but it also accepts the importance of imagination, especially as expressed in literature, music, and the other arts. Under urban knowledge one can classify a good deal of sophistication and "know how," but the term clearly means more than that. Urban knowledge is "decent" or "adequate" only as it goes beyond mere familiarity with mechanical devices and approaches the dignity of a philosophy.

That such knowledge is rare in cities, as James West says, is obvious. To millions of underpaid and overworked laborers it is almost as unavailable as it is to the shiftless hill people of Plainville or the migrant woodchoppers of Roxborough. One has to look hard to find it in middle-class suburbs or, for that matter, in Park Avenue apartments. I need only call in the novelists as witnesses. Studs Lonigan, George F. Babbitt, J. Ward Moorhouse—did any of them have a decent urban knowledge? Yet admittedly something of the sort can be found in any large and in almost any small city.

The decent rural knowledge of the self-sustaining small town of the early nineteenth century was a different but not an inconsiderable matter. It began with direct intimacy with soil and woods and weather, with wild and domesticated animals, and with all the processes of plant and animal growth, and it included a knowledge of human nature based on direct and many-sided relationships. It also embraced a great range of practical information that was valuable in that setting and can no more be disposed of as trivial than can the "know how" of the city-dweller. The small-towner knew less about the world, but he knew more about his immediate surroundings, and it may be that his mode of life encouraged deeper and more original thought. One thing at least is certain: the small-towner of a hundred years ago was better equipped for the life he lived than is the city-dweller of today for his life.

Something of the old rural knowledge persists in Roxborough, as it does in all small towns, but it is rapidly disappearing, and in any case it is not adequate for survival in the contemporary world. I am sorry to see its decline, for I respect the farmer's familiarity with physical nature and the small-towner's familiarity with human nature. The old-fashioned farmer, who engaged in all the manifold processes of farming, had a culture of a not contemptible kind—unless, of course, the nose was too close to the grindstone. But this kind of knowledge, valuable as it is in its own right, is no longer enough.

I do not know how a decent urban knowledge is to be brought to the small towns. It would seem to be the task of formal education, but, as I shall point out later on, the educational system has its hands more than full, and we would be unwise to expect too much. Something can be done by a process of diffusion, especially if the city people who make their homes in small towns do not keep themselves apart from the natives. In a Connecticut town in which a number of writers and artists have taken residence, the church had an exhibit of arts and handicrafts that ranged from hand-painted china to surrealist drawings and from quilts to volumes of *avant-garde* poetry. Whatever the results, it was an experiment worth trying, and one, I suspect, that neither the artists and writers nor the natives would have been likely to undertake without the prodding of a cultural middleman, in this instance the local minister. This much is sure: the small towns need urban knowledge at least as much as they need urban comforts.

The third requirement is the least tangible of the three, but of central importance. I have tried to make it clear that I cannot view the process of suburbanization in itself with any enthusiasm. A Roxborough that is merely a place where people have houses is not a Roxborough that interests me. If Roxborough cannot provide jobs for its people, and it cannot, they must look for them elsewhere, and I can only hope that they find them, for otherwise there is no future for the town worth talking about. Nevertheless, I believe that the town can be a town even if it is not self-sufficient.

I am told that real estate developments and housing projects sometimes acquire a considerable degree of community feeling, and I am greatly encouraged that this is so. If groups of people who are more or less arbitrarily thrown together can come to feel that they have interests and purposes in common, surely it should not be difficult to establish such a spirit on the foundation of traditions that are as strong as Roxborough's. Roxborough was a community in the old-fashioned sense not so long ago, and, as I have tried to show, the sense of the community persists vividly in many minds. It is true that the composition of the town has changed more rapidly in recent years, and will change still more rapidly in years to come, but it is also true that many of the newcomers are attracted by the qualities of small-town life and want to be assimilated. Most people who come to a town such as Roxborough come for more than a house, even if it does have all the modern conveniences.

The difficulty with Roxborough is that it is neither one thing nor the other. The traditional feeling for the community, as I have tried to show, often results in a stubborn, irrational resistance to change. Just as old-timers have recently opposed the buying of fire-fighting equipment and the building of a firehouse, so in the twenties they opposed the building of a town hall, the installation of street lights, and the purchase of a snowplow. They are always talking about high taxes, but I suspect that their objections are as much sentimental as they are practical. Because their feeling for the community is oriented toward the past, and not unnaturally so, it is an immediate liability, but it could be converted into an asset.

I would be the last, however, to underestimate the difficulty of the task. Our experience has shown that a number of outsiders and a number of natives, sons and daughters of the old-timers who resist change, can work together for the benefit of the community, but this homogeneous and effective group has been created only at the expense of arousing strong opposition among the majority of natives. Given plenty of time, we might wear the opposition down, but quite possibly the process would be too slow to save Roxborough. By what bold strategy can we capture the imaginations of enough natives to direct the feeling for the community toward the future?

If the will were present, the means would be available. There is no single formula for the salvation of a small town. Sometimes progress comes through the political machinery, and sometimes through civic organizations. A well-placed individual—the owner of a factory, perhaps, or the owner of land that can be profitably developed—can do a great deal. Mere paternalism, however, though it can give a town the air of prosperity, never suffices in the long run. The leader who counts is the one who can win followers, not buy them.

The lesson the old-timers have to be taught, if they can learn no other, is that community spirit has its economic value. A run-down community attracts run-down people, and Roxborough in recent years has attracted too many families that have cost the town money, to put the matter in its lowest terms. I do not want Roxborough to become an exclusive residential section for the best people, and I am quite willing that we should have and assume responsibility for our share of the unfortunate, but I do not want to see the town saddled with a burden that is too much for it. I hope we can attract the kind of family that will inquire about the school system, will demand decent fire protection, and will want to know whether the town has a library and what recreational facilities there are for young people. Such people will never be a burden on the town, and they are quite likely to be an asset. Even if the old-timers do proceed to penalize them by raising their taxes—the usual way of welcoming self-respecting newcomers—they will put into the town more than they take out of it.

—∿—

To me the future of the small town is not a negligible matter. I know that the choice does not lie between cities like New York and towns of eight hundred. I have been happy in cities of twenty and twenty-five thousand, and I will even admit that a city of a hundred thousand—I would scarcely go higher than that—can offer opportunities for the decent development of the human being as a social animal. Actually, so far as my observations go, the town of four or five thousand, at any rate in the Northeast, seems close to ideal. It can sustain a greater variety of activity than a smaller town can, is more likely to produce and attract adequate leadership, and makes an easier adaptation to the demands of the larger society, but at the same time is not too big to constitute a real community. However, the Roxboroughs are not unimportant—there are millions of Plainvillers, as James West says—and a town of this size is in many ways a more interesting laboratory than the town with a population of five thousand.

Certain reviewers of *Plainville, U.S.A.* were depressed by the picture James West drew of the people in his Ozark town and seemed inclined to dismiss them as sub-human. "Thank God," they said in effect, "most Americans aren't like this!" My guess is that a large proportion of Americans are a good deal like the people in Plainville and the people in Roxborough, though some of them disguise themselves by wearing city clothes and using city jargon, and most of them manage to keep out of the way of the intellectuals. They are not, by and large, morons or incompetents, but equally they are not at all what the intellectuals think the "common man" ought to be.

Harvey Dakin always maintains that Roxborough is well below average, but I doubt it, and I have heard Roxborough held up in other towns as a model of community spirit and enterprise. Aside from the special qualities, good and bad, of the old-timers, the human material in the town is probably pretty close to the norm. Most people, I observe, conduct themselves astutely in the matters they are concerned with, but I also observe that they are not concerned with many matters that are demonstrably relevant to their lives. I have never caught sight of the "common man," but I have watched the behavior of a certain number of specific men and women in specific situations, and I am not convinced that what I have seen is unrepresentative.

While I have been working on this book, a study has been going on in Montana, an attempt "to find out so far as possible how the lives of the people in Montana and of their families and communities may be stabilized and enriched." In one little town of ninety families, forty men and women came out every week through the winter of 1944–45 to study their own community with the aid of members of the research staff. A larger town put on a series of plays under the general title, "Darby Looks at Itself." There have been other experiments of the same kind. Baker Brownell, Director of the Montana Study, wrote me at the time the project was begun that there was one problem with three aspects: "namely the disintegration of human personality, the intellectual segregation of different levels of people, the decline of the human community." Later he wrote, "The year has confirmed me in believing that this is the way to go. The difficulties are those at the beginning of a great problem not at the end of it." I think he states the problem well, and I believe he is tackling it the right way.

X

The Larger Society

The kind of socialism that I and my friends believed in back in the twenties rested on nineteenth century humanitarianism and a nineteenth century faith in the human intellect. We had been brought up to believe that a good society was a moral society, and the immorality of capitalism was apparent, we felt, to the most casual glance. But we did not despair at the sight of so much evil in the world, for we were sure that men had only to think about their problems in order to solve them. One of my professors used to argue that capitalism was sound just because it was an organic growth and not a fabrication of man's fallible mind. At the time I could see nothing in this but willful paradox. What in the world was intellect for if not to shatter social institutions to bits and mold them closer to the heart's desire?

I was not an active socialist in the twenties, nor were most of my friends, and for that reason the depression caught us not only intellectually unprepared but also morally at a disadvantage. Although the young intellectuals of the twenties were contemptuous of the money-makers, we did succumb in our own way to the extravagant spirit of the times. We, too, went on a self-indulgent spree, and we, too, woke up with a hangover. Economically, of course, we were less affected by the depression than the business men, but intellectually and morally we were harder hit than they. We began to atone for our sins by turning on capitalism and rending it.

The question for me and many of my contemporaries in 1930 and 1931 was not whether capitalism should be supplanted but how. The socialism we had believed in was purely evolutionary:

it was so reasonable a doctrine, we felt, that sooner or later almost everyone could be expected to see the light. In the early thirties conversion didn't seem so probable, and in any case there wasn't time for it. We began to read or reread Marx, who had said that the capitalist system would go from depression to depression, and who had been proved right when a thousand and one exponents of the new capitalism were proved wrong. In the spring of 1929 I had talked with one of the most enlightened of American capitalists, a member of President Hoover's Committee on Recent Social Trends, and he had assured me, in the light of the committee's findings, that there was not the slightest danger of a depression. He and his kind had been so horribly wrong that Marx and the Marxists seemed doubly right. Marx said not only that capitalism could not solve the problem of depressions but also that the capitalists would oppose any plan of social reorganization. Only the exploited classes, those who had nothing to lose but their chains, could be counted on to establish socialism. Only revolution could put an end to the immorality and inefficiency of the capitalist system.

Although Marx's argument came to seem to me as unanswerable as a proposition in geometry, I know well enough that conversion, in my case and others, was not a matter of pure logic. There was the emotional impact of the depression, the shock of the apple sellers, the shock of the sleeping men in subway entrances, the shock of the breadlines. And there was also the susceptibility of the intelligentsia to contagion. There was so much talk about Marx in those days that one had to read him or lose one's intellectual standing. Conversion did not come overnight; it was a matter of months and years, and there were doubts and relapses.

It was the Communist Party, not the Socialist Party, that attracted my generation. "Becoming a socialist right now," wrote John Dos Passos in 1932, "would have just about the same effect on anybody as drinking a bottle of near-beer." We were revolting not only against capitalism but also against a whole set of nineteenth century values. Humanitarianism and rationalism no longer seemed adequate. It is true that communism's ultimate aims were humanitarian, and perhaps it would have had little attraction for the intellectuals if they had not been. It is also true that Marxism claimed to be the only truly rationalist philosophy. Yet in the immediate situation communism proposed to meet violence with violence in an open struggle for power. "The world," said the young intellectual to himself, "is obviously not ruled by gentleness and reason, as my parents and teachers claimed. It is dominated by self-interest or, at any rate, by class-interest. The ruling class will never voluntarily surrender its power; it will yield to nothing but force." The times, in short, seemed to call for desperate remedies, and desperation was part of the communist stock in trade.

Then there was Russia. I never thought of myself as a Russophile, and certainly I quarreled enough with the comrades who expected the social revolution in America to follow with absolute fidelity the Russian model. But I was for Russia rather than against, and it seemed to me that Russia had at least demonstrated the feasibility of socialism. If socialism had had even a measure of success in backward Russia, I thought, what could it not achieve in America? At any rate there the Soviet Union was, living proof that revolutionaries might win the day.

In the autumn of 1932 a rather impressive number of intellectuals, myself among them, signed a statement endorsing the Communist Party's candidates. That was the highest point of revolutionary passion among the intelligentsia, and in the miserable, fearful winter that followed revolution seemed no dream. With spring, however, came the New Deal, showing that capitalism had some resiliency, and at the same time the Nazis captured Germany. As fascism proceeded to destroy political opposition, subjugate the trade unions, abolish free speech, and persecute the Jews, we saw—or thought we saw—the full horrors of counter-revolution. On the one hand, the chances of communist revolution dwindled, and, on the other, the dangers of fascism loomed blacker and blacker. It seemed only the part of wisdom to work with "all progressive elements," as the phrase then went, against fascism.

It was in 1935, when the popular front was fairly launched, that I joined the Communist Party. After 1939, when I left the party, I was told contemptuously by loyal communists that I was a fool to have been taken in by the democratic front maneuver. No doubt I was. I realized, of course, that the democratic front policy served the purposes of the Soviet Union, which was seeking to find allies among the capitalist democracies against the Nazi war machine, but it also seemed to me the only way to ward off the dangers of fascism. I still believed that socialism was inevitable and desirable, but I thought the fight against fascism came first. "Our side," I believed, having conquered fascism, would move towards socialism, and by defeating a counter-revolution we would be spared the necessity of making a revolution.

This was good democratic front doctrine, and was professed— and certainly believed—by all communists between 1935 and 1939. There was another belief, however, that was held by the leaders and perhaps by a majority of the members of the party: whatever the Soviet Union does is right. This dogma has a certain rationale. Communism, the orthodox say, won a great victory in Russia in October, 1917, and since that time the primary duty of communists has been to defend what was then won. When, therefore, the exigencies of foreign policy led the Soviet Union to sign a non-intervention pact with Nazi Germany, the orthodox hastened to justify the pact as best they could. They had said again and again that it could not happen; but that did not matter. Because I still believed in fighting fascism, I left the party.

The months and years after my resignation from the party were a period of revaluation. For one thing, bitterly as I hated fascism, I began to wonder if the orthodox communist account of it was adequate. It seemed unreasonable to describe fascism as a device for bolstering up capitalism when the Nazis had systematically altered the whole economy of Germany. It was true that they had not expropriated the means of production, as the Bolsheviks had done in Russia, and it was clear that they had been supported by a section of the capitalist class. But if certain capitalists, favorites of the new rulers, were allowed to reap large profits, they were not allowed to exercise the classical capitalist prerogatives. They were told by the government what to make, how much to charge, what they could pay their workers. In short, if Nazism wasn't socialist, it wasn't capitalist either, but a curious mongrel—a controlled economy with capitalist fringes.

This discovery didn't make me like fascism any better, but it did underline certain significant parallels between Communist Russia and Nazi Germany. In Russia, too, there was only one political party. In Russia, too, there was no freedom of speech. In Russia, too, trade unions were mere agencies of the state. I had always realized that both revolutions were made by minorities, but I had believed that the Bolsheviks were acting in the interests of the workers and peasants, whereas the Nazis were ruthless opportunists interested only in power. Now I saw that, even if the distinction were more or less valid, the fact remained that the Leninist technique of revolution was a two-edged weapon, one that could be used by either reactionaries or progressives. Furthermore, I became convinced that the Soviet state, instead of withering away as Lenin predicted, had taken on more and more of the characteristics associated with the totalitarian tyranny of fascism. The Communist Party had increasingly become a clique of the people in power, not an organization of the masses. Many socialist goals had been abandoned: not only was there great inequality of income; there was inequality of educational opportunities and inequality between the sexes. Finally, the humanitarianism that had played so large a part in the thinking of Marx and Engels—along with very different elements, it is true—had been increasingly ignored by Stalin, so that in the Russia, as in the Germany, of the early forties the primary appeal was nationalistic.

I could see that there were profound differences between Communist Russia and Nazi Germany. In its culture Russia still drew upon the fraternal and equalitarian ideals of the nineteenth century, whereas Germany had adopted a kind of synthetic barbarism. Far from accepting the racist doctrines of the Nazis, the Soviet Union had continued to show the world an example of freedom from racial discrimination. Moreover, one could hope that the Soviet government, having less to fear as its power in the world increased, might become less repressive. Yet the great lesson of history had to be learned: starting from almost completely divergent theories, the Bolshevik and the Nazi revolutions had come to adopt nearly parallel courses.

The conclusions I drew were and are disturbing. In backward Russia a small group of determined men had seized power in a moment of chaos. They had used that power to liquidate capitalism: Once that task was done, they did not relinquish power but, rather, extended it, establishing a more and more rigorous control over every aspect of national life. In Germany an equally small and equally determined group had taken advantage, not of backwardness but of an advanced stage of paralysis, brought on both by inner conflicts and by outward pressures. They, too, had extended their control. And under such leadership both nations had risen from weakness to astounding military strength.

Should one call this the managerial revolution? I cannot agree with all of James Burnham's generalizations, but I think he has discerned a significant thread in the historical pattern. We have seen nations collapse, just as Marx predicted they would, but in Italy and Germany the proletariat did not take power, and in Russia the proletariat does not have power. Social collapse has favored small minorities, not the masses of the exploited. These minorities, however, claim to rule in the interests of all the people, except for certain scapegoat groups such as the Jews in Germany and the capitalists and landlords in Russia. Their strategy is not merely to make the people do what they want them to do but also to make them want what they want them to want.

One can only conclude that the potentiality of totalitarianism exists in the very nature of a mass society. The functioning of the larger society requires the coordination of millions of lives, and the totalitarian countries demonstrate that the coordination can be achieved from the top down, if no other way. We in our own country have seen how special interests have coordinated great masses of people for special purposes. It is doubtful if the totalitarian rulers have improved much on the technics devised by American advertising agencies; they have merely had the power to apply these technics on a wider scale and to supplement them, when necessary, by the use of force.

Totalitarianism is a short-cut. Socialists have been pointing out for a hundred years that capitalism cannot organize the productive resources of the new industrial society. Laissez-faire theories—as revived in 1944 by Friedrich Hayek, for example— sound well, but they ignore the pressures within capitalism that destroy the free market. Laissez-faire capitalism systematically destroys itself, and a point is finally reached at which the state has to step in. Evolutionary socialism insists that the state can take over the means of production without suspending democratic processes, and revolutionary socialism foresees the eventual establishment of an equalitarian society in which voluntary cooperation will supplant every kind of forced coordination. The burden of proof, however, is increasingly on the socialists' side. On the one hand, the state shows no signs of withering away in Russia, and if one has to grant that there are extenuating circumstances, one has a strong suspicion that there always will be. On the other hand, it has not yet been demonstrated that gradualism will work. The United States, to be sure, may continue for a long time with its system of relatively free enterprise, the government extending its controls only as rapidly as necessary and with popular consent. Great Britain may achieve a peaceful transition to a kind of state socialism with a democratic base. Yet in either country a crisis, whether of internal or of external origin, would immediately raise the possibility of the adoption of the totalitarian short-cut, as a step to be taken either by the government in power or by some revolutionary group.

The mere existence of this short-cut is alarming, but perhaps in practice it is easy to exaggerate the threat of totalitarianism. Many lugubrious prophets insisted that the war would inevitably turn the United States into a totalitarian nation, but in fact civil liberties remained in a remarkably healthy state. Strong controls were established over both production and distribution, but by due process of law and with adequate protection of the rights of individuals. For war purposes, both the United States and England achieved a high degree of coordination without the destruction of democracy.

We find ourselves, then, faced with a prospect that is gloomy enough, but hope can find some small standing ground. Democracy is alive in the world after six years of war, and that is something. I have no illusions about the limitations of democracy in the United States, but I believe that what we have is too precious to be given up without a fight. I can approve of no reform, however attractive it may sound, if it is likely to break a path for totalitarianism. On the other hand, I am quite aware that there is no surer way of bringing on tyranny than to permit gross evils to stand unremedied. Decisions are difficult, but we are lucky in that we still have choices to make.

—⁓—

All this is a long way from Roxborough, and yet the central issue touches the town closely. Some of us want to make plans for Roxborough, but how can we when nobody has made plans for the region on which Roxborough depends? They would not have to be perfect plans, but if someone could say in a general way what the various industries in the area will be doing in the next five years, we could tell what our chances are of having a community center and what kind of school we ought to work for.

According to good American tradition, we ought to be willing to take a chance, but I shouldn't like to have to tell that to my neighbors, for most of them are convinced there will be a depression. They may well turn out to be wrong, but the fact remains that they have lost faith in the inevitable progress of the American economy. So have most people. Those who talk loudest about free enterprise think twice before they make investments. They blame their hesitancy on the administration, and try to convince themselves and others that they would dare anything if the government would let them alone, but they make it clear that they don't want to be let wholly alone, and in any case they know they won't be. The risk-taking spirit of the old-fashioned entrepreneur may not be dead, but it isn't exactly flourishing.

The free-market system has broken down, and it is futile to go on assuming that people will act according to the rules they followed in a very different situation. Laissez-faire theories did work for a little while, but they do not work now. The necessary coordination of the larger society can be achieved only through conscious control, through specific agencies that can guide the course of production and distribution. I have no doctrinaire desire to do away with capitalism as such; so far as I am concerned, it may remain so long as it proves compatible with the bare minimum of planning necessary to prevent our economic system from collapsing; but on that minimum I insist. Of course there are dangers, as I have pointed out, but planlessness has greater dangers. Though I have lost some of my youthful confidence in the efficacy of pure reason in human affairs, I know that reason is what we have to fall back on. "We should all really prefer," Karl Mannheim says, "to leave the great decisions of our time to fate. At bottom we are afraid to take the responsibility. But in the periods when change goes very deep we have no power to decide whether we wish to accept responsibility or not, to plan or not to plan."

Even at the risk of seeming to dodge the most vital problems, I am not going to discuss the technics of national planning. The job, at least at the outset, is simply to compensate for the inadequacies of free enterprise. The obvious aims are to prevent depressions, maintain a high level of employment, and use the enormous national productivity to eliminate poverty. I have read some of the books on planning, and I know how difficult it is both to make plans and to execute them, but after the extraordinary achievements of the war I do not believe the difficulties are insuperable. What concerns me is the relation of planning to democracy. That the wrong kind of planning can destroy democracy scarcely needs saying. What I am wondering is whether the right kind of planning can strengthen democracy by making possible a deeper participation in the affairs of the larger society.

I went to Tennessee in the spring of 1945 full of curiosity. I had read David Lilienthal's *TVA: Democracy on the March,* and I wanted to see for myself, in so far as I could, how this particular kind of planning worked. I saw immediately and beyond any doubt that on one plane the TVA was a tremendous success. The river has been mastered: the threat of floods has been eliminated, abundant power has been created, navigation has been improved. And this is a job that could not possibly have been undertaken by private enterprise or by any public unit smaller than the federal government.

Such technical achievements, however, have become commonplace in America and can really be taken for granted. What I wanted to examine were the social accomplishments that Lilienthal claims for the TVA. "I trust it is clear," he writes, "that the methods of TVA are calculated to promote that accountability of the manager and that diffusion of power which are the precise opposite and may well be an effective antidote to the 'managerial revolution.'" And: "Here is the life principle of democratic planning—an awakening in the whole people of a sense of this common moral purpose. Not one goal, but a direction. Not one plan, once and for all, but the conscious selection by the people of successive plans." This, Lilienthal maintains, is the kind of planning that actually extends the democratic rights of the people. According to him, the TVA's experts are not bureaucrats, making theoretical blueprints in isolation, but are servants of the people, working with them. Decisions are not handed down from Washington or Knoxville but are arrived at through consultation with all those affected. Decentralization is the rule, and the TVA works through existing local institutions instead of setting up machinery under its immediate control. "Is it inescapable," Lilienthal asks, "that such a task of resource development be carried on only by highly centralized government direction? Must it inevitably be run by a privileged elite of managers or experts or politicians? Yes, say the defeatists about democracy, the disillusioned and frustrated liberals, the believers in force, the disbelievers in men. . . . The experience in this valley gives the lie to such answers and to those who utter them."

I left the Tennessee Valley convinced that Lilienthal's basic claims are sound. The TVA officials I met were a long way from the bureaucrats of political satire. They were unpretentious, accessible, acutely interested in what they were doing and eager to discuss it. I liked the way they talked about their jobs and about the people of the valley. Those who were working directly with the people, whether they were concerned with erosion control, the wider use of electricity, labor policy, community planning, library service, or whatever the task might be, seemed to be the kind of men who would win respect and get cooperation in Roxborough or almost anywhere else. They were enthusiastic but patient, expert but not cocky.

But what do the people of the valley think about this extraordinary agency in their midst? Do they feel that it is in any sense theirs? In Clifton, so far as I could make out, they certainly don't. They are acutely conscious of the TVA, and almost all of them think it is a Good Thing—like religion or democracy. It has paid high prices for the land it has bought, has given employment to a certain number of people, has lowered the cost of electricity. Almost everyone approves, as almost everyone approves of Santa Claus. Few persons, however, seem to be aware of the substantial

aid the TVA has given to a program for the conservation of the
lumber resources of the county, and not many more are concerned with developing the recreational facilities that have been
made possible by the creation of Kentucky Lake. As for any feeling
of direct participation in the work of the TVA, any sense of this
agency as something that belongs to the people, I found not a sign.
I am sure that in many ways Clifton is unrepresentative. An
unbalanced community, it was not ready to make the most of
what the TVA offered. Dandridge, on the other hand, a town of
about the same size east of Knoxville, was quick to take advantage
of opportunities for improvement, and in the spring of 1945 was
looking forward to great progress. The larger community of
Guntersville, Alabama, has been almost transformed by the TVA,
and many farming areas not only have adopted new methods and
achieved new standards of living but have learned new ways of
cooperation. All through the valley there are people who know
how much they owe to the TVA. I am not sure how many of
them have the sense of democratic participation that Lilienthal
describes, but I am inclined to believe that some such sentiment
is slowly taking shape.

Irregular development is what one ought to expect when a
planning agency is determined to wait for popular participation,
and if my observations led me to suspect that Lilienthal's claims
are sometimes too large, they convinced me that his aims and his
methods are right. I said this, a day or two after I left the valley,
to a man who has devoted his life to the study of the small community and democracy. To my surprise, he scoffed at the idea
that the TVA was democratic. It pretended to be, he said, but in
fact it imposed its will on the people, and what was more, he assured me, no such project could be democratic. I asked him what
he meant by democracy, and was given an eloquent and detailed
description of popular participation at every stage of planning
and doing. It was an attractive ideal, but it could be made a reality only in a community of individuals who had a wide range of
expert knowledge, a boundless interest in public affairs, and

unlimited time. When I said this, the expert smiled: "Oh, I'm not criticizing the TVA for failing to be democratic; it's the pretense I object to." And he went on to describe the rather drastic program of compulsion that he himself would be willing to adopt.

The experience was a useful warning, for it made me realize that insistence on some theoretical conception of pure democracy can result in the negation of democratic practice. It may be true that the TVA is sometimes concerned with the appearance rather than the substance of democracy, but even this is preferable to an outright abandonment of the attempt to enlist the interest and support of the people. On the other hand, it is unfortunate if the members of the TVA staff are fooling themselves. "Out of my experience in the valley," Lilienthal has written, "I am as acutely aware as anyone could be of the difficulties of securing the active participation of citizens at the grass roots. I know 'what a task' (again using the words of de Tocqueville) it is 'to persuade men to busy themselves about their own affairs.' But our experience here has in it more of encouragement than of despair. For in this valley, in almost every village and town and city, in every rural community, there has proved to be a rich reservoir of citizen talent for public service." I am sure there are people everywhere who can be counted on, and I have no doubt that greater and greater human resources can be developed, but my observations in the valley, such as they were, did not disclose what I would care to call "a rich reservoir."

Democracy and planning are compatible only if democracy is planned for. Two mistakes seem equally dangerous. The first and more obvious is the imposing of a plan without consideration of the people involved. The second is waiting for the people to come forward and offer to participate. I was not in the valley long enough to make my judgment of the TVA worth much, but I am willing to gamble on my knowledge of Roxborough, and it seems to me purely romantic to assume that any large number of people will continuously devote any large amount of time to public affairs. If it is important to secure their participation—and nothing seems to me more important—it is necessary to devise ways and means of getting it. That the TVA is trying to do, and I am willing to give it A plus for effort.

The task is one of extraordinary and continuing difficulty, but at the very least the TVA has demonstrated that representative government of the American type can adopt a large-scale plan for the conservation and development of natural resources without any impairment of constitutional rights. And it has demonstrated more than that, though perhaps not quite so much as David Lilienthal thinks. From the beginning it took people as well as things into account, and it has thus given the world some idea of what a plan for democracy might be.

—◆◆◆—

Looking at Roxborough, I have tried to imagine what would happen to the small-town mind in an age of planning. The small-town tradition of resistance to authority, though it has its unfortunate aspects, might turn out to be a valuable bulwark against totalitarianism. The small town has its own kind of conformity, and the fear of public opinion is stronger than it is in cities, but small-town people are not accustomed to acting in masses, and I cannot picture my neighbors lining up dutifully to salute a Fuehrer. Not many are so violently insistent on independence of thought, word, and action as Stan Cutter and Harvey Dakin, but Stan and Harvey are admired for just these qualities. They sometimes seem to me frontiersmen at heart, and there is something to be said for, as well as against, the persistence of the frontier spirit.

Defiant individualism, however, though a conceivable defense against totalitarianism, is also an obvious obstacle in the way of democratic planning. The distrust of officials may be healthy, but the distrust of government is not. For one thing, it provides an easy excuse for lack of participation. For another, it is likely to involve the individual sooner or later in exactly the kind of

personal dependence he is anxious to avoid. The man who dis-
trusts the processes of law, whether rightly or wrongly, is tempted
to turn for help to some person with influence, and the big shot
naturally expects a return for the favors he grants. Roxborough
furnishes plenty of examples of this type of relationship, and
some of the men who talk most loudly about their independence—not Harvey Dakin, by the way, or Stan Cutter—are kept
on a short leash.

The self-reliant spirit of the frontier or of the nineteenth century farming community was by no means hostile to the competitive spirit of an industrial age, and, as has already been
observed, it is no wonder that many small-town boys made good
in the big cities. The competitive spirit has continued to dominate American mores, manifesting itself most strangely in the
midst of a great national crisis. In most societies the individual
can be counted on to look out for himself, but it is the peculiar
faith of capitalist society that the acquisitive impulses are virtues.
The contradiction between the lofty sentiments that people more
or less sincerely profess in time of war and the practices in which
they customarily engage imposes a sharp strain. Roxborough
people behaved, I imagine, about like the average. They accepted many inconveniences with only a formal amount of complaint, but when they began to see that others were getting what
they were denied, the competitive spirit boiled up in them, and
they, too—some of them, that is—went after what they wanted.
We argued the point one day with a man who had two sons in
the service. "I'm not taking anything away from my boys," he
said. "Uncle Sam is looking after them, and they're getting plenty. But if those damned Jews can have all the meat they want, I
don't see why I can't."

I hope the advocates of planning have carefully studied the op-
erations of wartime rationing. In the more or less free market of
capitalism goods are valuable when they are scarce, and people
nurtured in a free-market psychology automatically crave whatever is hard to get. It is also in accordance with capitalistic ethics

that people should be resigned when they can't buy goods because of lack of money but, should be indignant when balked by government restrictions. If a planned society can deliver the goods and deliver them in abundance, it will have a chance of success, but a people who could barely tolerate the necessary shortages of war will have little patience with apparently arbitrary shortages in peace.

Is there any antidote to the competitive spirit? Certain kinds of cooperation did develop spontaneously in the farming communities of the past. In a subsistence economy it was natural for men to exchange work, and house-raisings and other bees were social events as well as the solution of an economic problem. Such cooperative activities easily existed in a community that was nevertheless predominantly individualistic. As money became more common, however, a man paid for the work he couldn't do himself, and relationships were that much less personal. There is still a good deal of neighborliness in the small towns, and many services are rendered free that in a city would be paid for. But neighborliness operates only in a narrow circle. The affairs of the larger society are strictly impersonal, and in relation to them, as I have said, the individualism of the small-towner operates with uncurbed voracity.

There is only one way in which the people of Roxborough—and the people of the United States, for that matter—can be reconciled to the larger society, and that is through understanding. The need for understanding is inherent in the very character of the larger society because it substitutes impersonal for personal relationships. The modern worker on an assembly line has often been contrasted with the old-fashioned craftsman, who made his product from start to finish, knew all about it, and knew it was his. The assembly-line laborer can know what he is doing only if he takes the trouble to study the whole process of which he is a tiny part. So the people of Roxborough can know the shape of their world only if they study it; they cannot get the feel of it, as their ancestors did, through the experiences of daily living.

If I say that most people in Roxborough seem appallingly ig-
norant of the character of the larger society, that is not to suggest
that I or anyone else thoroughly understands it. Thurman
Arnold has said that modern man lives by faith—faith that the
complicated machinery of production will keep running and supply his wants. Modern man has to have faith because he doesn't
know—doesn't know how the corporation is organized that supplies his daily bread, what chemical formulae it relies upon, where
the ingredients of the bread come from, how the finished product is distributed. He has faith that if he has his twelve cents the
bread will be forthcoming, and by and large it is. What do I know
about the internal combustion engine? For me the shortest ride
is an act of faith. And Stan Cutter, who can put an engine
through its paces, has to take for granted the organization by
which the engine is manufactured.

Obviously one can't be omniscient, and fortunately one does-
n't have to be, for up to a point one can trust the experts. It is
not the processes that matter but the ends for which they are
used. The citizen may rely on the expert to tell him what atomic energy can do, so long as he is in a position to tell the expert
what, of the things it can do, it should do. What the citizen
needs, in other words, is not so much a knowledge of the atom
as a knowledge of society.

And it is that kind of knowledge that most people in Roxborough don't seem to have. They can't place Roxborough, so to
speak, in either time or place. Foreign countries are foreign countries, and the past is the past, an indefinite expanse of barbarism
before the days of the automobile and electricity. Roxborough
people have opinions, to be sure, on many subjects, but these are
usually snap judgments, caught from some newspaper editorial
or, more likely, from some radio commentator. The opinions seldom rest on sustained thinking, and if there is any thinking, it is
seldom based on adequate information. I don't believe for a moment that my fellow-citizens are stupid, but they haven't any very
acute awareness of the world they live in. They don't know, ex-

cept in the most formal sense, how big it is, and, in spite of the war's drastic lessons, they don't begin to feel how interrelated its parts are. They aren't conscious of the larger society as a reality. It solves nothing to say that my neighbors are small-towners, farmers, hill-billies. One has only to read the most popular newspapers, listen to the most popular radio programs, or see the most popular movies, to realize that large numbers of the American people are not mature citizens of the larger society. Their backwardness, indeed, is a common-place not only of sociology but also of practical politics and practical business. It is, however, a commonplace that the detached urban intellectual can manage to ignore when he chooses to talk about the common man and grass roots democracy. It cannot be easily ignored in the Roxboroughs.

—w—

To be sure, knowledge is not the all-sufficient remedy. The persons who come closest to grasping the complexities of the larger society, instead of being well integrated and purposeful, are the very ones who are seized by the paralysis of doubt. When journalists refer, as they rather frequently do, to the schizoid personality of our time, it is the intelligentsia they have in mind. It is the intellectual who feels the shadow that falls "between the desire and the spasm, between the potency and the existence, between the essence and the descent." Never have the potentialities of a good society seemed more abundant than they seem today, and seldom—perhaps only in the final throes of the dead civilizations—has the world looked so bleak. Never has so much power been made available to the individual, and never has the individual felt himself so completely at the mercy of forces beyond his control. Even before the invention of the atomic bomb, the destructiveness of war surpassed the destructiveness of flood or famine, earthquake or pestilence. Life is in man's hands. He gives, with all the miracles of medicine, and takes away, with all the horrors of war. It is no wonder that those who understand, however vaguely, their guilt for the past and their responsibility for the future are sick at heart.

The disease manifests itself most obviously among the intellectuals, but it is not confined to them. The men who talk together in Roxborough's general store or as they eat their lunches in one of Troy's factories cannot say so clearly what it is they feel, but it would be wrong to assume that they are at ease. I remember the grimness that underlay the celebration of Japan's surrender. No one was naive enough to assume that this put an end to our problems. On the contrary, every individual, as he went through the motions of jubilation, was trying to come to terms with a disturbing vision of the future. The doubts showed themselves in mild understatement: "Well, guess I'll get a chance to patch the roof before snow flies," or, "I was getting kind of sick of that place anyhow."

After the bomb fell on Hiroshima, most of my neighbors were unmoved by all that the radio commentators babbled about the marvelous new world of atomic energy. One young mechanic said excitedly that it was wonderful: things were being discovered in the twentieth century that they hadn't been expecting until the twenty-fifth, when he wouldn't be alive to see them. But Stan Cutter said, "They ought to have just one more of them eggs ready to drop on the Japs if they don't behave, and then they ought to forget the whole thing." For once, I think, Stan spoke for the majority. When the miraculous new automobile with sealed-in atomic energy appears on the market, nobody will be more eager than Stan to try it, and perhaps by that time he will have forgotten his misgivings. I suspect, however, that even then his mind will retain a suspicion that men are playing with forces they cannot control.

Some of Roxborough's old-timers seem securely immured in their sense of the past, but I wonder if even they do not have the feeling that the earth may open at their feet. I am sure that my contemporaries and juniors know they live in the shadow of disaster. Their fears, of course, are buried deep, and it is difficult to tell how strong they are. How much would it take to make them unbearable? Remembering what certain neurotic intellectuals were able to do with the neurotic people of Germany, one asks that question with fear and trembling.

For hundreds of thousands of years, all but a tiny fraction of his life on earth, man was almost completely at the mercy of natural forces. Seeing no possibility of anything else, he came to terms with his insecurity. As science extended man's control over nature, optimists celebrated the release from fear. But the new fear has thus far proved harder to live with than the old fear. The power of nature was the power of God or gods, but the power of man is the power of man. The hero of modern fiction, as critics have observed, is the man to whom things are done—and not by Pallas Athene or Neptune or Yahweh or even Fate, but by something called social forces, something purely human and yet as impersonal and relentless as Kismet or the Norns.

By now it is quite clear that the problem of the reintegration of human personality is inseparable from the problem of the integration of society. If, that is, the individual could feel that social forces were under control, and in some real sense under *his* control, the new fears could be conquered. Anarchy cannot be long endured, and, on the other hand, manipulation of social forces from the top will only widen the schism in society, to use Toynbee's terminology, and the schism in the soul.

But what, in practice, does democratic control of social forces mean? Beyond a certain point popular participation in the making and executing of plans for the larger society is unthinkable. The problem is to discover that point—and reach it. This involves not merely the attainment of a higher level of understanding but also the achievement of some sort of common purpose. If people could agree on what they wanted, there is a good chance that they would equip themselves to get it.

Let us not deceive ourselves by thinking that it would be easy for the people of the world, or the people of the United States, to arrive at a common purpose, even in the most general terms.

The absence of such a purpose is the very heart of our modern dilemma. It may be wrong, however, to assume that we cannot regain our sense of direction unless some great evangelical movement sweeps through the world to change the hearts of men. We might begin more humbly, more experimentally. Of course we may be too late, but we can only try.

Perhaps the first step is to make sure that such plans as we adopt for the larger society make room for plenty of experimentation. In other words, as Lilienthal has pointed out, decentralization is essential to any democratic program of planning. Beyond any doubt, there must be a plan for the nation and eventually a plan for the world, but already enough planning has been done to prove that a plan can provide for a maximum or a minimum of conformity. The Russian planners, for instance, have insisted on a high degree of economic and political coordination, but they have permitted certain kinds of cultural diversity. The TVA necessarily has a unified plan for flood control through the valley, but in less essential matters decisions are made by or in cooperation with established units of local government. Upon the overall plan the individual can exert only a tiny, though important, influence; on lower levels his participation can be immediate.

We are back to our old problem, the community. For many years radicals have criticized the geographical basis of representation, and urged that men should vote as members of an industry, not as inhabitants of a particular area. The increasing importance of economic function in the larger society makes industrial representation desirable. Moreover, decentralization ought to be planned to give the workers in a particular factory the greatest possible amount of self-government. But the division of society on an economic basis is no more than a useful supplement to the geographical division. The importance of a man's economic function is enormous, but it is a mistake to assume that a man can be reduced to his job. The living community, with its many-sided relationships, remains the natural seedbed for social growth.

Perhaps because the United States was so recently a nation of small towns, even city-dwellers tend to create for themselves units of some comprehensible size, and in the largest cities neighborhoods sometimes develop local institutions and a fierce local pride. The neighborhood is a poor substitute for the community, but I hope that city planning will make more rather than less of all possible subdivisions of Megalapolis. The planned city of the future might be, among other things, a congeries of neighborhoods, in each of which the residents exercise as much power as is compatible with the welfare of the city as a whole.

Planned decentralization is practical, for the people on the spot by and large know what they need and, if they don't, they had better be left to learn from their own mistakes. Beyond that, participation in local affairs can prepare men and women for participation in the affairs of the larger society. It is quite true that the forces men are afraid of are national or worldwide in their scope, and it is consequently true that we need a common purpose that embraces the nation and, as soon as may be, the world. Nevertheless, if men feel that they are dealing successfully with the immediate environment; and if they begin to perceive how interknit local problems are with those of larger groups, they may grow into intelligent citizenship. We can only hope that the level of interest and the level of knowledge may be raised by a tiny margin, but that margin may be the difference between democracy and totalitarianism. We can only expect an awkward groping toward a common purpose, but even the bare beginnings of purposeful action may prove an antidote to corruption and despair.

If there can be no plan for a Roxborough without a plan for the region, which will depend in turn on a plan for the larger society, it may also be true that there can be no successful master plan that does not give scope for regional planning and no successful regional plan that leaves the Roxboroughs out of account. I know there is no clamor in Roxborough for a community plan. As things stand, there would be only apathetic support for any kind of plan and a great deal of bitter, unreasonable opposition.

This is the way things are, and there is no sense in pretending otherwise. All I can say is that we would do well to work on the problem at both ends. As I stated at the beginning of this chapter, I have long recognized the importance of the "big" end of the problem. Now I have come to see the importance of the "little" end and to feel that it is nearer my size.

XI

The Burden on the Schools

If there is one conclusion to be drawn from our investigation of the mind of Roxborough, it is that universal compulsory education hasn't been a great success. The testimony of the Sole Trustee of Common School District Number One is thus added to the lamentations, exhortations, and prescriptions of a host of weightier authorities. Most American institutions are currently subject to criticism, but in no profession or trade is self-criticism so prevalent as it is among teachers. To hear what is wrong with education, all one has to do is ask an educator.

In my capacity as trustee, I am principally concerned with elementary education. During most of Roxborough's existence grammar school was, to all intents and purposes, the sum total of education, and even at the present time it is true that few residents who are over thirty have gone beyond the eighth grade. Every spring, when the question of the transportation of high school pupils comes up, there ate old-timers to grumble over the cost and say that grammar school was enough for them.

The old-timers think that I am an advocate of all kinds of expensive educational frills and of everything that is modern and therefore bad in our school curriculum, but as a matter of fact there cannot be many persons in the town who are more appreciative than I am of the education the old-timers and their parents received. If the aim of education is to prepare a child for the life he will live as an adult, there is little doubt that the education children received in 1845 was better than that provided a century later. Most of the 1845 education, however, was obtained outside the school. All the teacher had to do was to give pupils the three basic tools—reading, writing, and arithmetic.

Watching Stan Cutter's eight-year-old, son, on the days when he tags his grandfather, I can appreciate the educational values of a farm. Mr. Cutter loves to talk about what he is doing, but even if he were as taciturn as some farmers I know, Little Mark is observant enough to educate himself. At eight Little Mark knows most of what there is to be known about plowing and dragging a garden, planting the various seeds, cultivating and harvesting the crops. He understands the care of livestock, and has an intimate and accurate knowledge of the processes of reproduction. He can skin a chipmunk, and knows, at least in theory, how to dress a chicken. He has taken care of both baby rabbits and baby skunks, and he can recognize deer tracks. He is only moderately handy with tools, but he goes at a job of carpentry the right way. If he finds us engaged in some kind of tinkering around the place, he usually has suggestions to make, and the suggestions are worth listening to.

A hundred years ago a boy brought up as Little Mark is being brought up would have been given chores to do and then more chores, and by the time he was twelve or fourteen he would have a vocation. Such training, as has been demonstrated times without number, fits a boy not only for farming but for much else. In the Tennessee Valley farm boys, confronted with the most complicated machinery, catch on at once. And why not? They have learned to use their eyes, and have acquired an insatiable curiosity about processes. If there were ten right ways of doing a thing and only one wrong way, I would probably try the wrong way first. My eight-year-old neighbor finds the right way—and usually there is only one right way—with a minimum of hesitation.

The training a boy received on a farm in the old days was not only training for a vocation; it was an initiation into life. Today the very same training cannot achieve the same results. Little Mark, for instance, is exposed to half a dozen different philosophies. His grandfather expounds, with some modifications, the values of the past. His father tries to impart to the boy his own defiant individualism and his love of machinery. In our home he encounters middle-class standards of speech and manners together with the special values of the professional intellectuals. Being an astute boy, he is acutely conscious of these various Weltanschauungs, and is remarkably successful in adapting himself to each in turn. He is also aware that there are considerable differences in the backgrounds of his schoolmates, and he perceives that the official values of the classroom are quite different from those of the playground.

It would be easy to exaggerate the unity of a town like Roxborough in the middle of the nineteenth century, and yet it is perfectly patent that the John Cutter of the Civil War letters and the George Holcomb of the diary were never subjected to such heterogeneous influences as bear upon Little Mark. No doubt there was a gulf between generations, but they were not so sharply set apart as are Little Mark's parents and grandparents, and there could have been no influence as drastically foreign as that of the Hickses. Home, school, and church were in at least general agreement, and the whole effect of life in the community was to enforce the accepted values.

The little school in the village has some twenty-five pupils, and it is supposed to do for these boys and girls a great deal that other institutions, particularly the farm-home, did for their great-grandparents. What boys and girls currently learn outside of school, whether they live in the city or the country, is no doubt important, but it is not so directly connected with what they need to know. There is only a slight chance, for instance, that Little Mark will be a farmer, and though the boy is acquiring traits that will always prove valuable, he is going to need another kind of training as well if he is not to feel ill at ease in the world in which he will be living. Even the boys who grow up on the farms of the West and South, and who have every intention of becoming farmers, are bound to learn that specialized farming requires scientific knowledge as well as practical apprenticeship. The experiences of childhood and youth have a lower educational value in the twentieth century than they had in the nineteenth, and the schools are supposed to make up the difference.

It would be unfair to suggest that educators are unaware of their responsibility. Certainly the department of education of New York State knows that the schools have had thrust upon them the job of introducing children, whether rural or urban, to the larger society.[1] One of their methods is the much discussed, much criticized program of social studies. I am not impressed when the old-timers boast of the names of state capitals and the dates of battles that they had to memorize, for the old-fashioned geography and history were the frills of their day. The program of social studies, on the other hand, is a serious attempt to give children a working knowledge of the modern world, a knowledge that is at least as necessary for them as reading, writing, and arithmetic are.

The program of social studies is perhaps the chief contribution of educators to the fulfillment of new tasks, and both intelligence and imagination have gone into the shaping of it, but it is not exactly a success. In saying so, I am not relying merely on what I have seen of the products of the high schools attended by Roxborough boys and girls; I have taught graduates of high schools and preparatory schools all over the country, and it is perfectly clear that with most of them social studies haven't taken. That they are less familiar with dates than my generation or my father's isn't important; what bothers me is that they don't know their way round. I have read the textbooks they have studied, and I know that if they had absorbed even a small part of what these books contain, they could not be wholly at a loss in the modern world. They just didn't get it.

Part of the trouble lies in the fact that most teachers aren't as good as the courses the state education department draws up and

<hr>

[1] See, for example, the publications of the Regents' Inquiry into the Character and Cost of Public Education in the State of New York, especially the summary volume, *Education for American Life,* written by Luther H. Gulick (New York, 1938). On page 5 of this volume there is an excellent brief statement of basic causes of educational shortcomings.

the books they recommend. There was, for example, a teacher in a nearby town who devoted the whole senior year in social studies to the Constitution, and failed to give even her brighter students an inkling of the significance of that document. Then there was the man I saw in action in a Tennessee town. The subject for the day was cooperatives, and the students had read a brief but adequate chapter in a moderately enlightened textbook. The teacher asked a series of minute questions, and the girls and even the boys drawled out a surprising amount of specific information and were given good grades in his little black book. The effect of his quizzing, however, was to obscure all distinction between producers' and consumers' cooperatives, and by the end of the hour it was obvious that one searching question would have set the class to writhing in confusion. What the end of the hour actually brought forth was an impassioned speech against cooperatives as a vicious importation from Europe.

Looking through the social studies texts that are in current use, one sees how valiantly the writers have tried to take all kinds of childhood experience into account—and how drastically they have failed. The failure is inevitable, and the teacher has to bridge the gap between the pupils and the books. If a teacher could be found with the erudition of Dr. Rugg and the intimate knowledge of local and family conditions that our Mrs. S. has, such a teacher might make social studies real for Little Mark and his companions. But that is a good deal to expect of the underpaid, overworked women who teach in grammar schools here and everywhere else.

The failure of the social studies program is related to a dozen other problems. There is almost no limit to what the schools are expected to do. They are not only supposed to provide the child with the necessary tools of communication and give him an introduction to the modern world, they are also expected to instill in him the desire to learn. Increasingly, moreover, they are being asked to take over the task of moral training, which the home and the church formerly united in handling. I remember a PTA discussion of child delinquency, in the course of which two members, both of them parents and both of them churchgoers, maintained that the only solution was for the schools to teach children what was right and what was wrong. It is true enough that in many homes children do not receive adequate moral instruction, but the more jobs the schools undertake, the less likely they are to do any of them well.

In addition to everything else, the grammar school teacher has the urgent task of preparing her pupils to enter high school. This was not true in the old days. Even in a city the size of Boston, when my mother and father were young, high school was still a privilege, and it was up to the individual pupil, with or without parental pressure, to get himself in and see that he stayed. Now boys and girls have to remain in school until they are sixteen, and it is up to their teachers to push them into high school if it can possibly be done. Conscientious students no doubt worry about "Regents," but there are others, many of them, who are content to let the teacher do the worrying.

It was possible to set the working age at sixteen because boys and girls had proved to be no economic asset in the industrial, urban society of the twentieth century, and it was necessary to extend the period of compulsory schooling because the schools had become responsible for an increasingly large segment of the child's preparation for life. The change was highly desirable, but it has resulted in the demoralization of the high schools. In the eighteen-eighties the better high schools dropped backward students with a ruthlessness that only the first-rate law and medical schools exhibit today. It is likely that this method threw into outer darkness a host of boys and girls whose feet, with a little coaxing, might have been set upon the paths of light, but it did protect the interests of the more serious and more intelligent students. They, at least, got what their instructors had to give. But between 1870 and 1940, a period in which the population trebled, the number of pupils in secondary schools rose from 80,000 to 7,000,000. Today there are ninety students in high school for every one who attended in 1870. Who can be surprised if some of the ninety don't want to be there at all and if many of the others have to be shown? The mere increase in numbers has created a problem, but that is nothing compared to the crisis that has been precipitated by the character of the new material.

Anyone who has dealt with college freshmen is bound to be conscious of the deterioration of high school education. Almost any college English teacher, for example, will tell you that the majority of freshmen cannot write legibly, spell correctly, or punctuate a sentence. Teachers of history, mathematics, and the sciences agree that the first college year has to be devoted in the main to covering ground that is theoretically the responsibility of the secondary school. I myself saw the change taking place at the end of the first World War. Half a dozen classmates and I—the majority of those who had any desire to go to college—passed college board exams at the conclusion of the regular high school course and without any special coaching. Within five years, however, it was generally accepted that graduates of that particular high school needed a year elsewhere before they could face college boards. The abolition of college board examinations was in part a tribute to the efficiency of the cramming schools, but it was also an admission that the majority of secondary schools could no longer get their pupils over the hurdle. The standards of the college board were always arbitrary, and the whole system had become a horrible incubus long before its demise, but it was originally a success in that it did admit to the colleges more or less the kind of material they wanted and did keep out most of the material they didn't want. The colleges once were able to say, "This is what we are looking for," and the secondary schools delivered the goods. Now the colleges are saying, "We'll take the best you have, and do what we can with it."

Secondary education cannot be called a failure because it is unable to do one of its jobs, one in which only a minority of pupils are interested. The high schools, however, are having no greater success with students who do not intend to go further.

My mother attended the Girls' High School and my father the English High School in the Boston of the eighteen-eighties. Neither school prepared students for college, that function being left to the so-called Latin schools. Both my parents acquired the ability to express themselves clearly and correctly, learned as much of algebra and geometry as they were ever called upon to use, became familiar with the outlines of American and English history, and made some acquaintance with a foreign language. High school gave them a certain cultural advantage over those contemporaries—the majority, of course—who went no further than the ninth grade, and it gave them some useful tools. I am ready to admit that Boston schools were better than most in the eighties, but the deterioration of high school education remains a fact, and not only in Boston.

The whole character of the problem has changed. A New England banker once said to me, "People tell me that high school pupils nowadays don't know what they want to do. We didn't always know what we wanted to do. But we knew damned well what we ought to want." In the later nineteenth century a child went to high school because either he or his parents believed strongly that a high school education was economically, socially, or morally valuable. In the middle of the twentieth century high school is something that society forces upon the majority of students, and parents are likely to be as skeptical as pupils. They are glad to have their children out of the way, and probably most of them have a vague hope that some practical good will result, but they insist on leaving to the schools the full responsibility for what happens.

Some decades ago educators began to ask what could be done for these boys and girls who were, willy-nilly, kept in school at the public expense. The first answer was the obvious one: if they could not be given an education, in the traditional sense of the term, why not give them vocational training? For some boys and girls vocational training has worked very well, and I can think of several Roxborough young men who owe their good jobs in some measure to the shop courses they took in high school. There has been a tendency, however, for the courses in industry, agriculture, and domestic arts to become mere catch-ails for pupils who have done poorly in other classes. Shopwork is no better than Latin for a boy who isn't interested, and a teacher of vocational courses finds it as difficult as any other teacher to do his best for the students with interest and aptitude when his time is taken up with a multitude who have neither. Moreover, vocational training has turned out to be rather less practical than its advocates promised. On the one hand, the lesser skills can be picked up in a factory in a week or so. On the other, the complexities of the new technology are beyond the high school range, as New York State has recognized in its plan to establish a number of industrial and agricultural schools to give two-year courses to high school graduates.

Vocational training in high school has always been an evasion of the basic problem of secondary education for the seven million. Instead of becoming gradually more useful to his parents, and thus working himself into a way of life, the modern child is kept dependent until a relatively late age, and then is abruptly plunged into a complex and impersonal system of production and distribution. What he needs is not a set of specific skills but some preparation of mind and body for the plunge.

In some degree high school does provide that preparation, and therefore it is not a complete failure. By and large, however, the high school does its job, not by the courses it offers but by the opportunities it provides for the creation of a society of adolescents. From the Roxborough vantage point, this function is clearly seen, for it is only in high school that Roxborough boys and girls begin to meet contemporaries from strikingly different backgrounds and learn to adjust themselves to them. But the city child also has plenty to learn about the more complicated social structure of his environment, and in the ordinary contacts of high school, as well as in the multitude of extra-curricular activities, he receives his initiation. High school politics teach lessons that are learned by students who have flunked social studies. Athletic, musical, dramatic, literary, and managerial talents are discovered and evaluated. Any high school reproduces some of the characteristics of the larger society, and to that extent it gives an education.

But the very success of the high schools in providing a field for the practice of social adjustment underlines the confusion in education. What connection is there between what the pupil learns and what he does? In class elections the student plays the political game with a realism that Thurman Arnold would approve of, but does anyone ever point out to him the parallels between his behavior and the actions of the big shots, the ward-heelers, and the common voters of his city? Certainly it does not occur to him to apply in high school affairs the principles of good government he finds set forth in his social studies textbook, and no one bothers to call his attention to the chasm between theory and practice, much less to try to explain its existence. He finds his way about the microcosm of high school society, and is left to apply the same pragmatic and deeply inadequate approach to the fragments of the macrocosm with which he may subsequently come in contact.

There are, of course, high school teachers who perform miracles, and there might be a great deal more good teaching if educators were to become convinced of the importance of secondary education, if high school teachers would band together and insist on conditions that would permit them to do their job, and if school boards and taxpayers would learn that education can't be purchased over the bargain counter. Good teaching, however, wonderful as its results can be, will not solve the problem so long as there is no agreement on the aims of education.

This is the crux of the educational dilemma, and particularly on the college plane. In part, of course, the problem of the college is merely an extension of the high school problem, and failure to recognize that fact is responsible for the fatuousness of some of the talk about liberal education. The flood that had inundated the high schools swept into the colleges in the nineteen-twenties, and the new generations of freshmen were less well prepared than their predecessors had been, at any rate for the traditional purposes of the colleges. Since no one knew what the place of the colleges in the larger society ought to be, the situation was met by a series of hasty improvisations. Many large state universities, eager to produce results that fund-voting legislators would understand, began to offer a lavish variety of vocational courses. Sometimes these courses serve their specific purposes, but more often they are catch-alls, like the vocational courses in high school. That is, they furnish an excuse for keeping a student in college. His real reason for being there, of course, is to have a good time, play football, make friends of both sexes, and discover his place in the society of his contemporaries. Her real reason is to get a husband.

Nowhere is the schizoid character of modern American life more apparent than in the popular attitude towards education, particularly higher education. While I was an undergraduate, I worked for two or three summers in a large factory. The other college boys and I were looked on as freaks and as fair game for jibes and practical jokes, but at the same time it was assumed, on the whole without much justice, that we participated in those glamorous aspects of college life that the newspapers write about, and we were envied. We were regarded as utterly impractical, and yet we were supposed to know things that other people didn't know—and might very well like to—and to be able to do things that other people couldn't do. The general consensus was that college education was useless and that all college graduates got rich.

Our home in Roxborough once belonged to a professor of civil engineering. That would seem to be an eminently practical subject, but the legends of the man's impracticality—the typical impracticality of a college professor—have survived him by at least a decade. Even more fantastic stories have grown up around another summer visitor, a scientist of some prominence. The

Hicks saga will eventually be stupendous. "You're the smartest man in town," a politician said to me recently, "and you've done as much for the town as anyone, and nobody's got any use for you. I say you're a chump." Men who work with their hands almost always look with a mixture of resentment and contempt on the man who earns a living without doing manual labor, and people who haven't been to college are always aware that those who have are different, and are always afraid that they may be right. Belief that the educated man is impractical soothes the ego, though it does not quite restore self-confidence.

College students increasingly come from homes in which there is this split. My parents were determined for me to go to college because they believed in education, and their faith, though it may have been naive, was strong. Faith in education has declined in a quarter of a century, and more and more college students come from sections of the population that that faith has never reached. Men who scoff at the college graduates they meet in their factories or offices insist on sending their children to college, and boast about them intolerably once they are there. Education is useless, and yet college is the key to success.

At first glance it would seem that the change in the college population had given the liberal arts colleges their great opportunity: the young barbarians were delivered into the hands of the civilized minority. It can scarcely be said, however, that the barbarians have been converted in large numbers. For one thing, college teaching has rarely attracted pioneers or crusaders. It has attracted rather gentle, often timid individuals, who are either very much wrapped up in special studies or merely find the academic life a safe and pleasant one. They are saddened by the fact that students prefer football to their courses, but it seldom occurs to them that the courses may be at fault. On the contrary, each holds tenaciously to the courses he gives in his little specialty and fights for the right to give more.

However, it is as true of the colleges as it is of the high schools that the problem is not merely one of personnel. For some years it has been customary to blame all the evils of higher education on President Eliot, and it does seem as if the elective system was peculiarly ill-adapted to the conditions created by the new influx of students. Harvard, however, began repairing the damage as early as 1910, and all sorts of modifications and compromises have been devised since then. But in spite of fields of concentration, tutorial systems, special handling of honor students, orientation courses, comprehensive examinations, and all the rest, nobody has been satisfied with the results of college education. It was inevitable, of course, that someone should repudiate the elective system lock, stock, and barrel, and St. John's hundred best books seem to a few educators the way of salvation. Most college faculties were frantically revising their curricula for post-war purposes when Japan surrendered, and though few colleges are willing to go all the way with St. John's, there is a general tendency to set up compulsory courses wherein students will be exposed to the best that has been thought and said. Almost any plan is preferable to chaos, and the process of adopting a plan does compel some thought about the purposes of education. Moreover, most of the plans I have seen have said or implied that teaching should no longer be subordinated to research, and have otherwise suggested that colleges should be conducted for the benefit of the student body rather than the faculty. On a good many campuses there are encouraging changes in sight; whether they will prove adequate to the crisis remains to be seen.

Two questions have to be asked at every stage of the educational process. First, how can we contrive to equip every student for citizenship in the larger society? Second, how can we do this while giving exceptional students the opportunities they deserve? The colleges may be discovering how to do more for both the masses and the minorities, but there will still remain the necessity of vast reforms in elementary and secondary education. And permeating every educational problem, from kindergarten to graduate school, is the question of values. How can the purpose of education be defined in a society that has lost its sense of direction?

One way of approaching the subject is to study the school and the community together. Even Harvard—that "fenced-in oasis in the midst of the Cambridge jungle," as one of its professors describes it—has admitted in the report of its faculty committee, *General Education in a Free Society,* that the community cannot be ignored. Twenty-five years ago some teacher of mine spoke of the English visitor who predicted that Cambridge and Boston mobs would burn the college down if Harvard persisted in its aloofness. That hasn't happened, and perhaps isn't likely to happen, but both the community and the college have paid a price in comparison with which the mere loss of physical property would be insignificant.

As a school trustee and member of a committee on school centralization, I am face to face with this question of the school and the community. After the first World War, New York State attacked the problem of rural and small-town education by providing rather generous subsidies for central schools. So that a school may be of an efficient size, a central school district usually embraces three or four or more towns. Transportation is provided, and though ten or twelve miles is the usual limit, some pupils are carried thirty or thirty-five. By now more than half the common school districts in the state have entered central districts and it seems to be only a matter of time before centralization is complete. Most of the central schools are well constructed and well equipped, and of course provide facilities that are out of the question for a town the size of Roxborough.

The great trouble is that many of the smaller communities are left without schools. Some authorities are not disturbed by this. People, they point out, are no longer restricted to the townships in which they happen to live, and the central district can become the community of the future. Unfortunately, however, things do not work out that way. In the first place, school districts are drawn up with due consideration for the distribution of population, the availability of roads, and so on, but without much thought for the habits of the people. Thus two towns may be put in the same district though they have little in common whereas each has significant ties with some other town. In the second place, town loyalty remains strong, and the mere existence of a central district does not create a larger loyalty. In Van Hornesville, in the western part of the state, an attempt has been made to coordinate churches, social organizations, and economic institutions, as well as the school system, and as a result a sense of the district as a community seems to have developed. This is something, however, that must be worked for. What ordinarily happens is that the central school becomes an asset to the town in which it is located and does little for the other towns in the district.

In the late thirties Roxborough was urged to join a central district that had already built a school in a town some ten miles to the southeast. I was in favor of the idea at the time, but I quickly discovered that most people in Roxborough felt that they had nothing in common with the people of this town. In all its practical affairs Roxborough looks west, towards Troy, and the citizens don't want to send their children "further back in the hills." More recently there has been talk of a new central district to the west of us, and though there are plenty of people who oppose the whole idea and want to keep the one-room schoolhouses, there is more sentiment for this plan than there ever was for the other.

Since Roxborough refuses to join the central district on the east, and since there is little likelihood that a district will be immediately formed on the west, we are stalemated, but sooner or later we are going to have to decide what to do. That Roxborough children will get a better education in a central district seems to me undebatable, but I want the central district to establish a branch school in Roxborough for the first six grades. A modern school, with some sort of small assembly room, with facilities for showing moving pictures, and with a kitchen and lunchroom, could become a center of community life. With such a school, the people of Roxborough might be interested in the activities of the district and come to feel part of it. But to take the schools out of Roxborough altogether would complete the disintegration of the community without creating loyalties to a larger area. As a matter of fact, state education department figures show that it would be cheaper to build and operate branch schools in this proposed district than it would be to transport the children to one central school. The department, however, is so committed to the idea of getting all the children under one roof that its subsidy for this plan would be larger and hence the tax rate would be lower. I should be discouraged if it were not that some members of the department have begun to lay more emphasis on saving the small community, even the very small community. I believe that in the future a way will be found to build a school in Roxborough, and until that time I hope the people will sit tight. They almost certainly will, for sitting tight is what they do best.

The concrete problems of the Roxborough schools bring us back to the question of planning. The state education department has issued a handbook[2] for the use of individuals and organizations interested in school problems. The first question asked is, "What will the community (city, village, or school district) be like in 1950?" The average citizen might well reply, "I wish to God I knew." However, as the manual goes on to explain, one can study population trends, survey housing conditions, query business men, and otherwise arrive at some sort of guess. The second question is, "What should education be like by 1950?" Here the committee has answers of its own for local groups to consider. "The education program," it suggests, "should insure that each child achieves: 1. Ability to read, write and speak the English language. 2. Ability to use mathematics required in the society of 1950. 3. Knowledge of the history of our country, its ideals, the development of our government and our way of living, the role of our country in the world today in

---

[2] "Problems Confronting Boards of Education, A Manual for Community Participation in Educational Planning," Albany, 1944.

relation to other countries. 4. Knowledge of the history and achievements of the scientific method in both the natural and social fields and the ability to use this method. 5. Basic health habits and knowledge; bodily stamina; coordination for efficient physical fitness; medical, dental and psychiatric care necessary for sound development. 6. Opportunity to choose wisely from a wide range of vocational opportunities (not limited to his local community) and basic training appropriate to his choice. 7. Appreciation of the great creative achievements of the people of the world in literature, music and art and a minimum skill of performance in some creative area. 8. Ability to participate effectively as a member of a significant group, defined as one in which the child experiences 'a strong feeling of belonging and a sense of loyalty.'" There follows a list of desirable services to preschool children, handicapped children, discharged soldiers and sailors, and so forth, and the committee then asks, "What educational deficiencies are indicated?" and, "How do we move from the present to the desired program?"

In how many communities could this manual be read without despair? At the end of its eight-point educational program the committee has left a space for additional items, and one is tempted to write in, "A reading knowledge of Greek, Hebrew, and Sanskrit; advanced courses in radar and atomic energy; the ability to play golf and polo; and a complete psychoanalysis." Yet, great as the distance is that separates the program from reality, it has its uses as a measure of the shortcomings of the schools. Certainly there is nothing it recommends that one would not like to see achieved.

But how is this perfection, or any approximation of it, to be brought about? As I have intimated, I do not believe that there can be any fundamental solution of educational problems until our civilization recovers its sense of direction, and this is unlikely to happen until western man learns to control his social environment. Yet when I was talking about planning, I said that there could be no democratic participation without some rise in the level of interest and knowledge. If, in other words, the schools were doing their job better, the chances of democratic planning would be brighter. One has to try to improve the schools by improving the community and improve the community by improving the schools.

However far away perfection may be, there is no lack of immediate opportunity for improvement in education. If the colleges are going to do better in the future, their ever more numerous product can be a leaven in society. It will be a pity, I think, if the colleges do not do their best to direct the energy and intelligence of their graduates into the service of the community. Not only as teachers but also as parents and citizens they can begin to reshape elementary and secondary education. But it will always be a mistake to rely on the schools alone: if the spirit of the community is not behind the school, reinforcing its values, the best teacher in the world, with the best curriculum in the world, will be engaged in an uneven contest.

If the democracies do not find a democratic way of reforming education, a totalitarian way is ready and waiting for the use of the dictators. Germany and Russia have developed efficient forms of mass indoctrination, and have demonstrated how easily youth can be shaped to the purposes of the state. American ingenuity, moreover, has devised tools perfectly suited to totalitarian use. Certain of the courses that the Army and Navy gave during the war were virtually teacherless. Each class did have an instructor, of course, but he was little more than a glorified proctor, for his chief duties were to take the attendance and play the proper phonograph records. Periodically he gave prescribed tests, which he marked with the aid of a mechanical device. A French minister of education once boasted that at any given moment he could tell what was being studied in each grade in each school in the country, but he had to rely on teachers, who are always fallible and may be heretical. The regimentation that now seems possible lacks only the refinement once suggested by Aldous Huxley—indoctrination of the subconscious during sleep.

That kind of regimentation may not be imminent, but it will come if totalitarianism comes. After all, a totalitarian society is merely one in which a plan is imposed upon society by a strategically situated minority. The minority can use force to bring about conformity, and always will, but there are limits to force in any society and particularly in industrial society. Force is useful for the seizure and consolidation of power, but the minority can maintain control only by inculcating the appropriate beliefs and desires. Propaganda serves in the short run, but only education can lay the basis for stability.

In education as everywhere else the danger of totalitarianism is obvious: it would be such an easy solution. All debate on the aims of education would automatically cease with the revolution, and millions of people would doubtless be relieved. Simultaneously the area of personal responsibility for the functioning of the larger community would be reduced to a minimum, and teachers could concentrate on a few simple principles formulated by the elite. It would be necessary for students to acquire the tools of communication, for totalitarianism, unlike earlier dictatorships, demands a literate public, and the sciences and the scientific method would remain important. History and literature, on the other hand, would become mere branches of mythology and propaganda. Academic curricula, in short, could be greatly simplified, and vocational courses would be shaped by the needs of the state, not by the desires of the pupils. Mechanical devices would minimize the importance of the individual teacher, and give the experts at the top almost perfect control. Finally, the state could take care of incentives by the kind of emotional atmosphere it created and by a carefully calculated system of rewards and punishments.

We have seen what the alternative is. The first step is the elimination of those individuals who have a vested interest in education as it is. I have said that educators are dissatisfied with the schools, and that is true of many and particularly of the more articulate ones. Their articulateness, however, should not lead us to forget the teachers and administrators and trustees who are keeping quiet because they hope to stay put. They are being badly battered just now, but they have not been dislodged from positions in which their talent for obstruction can be effectively employed.

The second step is the conscientious reconsideration of curricula all the way up and down. Even if education cannot carry all the burdens that have been laid upon it, the schools can do a better job than they are now doing. Educators consistently refuse to examine the actual functions of the schools in our society as it is at present constituted. Things being what they are, one can hardly blame them, but, until we know what kind of society we want and how we propose to get it, we had better concentrate on doing as well as possible the things we can do. If a school system cannot perform all the tasks suggested by the education department's manual—and not many school systems can—it had better decide what it can do and do that well. Since the big problems cannot be solved in terms of education alone, and must wait upon social reconstruction, the sensible thing is to tackle the little problems one after another.

But how is education to prepare the way for social reconstruction? This seems the heaviest burden of all, and certainly it would be if the schools were to take it on as their direct responsibility and theirs alone. Actually, however, the great social battles always have to be fought on many fronts simultaneously. If the schools can do some of their jobs a little more efficiently, that will be their share.

XII

The Duty of the Intellectuals

As I have said before, a growing awareness of the intellectual's limitations has not diminished but actually increased my respect for his particular talents. The question is whether these talents are being used to the best advantage of society. Certainly the position of the intellectual today is a dubious and unhappy one.

In earlier times the intellectuals had a privileged status, and naturally so in view of the debt that civilization owed to the minority who could keep records and use figures. But ever since the destruction of feudalism, the intellectual has had to compete in the marketplace, and as a rule intellectuals are now accorded special respect only in countries where some vestiges of the caste system remain. The increase of literacy has accelerated the decline in prestige, for the mere ability to read and write no longer inspires awe. More than that, the extension of education has heightened the competition within the intellectual class. Sometimes a society has more intellectuals than it can find employment for, and Konrad Heiden has attributed the rise of Nazism to the existence in Germany of a large group of frustrated intellectuals.

It might seem that the disintegration of the caste system should have had the effect of bringing the intellectuals closer to the rest of the people. With the breakdown of castes, however, has gone a great increase in specialization. This is one of the paradoxes of mass society: interdependence draws people together, but specialization drives them apart, and interdependence and specialization are inseparable aspects of the same phenomenon. Socially speaking, the distance between the intellectuals and the masses was greater two hundred years ago than it is now, but the functions of the intellectuals were more easily understood, or at any rate more readily accepted, than they are today. A caste system seems to the members of society a logical and inevitable scheme of social relationships, but relationships in a mass society fall into no recognizable pattern.

In *Good-Bye, Wisconsin* Glenway Wescott describes his return to his home after some years abroad. In the milk-train that took him to Milwaukee were two young workmen, one employed in a tannery, the other in a foundry. They kept looking at his cigarette-lighter, his gloves, his Basque beret, and finally they asked him where he worked. He didn't know what to answer. "If this were Europe I could have told them I was a writer, which would have been the end of it. One day years ago when I was wearing a rather pretentious black cape, I tipped a porter in a Munich railway station. 'Thank you kindly, Herr. poet,' he said." Wescott felt that there was an insuperable barrier between himself as a writer and the young workers, and of course there was. The porter's flattering salutation was, I suppose, an echo of caste feeling, an acceptance of differences. The American workmen, on the other hand, had no pigeonhole into which this exotic creature could be placed, and they were puzzled. What Wescott forgot is that they would have been equally puzzled if he had said that he was a pathologist or a bio-chemist or a cultural anthropologist. For that matter, did he have any clear idea of what a tanner did or an ironworker? And what if they had told him that they were jewelry lappers or monotype keyboard operators or pantograph engravers or practiced some of the other mysterious specialties that one finds listed in the want ads? Most vocations in this mass society are mysteries to most of us.

Scott Fitzgerald once said that the rich are different from the rest of us and that we have no real idea of the way they live. There are many obstacles to understanding in our society, and perhaps the barrier between intellectuals and nonintellectuals is not the most important, but it is real enough, and its effects are serious. If Glenway Wescott had happened to be an engraver, he would still have had difficulty in explaining to the young workmen what he did, but he would have got on with them a great deal better. If, on the other hand, his companions had turned out to be biochemists, he would have been bored by their shoptalk, but he and they would have found some common ground. By and large intellectuals mingle with intellectuals, and preferably with men who are interested in their particular fields or in fields that are closely related. Some intellectuals are forced by the work they do to come in contact with a variety of people, but others are able to withdraw into a small and congenial circle, and most of those who can do. Everyone knows about literary cliques and the closeknit social life of college faculties, but groups of technicians and managerial employees, both in government offices and in private businesses, are often just as effectively segregated.

Because I have seen more of writers than of other kinds of intellectual, I am particularly conscious of what has happened as a result of the concentration of the arts in New York City. The writer who lives outside New York cannot easily fail to realize that there is a great deal of life from which he is isolated, but the typical urban intellectual suffers from the delusion that he is at the very heart of America. His particular coterie, whether it is conservative or radical, arty or frankly commercial, looks and sounds and feels like the real thing. If he is successful, he may go lecturing and may convince himself that the bored eyes and explosive coughs and sweaty hands he encounters are the people. He may move in larger and larger circles—Hollywood and the radio and the kind of parties that get mentioned in the gossip columns. And all the time he remains an isolated urban intellectual, knowing little of what goes on in the minds of people whose opportunities and inclinations happen to have been different from his own.

It would be stupid to blame the intellectuals for a situation that all the complex forces of social change have created, but perhaps the intellectual does owe it to himself and to society to break through barriers, not build them up. This does not mean that a writer cannot be a good writer unless he runs for political office or assumes some other public role. The very meaning of participation differs from artist to artist. James Joyce, leaving Dublin in his early twenties, was so saturated with the life of the city that forty years could not put on paper a tithe of what he had to say. Proust devoted himself to a small segment of Parisian society and eventually withdrew into complete seclusion, but he had all his imagination needed to feed on. On the other hand, there are men like Shaw, who has almost continuously taken part in social and political movements. While it can be argued that Joyce is a greater writer than Shaw or vice versa, it cannot very well be maintained that either man would have done better writing if he had lived as the other lived.

I am willing to defend only two propositions. First, the isolated intellectual pays a price, and what he gets may or may not be worth what he pays. Second, the already calamitous situation of our society can only deteriorate further if the gulf between the intellectuals and other people continues to widen. The first point must remain a matter of personal judgment, though there are biographies and literary studies that support my contention. The second thesis scarcely needs to be demonstrated. We, collectively, know enough to make a decent society, but the knowledge is concentrated in too few heads. There is no pathway of confidence and sympathy between the intellectuals and the people along which knowledge can travel. And if the people are often badly informed, the intellectuals are just as often naive and narrow in their judgments.

No one can lay down laws for the kind and degree of participation. I have known more than one economist who became so interested in the labor movement that he abandoned research and became an organizer or an adviser to organizers. In any given instance more may have been gained than was lost, but I am sure that there was a loss. I have known teachers who became so deeply concerned with their pupils that they ceased to follow the advance of knowledge. This is a better reason than mere laziness for losing touch, and a less common phenomenon, but the young teacher had better be warned against the danger. I have known writers, especially in the thirties, who spent more time in committee meetings than they did at their typewriters. Very possibly the world is no poorer, but that cannot merely be taken for granted.

One cannot be surprised that participation as well as nonparticipation has its casualties, for this is what we ought to expect in a situation that makes adjustment difficult. If it were easy for intellectuals to strike the right balance, more of them would do it. Perhaps, as Arthur Koestler has suggested, the mere existence of an intellectual class makes for tension. Not all intellectuals are innovators and revolutionaries, but innovators and revolutionaries are usually intellectuals. Roxborough old-timers believe that once a man has a little book learning he is never satisfied with things as they are, and up to a point they are right, for even if the intellectuals do not bring change about, they point out the consequences of change, and that seems just as bad. Until the whole character of society is so altered that the distinction between intellectual and nonintellectual is pretty well blurred, friction can be expected. But there can be less friction rather than more.

The experiences described in this book are not presented as a model for others to follow. I doubt if I am representative, and I hope that Roxborough is not. Some of my friends tell me that I am wasting my time in attending meetings, running dances, getting signatures, cataloging books, and doing all the scores of more or less arduous and more or less dull jobs that constitute my participation in the life of the town. As they frankly admit, they hope that sooner or later I will get sick of the whole business, and maybe I will. As yet, however, I am unwilling to say that I am licked. What is more important, I do not think that I have learned all that the town has to teach me. One of my good friends—perhaps in part because he is my friend—was recently defeated in a contest for a minor office. Someone remarked that his campaign hadn't cost much. "Hell," he said, "I got a thousand dollars' worth of experience for $2.25." I, too, feel that I have been amply repaid—thus far at any rate—for all the time I have spent.

What I have learned will seem commonplace enough to many persons, and I am aware that I have said and can say little that hasn't been said before. It seems to me, however, that there are certain ideas that many persons profess to accept but that few act upon. One way of disposing of an awkward fact is to say, "Everybody knows that." Perhaps everybody does, but what difference does that make if nobody takes the knowledge into account?

There is nothing startling, for instance, in saying that many—perhaps most—of the people in a town like Roxborough live according to standards and concepts that were appropriate to an age of self-sufficiency but have little relevance in a mass society. Any urban intellectual will grant that there is a lag in rural areas, and when he has made the admission, he thinks he has solved the problem. But if one has to deal with James West's "millions of Plainvillers," not all of whom live in small towns, one finds that having a label for the phenomenon does not help much.

Urban intellectuals seem to forget that human nature does not permit the existence of a vacuum. Talk about a lag implies that something is missing, that there is a kind of unoccupied territory in the small-town mind for urban ideas to take over. In practice what one comes up against is a positive set of values. The people in Roxborough do not ask themselves whether they should accept certain city notions but whether they should abandon their familiar and tested way of life. Personally I have some sympathy with those who wish they could preserve the values of the self-sufficient small town, but it is not sympathy that matters as much as understanding. What I have to remember is that in asking these people to take something I am also asking them to give something up, and what they are asked to abandon seems just as important to them as what I am asking them to take seems to me.

If one realizes that one is dealing with a positive way of life, one cannot be surprised by unevenness in the rate of change.

To the five Antioch girls, all of them from urban or suburban backgrounds, Roxborough seemed an impoverished community. If a house did not have modern conveniences, the girls took it for granted that the owner was too poor to install them. It did not occur to them that a man might go without electricity or running water because these things did not seem essential to his way of life and because he wanted other things more—for instance, a bank account that would take care of him in his old age. Both mechanical devices and ways of thought are assimilated according to patterns that belong to the community, not according to urban ideas of what is necessary or proper. People pick up bits of slang from the radio, but their speech remains Roxborough speech. In fact, a person can take over a large number of urban traits without abandoning the small-town attitude toward life.

There is no lack of variety even in so small a town as Roxborough. At one extreme are the old-timers, living in their memories of the past, and at the other are the newcomers from the cities, more or less contemptuous of hill-billy ways. Yet some old-timers are proud of their electric appliances, while others say smugly that kerosene is good enough for them, and some newcomers slip effortlessly into the small town's habits of dress and speech and thought, as if that was what they had really wanted all the time. We have drawling hill-billies who have scarcely stepped outside the town, and drawling hill-billies who operate the most complicated types of machinery. We have alert, informed women living in houses that have no running water, and we have women whose homes are furnished from the best stores in Troy while their minds belong to the backwoods. We have stupid men who can parrot the phrases of the radio commentators, and wise men who can't get their tongues round a polysyllabic word.

Because so much of human nature is exposed to view, an intellectual can easily be fascinated by life in a small town, but his observations are unlikely to encourage optimism. He will quickly discover, for example, that the majority of the people are interested only in their own affairs and have little concern for the common good. He will learn that most public issues are confused by factionalism, prejudice, stupidity, and a most unenlightened selfishness. Unless he is fortunate in his choice of community, he will find, to his sorrow, that the townspeople are easier to exploit than they are to help. But if the intellectual thereupon decides that there is nothing to do with the small towns but liquidate them, and if he returns to his particular urban circle, vowing never again to leave it, he has learned only the poorer half of his lesson. Patience will teach him something not only about small-towners but also about city people and about himself.

In the past the small community was the seedbed of our American kind of democracy. In the future, if we are wise, the small community may become an experiment station for new democratic processes. At present it is merely something that has been pushed aside by the forces that are creating the larger society. Yet in some ways the great transformation that is taking place can be studied better from the margins of the larger society than from the center. I know that we are committed to a mass society worldwide in its scope, but I also know that in the whole sweep of history the small community has been the norm and cities and empires the exceptions. I am not suggesting that every small-town problem must be solved before the problems of the larger society can be tackled, but I do believe that some of the problems are the same, and that they can be most effectively handled, to begin with, on the small-town level.

If the intellectual chooses to live in a small town, that does not mean that his life must be lived in small-town terms. His value to the community, indeed, depends on his maintaining contact with the world of the mind. But that is easy to do, both in body and in spirit. Our friends come here, and we visit them. We get to New York now and then for the theaters and the art galleries. And in any case, thanks to books and periodicals and records and the radio, we could live in the world of the mind if we never set foot outside of Roxborough. I think there are many urban intellectuals who listen to less good music and read fewer of the books that are worth reading than we manage to do here, and we have an active community life and a good deal of outdoor work into the bargain.

But I did not intend this to become a plea for the small town, for I am principally concerned with the general relationship between intellectuals and other people. This is not just a book about a small town but a book about a small town in a certain kind of world. If, as I believe, the intellectuals have the skills that are essential to the maintenance of intelligent control over social forces, then the issue of the struggle between democracy and totalitarianism depends on their decision, and it is their chief duty to make sure that they are with the people and the people with them.

I have not prettified my account of our participation in the life of a small town, and though the intellectual would encounter a different set of problems in a different situation, I doubt if he would find them easier to solve. It is no simple matter for the urban intellectual to find a point of significant contact with the world outside his circle. "What should I do," a college professor asked me, "join the Rotary Club, invite the grocer to dinner?" Well, he could do worse, but he could also do better. He has never canvassed in a political campaign, collected money for the community chest, or taken part in adult education. These things are little enough, as many intellectuals have found out, but they do establish contacts and can lead the way to more significant relationships. The truth is that this man does not want to weaken the barriers that protect him from interruptions and permit him to do the work he feels he is fitted to do. For him this isolation may be right, but he need not pretend that he could not escape if he desired to.

I have learned to moderate the optimism that once was so strong in me. I think it wholly likely that attempts at peaceful organization of the world may fail, with either anarchy or tyranny as the outcome of the resulting wars for world hegemony. I think it probable that democratic social planning will come, if it comes at all, only after further experiments in totalitarianism. But just as I no longer believe in the inevitable progress of mankind onward and upward forever, or in the operation of a dialectical materialism that guarantees the safe arrival of the classless society, so I do not believe in irresistible forces making for either chaos or despotism. I see no reason to assume that our problems cannot be solved. If they are solved, there will of course be other problems, but that is a different matter. All that we have to worry about is the battle that lies directly ahead—and, that is plenty. I have no formula for victory, but merely ideas about some of the ways in which we might make a start.

As I write this, I think of the meeting of the board of fire commissioners that I must attend in a few hours. The outcome may be good or bad; all I can predict is that a considerable amount of time will be wasted in unnecessary talk. However, it. appears to be my job as much as it is any man's. I know that the board would be in bad shape if all the members had my particular limitations, but there are contributions that a person with my background can sometimes make. So I shall go to the meeting, and no doubt I'll be bored, and perhaps I'll be displeased with the outcome, but I may learn something and I may do something. As a matter of fact, I expect to enjoy parts of the evening, as I have enjoyed parts—and rather large parts—of the whole experience with which this book has dealt.

A Granville Hicks Bibliography

Aaron, Daniel. *Writers on the Left*. New York: Oxford University Press, 1977.

Bicker, Robert J. *Granville Hicks: An Annotated Bibliography, February, 1927 to June, 1967, with a Supplement to June, 1968*. Emporia, KS: Emporia State Research Studies, 1968.

Broderick, Warren F. "Granville Hicks: Champion of the Small Town." *Hudson Valley Regional Review* 18, no. 1 (March, 2001): 1-30.

"City vs. Country." *Life Magazine*, 17 March 1947, 96–98.

Hicks, Granville. *Behold Trouble*. New York: Macmillan, 1944.

———. *Eight Ways of Looking at Christianity*. New York: Macmillan, 1926.

———. *Figures of Transition: A Study of British Literature at the End of the Nineteenth Century*. New York: Macmillan, 1939.

———. *The First To Awaken*. New York: Modern Age Books, 1940.

———. *Granville Hicks in the New Masses*. Edited by Jack Robbins. Port Washington, NY: Kennikat Press, 1974.

———. *The Great Tradition: An Interpretation of American Literature Since the Civil War*. New York: Macmillan, 1933.

———. *I Like America*. New York: Modern Age Books, 1938.

———. "Is the Small Town Doomed." Unpublished article, 1956. Granville Hicks Papers, Syracuse University Library.

———. *James Gould Cozzens*. Minneapolis: University of Minnesota Press, 1966.

———. *John Reed: The Making of a Revolutionary*. New York: Macmillan, 1936.

———. *Literary Horizons: A Quarter Century of American Fiction*. New York: New York University Press, 1970.

———. "The Mind of a Small Town." *The American Mercury* LXIII, no. 272 (August 1946): 154–160.

———. *Only One Storm*. New York: Macmillan, 1942.

———. *Part of the Truth: An Autobiography.* New York: Harcourt, Brace & World, 1965.

———. "A Place in the Country." Unpublished article, 1952. Granville Hicks Papers, Syracuse University Library.

———. "Reflections of a Small-Towner." *Georgia Review* I, no. 2 (Summer 1947): 142–152.

———. "Roxborough: Post-Truman." *Commentary* 15, no. 3 (March 1953): 227–235.

———. *Small Town.* New York: Macmillan, 1946.

———. *There Was a Man In Our Town.* New York: Viking, 1952.

———. *Where We Came Out.* New York: Viking, 1954.

Hicks, Granville, ed. *The Living Novel: A Symposium.* New York: Macmillan, 1957.

———. *Proletarian Literature in the United States.* New York: International Publishers, 1935.

Hicks, Granville, and Lynd Ward. *One of Us: The Story of John Reed.* New York: Equinox Cooperative Press, 1935.

Lerner, Max. *America as a Civilization: Life and Thought in the United States Today.* New York: Simon & Schuster, 1957.

Levenson, Leah, and Jerry Natterstad. *Granville Hicks: The Individual in Mass Society.* Philadelphia: Temple University Press, 1993.

Lingeman, Richard. *Small Town America: A Narrative History.* New York: G. P. Putnams' Sons, 1980.

Long, Terry L. *Granville Hicks.* Boston: Twayne Publishers, 1981.

Nisbet, Robert. *The Quest for Community: a Study in the Ethics of Order and Freedom.* New York: Oxford University Press, 1953.

Pells, Richard. *The Liberal Mind in a Conservative Age: American Intellectuals in the 1940s and 1950s.* New York: Harper & Row, 1985.

———. *Radical Visions and American Dreams: Culture and Social Thought in the Depression Years.* New York: Harper & Row, 1973.

Rideout, Walter. *The Radical Novel in the United States, 1900–1954: Some Interrelations of Literature and Society.* New York: Hill & Wang, 1956.

Rovere, Richard. *Final Reports: Personal Reflections on Policy and History in Our Time.* New York: Doubleday, 1984.

"Would You Rather Live in a Small Town or a Big City?," *Town Meeting* (Bulletin of America's *Town Meeting of the Air*) 12, no. 35 (December 26, 1946): 3–24.

Index

Intellectuals
    American life and, 237–38
    on "common man," 203, 221
    Depression's influence on, 204
    duty of, 247–56
    Hicks as, xxv, xxxv, 13–33, 34–35, 39
    idea loyalty of, 147
    inadequacy of, 137
    inspiring new, 42
    isolation of, 249, 250, 255
    as leaders, 169
    old-timers v., 94
    in politics, 179–80
    resentment against, 15–16
    segregation of, 203
    small-town mind v., 101, 119
    socialism and, 204
    status, 247
    urban/city v. small-town, 11–12,
        156, 249, 254–55
    use of word, 16*n*1
    writers as, 248–51
Intelligence
    knowledge v., 147
    value of, 147
Interior monologues, 98
Irwin, Ohio, 181–82, 181*n*1, 186, 189, 191
Isolation
    of intellectual, 249, 250, 255
    of Roxborough, 54–55, 85
    of small towns, 183–84

Jackson, Charles, xxix–xxx
Jackson, Kenneth, x
Japan, bombing/surrendering of,
    221–22, 239
Jewish people
    anti-Semitism targeting, 6, 16, 102–3
    Nazi Germany and, 116, 206–9
Jobs. *See also* Employment; Unem-
    ployment
    city, 10, 36, 64, 69, 70, 71–72, 75,
        76, 102–4, 175
    during Depression, 72–73, 80, 84
    providing, 200
    during World War II, 80, 85, 196

*John Reed: The Making of a Revolu-
    tionary* (Hicks), xvii, xxii
Josephs, Sam, 166, 190–91
Joyce, James, 250
Justices, election of, 172–73

Kay, Old Doc, 24–25
Knowledge
    of economy, 117–18
    intelligence v., 147
    of machinery, 105–7, 119, 228, 229
    of philosophy, 113
    of religion, 113–14
    of society, 220–21, 250
    society and, 250
    urban v. rural, 198–200
Ku-Klux Klan, 154
Kunstler, James, xviii–xix

Ladd, Everett, xxvii–xxviii
Laissez-faire theories, 210, 212
Landaff, New Hampshire, 185–86, 187,
    188
Lawlessness, 145
Law, regard for, 126, 145
Leadership
    intellectuals and, 169
    question of, 168–70
    Roxborough natives v. outsiders
        in, 127–29
League of Nations, 21
Leaving Roxborough
    after marriage, 80–83
    farms, 64
    fear of, 82–83
    for work, 10, 36, 64, 69, 70, 75–76,
        76, 102–4, 175
    Library, free, 41, 112
    Hick's role in, xxi, xxxiv, 5, 6, 8,
        48, 49, 161–62
Life magazine, xxx
Lilienthal, David, 213–17
Locality
    autonomy of, xxxi
    in democracy, 43, 221
    in factory ownership, 186